THE
OTHER SIDE
OF ME

THE
OTHER SIDE
OF ME

SIDNEY
SHELDON

WARNER BOOKS

NEW YORK   BOSTON

Warner Books

Time Warner Book Group
1271 Avenue of the Americas, New York, NY 10020
Visit our Web site at www.twbookmark.com.

Printed in the United States of America

First Edition: November 2005
10   9   8   7   6   5   4   3   2   1

Library of Congress Cataloging-in-Publication Data

Sheldon, Sidney.
    The other side of me / Sidney Sheldon.— 1st ed.
        p.   cm.
    Summary : "Memoir of entertainment legend Sidney Sheldon, now 88 years old, an
Academy Award-winning screenwriter and creator of many television hits"—Provided
by publisher.
    ISBN 0-446-53267-3 — ISBN 0-446-57895-9 (lg. print ed.)
  1. Sheldon, Sidney. 2. Novelists, American—20th century—Biography. 3. Television
writers—United States—Biography. 4. Screenwriters—United States—Biography. I.
Title.
    PS3569.H3927Z47 2005
    813'.54—dc22   2005016215

For my beloved granddaughters,

Lizy and Rebecca

so that they will know what a

magical journey I had

THE
OTHER SIDE
OF ME

"He that has no fools, knaves nor beggars in his family was begot by a flash of lightning."
—*Thomas Fuller*
17th century English clergyman

CHAPTER

1

At the age of seventeen, working as a delivery boy at Afremow's drugstore in Chicago was the perfect job, because it made it possible for me to steal enough sleeping pills to commit suicide. I was not certain exactly how many pills I would need, so I arbitrarily decided on twenty, and I was careful to pocket only a few at a time so as not to arouse the suspicion of our pharmacist. I had read that whiskey and sleeping pills were a deadly combination, and I intended to mix them, to make sure I would die.

It was Saturday—the Saturday I had been waiting for. My parents would be away for the weekend and my brother, Richard, was staying at a friend's. Our apartment would be deserted, so there would be no one there to interfere with my plan.

At six o'clock, the pharmacist called out, "Closing time."

He had no idea how right he was. It was time to close out all the things that were wrong with my life. I knew it wasn't just me. It was the whole country.

The year was 1934, and America was going through a devastating crisis. The stock market had crashed five years before and thousands of banks had failed. Businesses were folding everywhere. More than thirteen million people had lost their jobs and were desperate. Wages had plunged to as low as a nickel an hour. A million vagabonds, including two hundred thousand children, were roaming the country. We were in the grip of a disastrous depression. Former millionaires were committing suicide, and executives were selling apples in the streets.

The most popular song was "Gloomy Sunday." I had memorized some of the lyrics:

Gloomy is Sunday
With shadows I spend it all
My heart and I
Have decided to end it all

The world was bleak, and it fit my mood perfectly. I had reached the depths of despair. I could see no rhyme or reason for my existence. I felt dislocated and lost. I was miserable and desperately longing for something that I couldn't define or name.

We lived near Lake Michigan, only a few blocks from the shore, and one night I walked down there to try to calm myself. It was a windy night, and the sky was filled with clouds.

I looked up and said, "If there is a God, show yourself to me."

And as I stood there staring at the sky, the clouds merged together, forming a huge face. There was a sudden flash of lightning that gave the face blazing eyes. I ran all the way home in a panic.

I lived with my family in a small, third-floor apartment

in Rogers Park. The great showman Mike Todd said that he was often broke but he never felt poor. I, however, felt poor all the time because we were living in the demeaning kind of grinding poverty where, in a freezing winter, you had to keep the radiator off to save money and you learned to turn the lights out when not in use. You squeezed the last drops out of the ketchup bottle and the last dab of toothpaste out of the tube. But I was about to escape all that.

When I arrived at our dreary apartment, it was deserted. My parents had already left for the weekend and my brother had gone. There was no one to stop me from what I intended to do.

I walked into the little bedroom that Richard and I shared and I carefully removed the bag of sleeping pills I had hidden under the dresser. Next, I went into the kitchen, took a bottle of bourbon from the shelf where my father kept it, and carried it back to the bedroom. I looked at the pills and the bourbon and I wondered how long it would take for them to work. I poured some whiskey into a glass and raised it to my lips. I would not let myself think about what I was doing. I took a swallow of the whiskey, and the acrid taste of it made me choke. I picked up a handful of sleeping pills and started to raise them to my mouth, when a voice said, "What are you doing?"

I spun around, spilling some of the whiskey and dropping some of the pills.

My father was standing in the bedroom doorway. He moved closer. "I didn't know you drank."

I looked at him, stunned. "I—I thought you were gone."

"I forgot something. I'll ask you again: What are you doing?" He took the glass of whiskey from my hand.

My mind was racing. "Nothing—nothing."

He was frowning. "This isn't like you, Sidney. What's wrong?" He saw the pile of sleeping pills. "My God! What's going on here? What are these?"

No plausible lie came to my mind. I said defiantly, "They're sleeping pills."

"Why?"

"I'm going to—to commit suicide."

There was a silence. Then my father said, "I had no idea you were so unhappy."

"You can't stop me, because if you stop me now I'll do it tomorrow."

He stood there, studying me. "It's your life. You can do anything you want with it." He hesitated. "If you're not in too big a hurry, why don't we go for a little walk?"

I knew exactly what he was thinking. My father was a salesman. He was going to try to talk me out of my plan, but he didn't have a chance. I knew what I was going to do. I said, "All right."

"Put on a coat. You don't want to catch cold."

The irony of that made me smile.

Five minutes later, my father and I were headed down windswept streets that were empty of pedestrians because of the freezing temperature.

After a long silence, my father said, "Tell me about it, son. Why do you want to commit suicide?"

Where could I begin? How could I explain to him how lonely and trapped I felt? I desperately wanted a better life—but there was no better life for me. I wanted a wonderful future and there was no wonderful future. I had glowing daydreams, but at the end of the day, I was a delivery boy working in a drugstore.

My fantasy was to go to college, but there was no money for that. My dream had been to become a writer.

I had written dozens of short stories and sent them to *Story* magazine, *Collier's*, and *The Saturday Evening Post*, and I had gotten back printed rejections. I had finally decided I couldn't spend the rest of my life in this suffocating misery.

My father was talking to me. "... and there are so many beautiful places in the world you haven't seen ..."

I tuned him out. *If he leaves tonight, I can go on with my plan.*

"... you'd love Rome ..."

If he tries to stop me now, I'll do it when he leaves. I was busy with my thoughts, barely listening to what he was saying.

"Sidney, you told me that you wanted to be a writer more than anything in the world."

He suddenly had my attention. "That was yesterday."

"What about tomorrow?"

I looked at him, puzzled. "What?"

"You don't know what can happen tomorrow. Life is like a novel, isn't it? It's filled with suspense. You have no idea what's going to happen until you turn the page."

"I know what's going to happen. Nothing."

"You don't really know that, do you? Every day is a different page, Sidney, and they can be full of surprises. You'll never know what's next until you turn the page."

I thought about that. He did have a point. Every tomorrow *was* like the next page of a novel.

We turned the corner and walked down a deserted street. "If you really want to commit suicide, Sidney, I understand. But I'd hate to see you close the book too soon and miss all the excitement that could happen to you on the next page—the page *you're* going to write."

Don't close the book too soon ... Was I closing it too soon? Something wonderful could *happen tomorrow.*

Either my father was a superb salesman or I wasn't fully committed to ending my life, because by the end of the next block, I had decided to postpone my plan.

But I intended to keep my options open.

CHAPTER

2

I was born in Chicago, on a kitchen table that I made with my own hands. At least, my mother, Natalie, insisted it was so. Natalie was my North Star, my comforter, my protector. I was her first child and she never got over the miracle of birth. She could not talk about me without the aid of a thesaurus. I was brilliant, talented, handsome, and witty—and that was before I was six months old.

I never addressed my parents as "mother" and "father." They preferred that I called them "Natalie" and "Otto," possibly because it made them feel younger.

Natalie Marcus was born in Slavitka, Russia, near Odessa, during the reign of the czars. When she was ten years old, she escaped a Russian pogrom against Jews, and was brought to America by her mother, Anna.

Natalie was a beauty. She was five foot five tall, with soft brown hair, intelligent gray eyes, and lovely features. She had the soul of a romantic and a rich inner life. She had no formal education, but she had taught herself to read. She loved classical music and books. Her dream was to marry a prince and travel around the world.

Her prince turned out to be Otto Schechtel, a Chicago street fighter who had dropped out of school after the sixth grade. Otto was handsome and charming, and it was easy to see why Natalie had been attracted to him. They were both dreamers, but they had different dreams. Natalie dreamed of a romantic world, with castles in Spain and moonlit gondola rides in Venice, while Otto's fantasies consisted of impractical get-rich-quick schemes. Someone said that all it took to be a successful writer was paper and a pen and a dysfunctional family. I was raised by two such families.

In this corner I would like to present the Marcus clan: two brothers, Sam and Al, and three sisters, Pauline, Natalie, and Fran.

And in the opposite corner, we have the Schechtels, five sisters and two brothers: Harry and Otto, and Rose, Bess, Emma, Mildred, and Tillie.

The Schechtels were extroverts, informal and street-smart. The Marcuses were introverted and reserved. The two families were not only dissimilar; they had absolutely nothing in common. And so, fate decided to amuse itself.

Harry Schechtel married Pauline Marcus. Otto Schechtel married Natalie Marcus. Tillie Schechtel married Al Marcus. And if that were not enough, Sam Marcus married Pauline's best friend. It was a marital feeding frenzy.

Otto's older brother, Harry, was the most formidable member of the Schechtel clan. He was five foot ten, muscular and powerful, with a commanding personality. If we had been Italian, he would have been the consigliere. He was the one that Otto and the others went to for advice. Harry and Pauline had four young boys—Seymour,

Eddie, Howard, and Steve. Seymour was only six months older than I, but he always seemed older than his age.

In the Marcus family, Al was the charmer, good-looking and amusing, the family bon vivant. He liked to gamble and flirt. Sam Marcus was the solemn elder statesman who disapproved of the Schechtels' lifestyle. Sam's business was running checkroom concessions in various Chicago hotels.

Sometimes when my uncles got together, they would go into a corner and talk about a mysterious thing called sex. It sounded wonderful. I prayed that it wouldn't go away before I grew up.

Otto was a spendthrift who enjoyed throwing money around, whether he had it or not. He would often invite a dozen guests to an expensive restaurant, and when the bill came, borrow the money from one of them to pay the tab.

Natalie could not stand borrowing or owing money. She had a strong sense of responsibility. As I grew older, I began to realize how totally unsuited they were for each other. My mother was miserable, married to a man she had no respect for, living an inner life that he could not understand. My father had married a fairytale princess, only to find himself bewildered when the honeymoon ended.

They argued constantly, but these were not normal arguments; they were bitter and vicious. They found each other's weak points and tore at them. The arguing became so savage that I would run out of the house to the public library, where I escaped to the peaceful and serene worlds of the Hardy Boys and the Tom Swift books.

One day when I got home from school, Otto and Natalie were screaming obscenities at each other. I decided I couldn't stand it any longer. I needed help. I went to my Aunt Pauline, Natalie's sister. She was a sweet, loving dumpling of a woman, pragmatic and intelligent.

When I arrived, Pauline took one look at me and said, "What's the matter?"

I was in tears. "It's Nat and Otto. They fight all the time. I don't know what to do."

Pauline frowned. "They're fighting in front of you?"

I nodded.

"All right. I'll tell you what you do. They both love you, Sidney, and they don't want to hurt you, so the next time they start to fight, you go up to them and tell them that you don't want them to ever fight in front of you again. Will you do that?"

I nodded. "Yes."

Aunt Pauline's advice worked.

Natalie and Otto were in the middle of a shouting match when I walked up to them and said, "Don't do this to me. Please don't fight in front of me."

They were both immediately contrite. Natalie said, "Of course. You're right, darling. It won't happen again."

And Otto said, "I'm sorry, Sidney. We have no right to put our problems on you."

After that, the arguments continued, but at least they were muffled by the bedroom walls.

We were constantly on the move from city to city, with Otto looking for work. When someone would ask me what my father did for a living, my answer always depended on where we were. In Texas, he worked in a jewelry store; in Chicago, it was a clothing store; in Arizona, it was a depleted silver mine; in Los Angeles, he sold siding.

Twice a year, Otto would take me shopping for clothes. The "shop" was a truck parked in an alley, filled with beautiful suits. They were so new that they still had their price tags on them and they were remarkably inexpensive.

In 1925, my brother, Richard, was born. I was eight years old. We were living in Gary, Indiana, at that time, and I remember how thrilled I was to have a brother, an ally against the dark forces of my life. It was one of the most exciting events of my life. I had big plans for us, and I was looking forward to all the things we were going to do together as he got older. Meanwhile, I raced him around Gary in his buggy.

During the Depression, our financial situation was something out of *Alice in Wonderland*. Otto would be away, working on one of his fantasy mega-deals, while Natalie, Richard, and I lived in a dreary, cramped apartment. Suddenly Otto would appear and announce that he had just made a deal that paid him a thousand dollars a week. Before we knew it, we would be living in a grand penthouse in another city. It seemed like a dream.

It always turned out to be a dream, because a few months later, Otto's deal would have vanished and we would be back living in a little apartment again, in a different city.

I felt like a displaced person. If we had had a family crest, it would have been a picture of a moving van. Before I was seventeen, I had lived in eight cities and attended eight grammar schools and three high schools. I was always the new kid on the block—an outsider.

Otto was a great salesman and when I started at a new school, in another city, he would always take me to see the principal on the first day, and almost invariably he would talk him into promoting me a grade. The result of that was that I was always the youngest boy in the class, creating another barrier to making friends. Consequently I became shy, pretending that I enjoyed being a loner. It was a very disruptive life. Each time I would start to make friends, it was time to say goodbye.

Where the money came from I don't know, but Natalie bought a little secondhand spinet piano, and she insisted I start taking piano lessons.

"Why?" Otto asked.

"You'll see," Natalie said. "Sidney even has the hands of a musician."

I enjoyed the lessons, but they ended a few months later, when we moved to Detroit.

Otto's proudest boast was that he never read a book in his life. It was Natalie who instilled the love of reading in me. Otto was concerned because I enjoyed sitting at home, reading books I took from the public library, when I could have been out on the street, playing baseball.

"You're going to ruin your eyes," he would keep saying. "Why can't you be like your cousin Seymour? He plays football with the boys."

My Uncle Harry went further. I overheard him saying to my father, "Sidney reads too much. He's going to come to a bad end."

When I was ten years old, I made matters worse by starting to write. There was a poetry contest in *Wee Wisdom*, a children's magazine. I wrote a poem and asked Otto to send it to the magazine to enter it in the contest.

The fact that I was writing made Otto nervous. The fact that I was writing poetry made him *very* nervous. I later learned that because he did not want to be embarrassed when the magazine rejected my poem, he took my name off it, substituted my Uncle Al's name, and sent it in to the magazine.

Two weeks later, Otto was having lunch with Al.

"The damnedest thing happened, Otto. Why would *Wee Wisdom* magazine send me a check for five dollars?"

Thus, my first professional writing was published under the name of Al Marcus.

One day, my mother came running into the apartment, breathless. She hugged me and exclaimed, "Sidney, I've just come from Bea Factor. She says you're going to be world-famous! Isn't that wonderful?"

Bea Factor was a friend who was reputed to be a psychic and there were many acquaintances of hers who verified it.

To me, it was wonderful that my mother believed her.

In the twenties and thirties, Chicago was a city of noisy elevated trains, horse-drawn ice wagons, crowded beaches, strip clubs, the smell of the stockyards, and the St. Valentine's Day Massacre, where seven mobsters were lined up against a wall in a garage and machine-gunned down.

The school system was run like the city—tough and aggressive. Instead of "show and tell," it was "throw and tell." And it wasn't the students who were throwing things; it was the teachers. One morning, when I was in third grade, a teacher was displeased by something a pupil said. She picked up one of the heavy glass inkwells that were set on each desk and hurled it across the room at the student. If it had hit him in the head, it would have killed him. I was too terrified to return to school that afternoon.

My favorite subject in school was English. Part of the

class assignment was taking turns reading aloud from a book called the *Elgin Reader* that contained short stories. We would turn to a story by Poe or O'Henry or Tarkington, and I would dream that one day the teacher would say, "Turn to page twenty in your reader," and lo and behold, there would be a story written by me. Where that dream came from, I do not know. Perhaps it was an atavistic throwback to some long-gone ancestor.

The tenth floor of the Sovereign Hotel was the neighborhood's ole swimmin' hole. Whenever possible, I would take Richard there to play in the pool. He was five years old.

On this particular day, I deposited him in the shallow end and I swam to the deep end. While I was talking to some people, Richard got out of the pool, looking for me. He came to the deep end of the pool, slipped and fell in. He went straight to the bottom. I saw what had happened, dove down, and pulled him up.

No more ole swimmin' hole for us.

When I was twelve years old, in the seventh grade at Marshall Field grammar school, in Chicago, I was in an English class where we were allowed to work on our own projects. I decided to write a play about a detective investigating a murder. When it was finished, I turned it in to my teacher. She read the play, called me to her desk, and said, "I think this is really good, Sidney. Would you like to stage it?"

Would I! "Yes, ma'am."

"I'll arrange for you to put it on in the main auditorium."

And suddenly I remembered Natalie's excitement

about Bea Factor's prediction. *Sidney is going to be world-famous.*

I was filled with excitement. This was the beginning. When the class heard the news, everyone wanted to be cast in the play. I decided that not only would I produce it and direct it, but I would also star in it. I had never directed before, of course, but I knew exactly what I wanted.

I began casting. I was allowed to rehearse after school in the huge auditorium and soon my play was the talk of the school. I was given all the props I asked for: couches, chairs, tables, a telephone . . .

It was one of the happiest times of my life. I knew without question that this was the beginning of a wonderful career. If I could write a successful play at my age, there was no limit to how far I could go. I would have plays on Broadway with my name in lights.

I held a final dress rehearsal with my classmates who had been cast by me, and the rehearsal went perfectly.

I went to my teacher. "I'm ready," I said. "When would you like me to put the play on?"

She was beaming at me. "Why don't we do it tomorrow?"

I got no sleep that night. I felt that my whole future depended on the success of the play. Lying in bed, I went over it scene by scene, looking for flaws. I could find none. The dialogue was excellent, the plot moved swiftly, and the play had an unexpected twist at the end. Everyone was going to love it.

The next morning, when I arrived at school, my teacher had a surprise for me.

"I've arranged to have all the English classes dismissed so that they can come down to the auditorium to see your play."

I could not believe it. This was going to be a far bigger triumph than I had imagined.

At ten o'clock in the morning, the huge auditorium was filled. Not only were all the students in the English classes there, but the principal and teachers who had heard about my play were present, eager to see the work of the child prodigy.

In the midst of all this excitement, I was calm. *Very* calm. It seemed only natural that this was happening to me at such an early age. *You're going to be world-famous.*

It was show time. The conversations in the auditorium began to die down and the theater became hushed. The set consisted of a simple living room where a boy and girl were playing a husband and wife whose friend had been murdered. They were seated next to each other on a sofa.

I was playing the detective investigating the murder. I stood in the wings, ready to make my entrance. My cue was the boy on stage looking at his watch and saying, "The inspector should be here soon." But instead of "soon," he started to say "any minute," and he caught himself and tried to change "minute" to "soon." What came out was, "The inspector should be here any minsoon." He quickly corrected himself, but it was too late. *Minsoon?* That was the funniest sound I had ever heard. It was so funny, I had to laugh. And I could not stop. The more I thought about it, the louder I laughed.

The boy and girl on the stage were staring at me in the wings, waiting for me to make my entrance. I could not move because I was laughing too hard. I was helpless. The laughing took over completely and I became more and more hysterical.

The play had come to a standstill before it started.

After what seemed an eternity, from the auditorium I

heard my teacher's voice calling, "Sidney, come out here."

I forced myself to leave the shelter of the wings and stumble out to the center of the stage. My teacher was in the middle of the auditorium, on her feet, listening to my frenzied outburst. "Stop it," she commanded.

But how could I? *Minsoon?*

The audience began getting up and drifting out of the auditorium and I watched them go, pretending that I was laughing because I wanted to, pretending that what was happening was not important.

Pretending that I did not want to die.

CHAPTER

3

By 1930, the Depression had gotten deeper and was squeezing the economic life out of the country. Bread lines had increased and unemployment was pandemic. There were riots in the streets.

I had graduated from Marshall Field grammar school in Chicago, and had a job at Afremow's drugstore. Natalie was working as a cashier at a roller derby, a new craze that took place in large roller dome arenas with huge circular wooden rinks where intrepid men on roller skates raced around the rink, knocking down their rivals and committing as much mayhem as they could while the audience cheered them on.

Otto, meanwhile, was traveling around the country putting together his hypothetical mega-deals.

Intermittently, he would come home from the road filled with enthusiasm.

"I have a good feeling about this. I just made a deal that's going to put us on easy street."

And we would pack up and move to Hammond, or Dallas, or Kirkland Junction, in Arizona.

"Kirkland *Junction*?"

"You'll love it there," Otto promised. "I bought a silver mine."

Kirkland turned out to be a small town, 104 miles from Phoenix, but that was not our destination. Kirkland *Junction* was a dilapidated gas station, and we ended up living in the back of it for three miserable months while Otto tried to corner the silver market. It turned out that there was no silver in the mine.

We were saved by a phone call from Uncle Harry.

"How's the silver mine?" Harry asked.

"Not good," Otto said.

"Don't worry about it. I'm in Denver. I have a great stock brokerage company going. I want you to join me."

"We're on our way," Otto told him. He hung up and turned to Natalie, Richard, and me. "We're moving to Denver. I have a good feeling about this."

Denver turned out to be a delight. It was pristine and beautiful, with cool breezes sweeping down from the snowcapped mountains through the city. I loved it.

Harry and Pauline had found a luxurious, two-story mansion in an elegant section of Denver. The back of their home looked out on an enormous, verdant piece of land called Cheeseman Park. My cousins, Seymour, Howard, Eddie, and Steve, were glad to see us, and we were delighted to see them.

Seymour was driving a bright red Pierce Arrow and dating girls older than himself. Eddie had been given a saddle horse for his birthday. Howard was winning junior tennis matches. The moneyed atmosphere in their lives was a far cry from our dreary existence in Chicago.

"Are we going to live with Harry and Pauline?" I asked.

"No." They had a surprise for me. "We're going to buy a home here."

When I saw the house they were going to buy, I could hardly believe it. It was large, with a lovely garden, in a quiet suburb on Marion Street. The rooms were large, beautiful, and welcoming. The furniture was fresh and lovely, far different from the musty furniture in the apartments I had lived in all my life. This was more than a house. This was a home. The moment I walked in the front door, I felt that my life had changed, that I finally had roots. There would be no more moving around the country every few months, changing apartments and schools.

Otto is going to buy this house. I'm going to get married here and my children will grow up here . . .

For the first time in my memory, money was plentiful. Harry's business was doing so well that he now owned three brokerage firms.

In the fall of 1930, at the age of thirteen, I enrolled at East High School and it turned out to be a very pleasant experience. The teachers in Denver were friendly and helpful. There was no throwing of inkwells at students. I was starting to make friends at school, and I enjoyed the thought of going home to the beautiful house that was soon to be ours. Natalie and Otto seemed to have settled most of their personal problems, which made life even sweeter.

One day, during a gym class, I slipped, hurt my spine, and tore something loose. The pain was excruciating. I lay on the floor, unable to move. They carried me to the school doctor's office.

When he was through examining me, I asked, "Am I going to be crippled?"

"No," he assured me. "One of your discs has torn

loose and it's pressing against your spinal cord. That's what's causing the pain. The treatment is very simple. All you have to do is lie still in bed for two or three days with hot packs to relax the muscles, and the disc will slip back into place. You'll be as good as new."

An ambulance took me home and the paramedics put me to bed. I lay there in pain, but just as the doctor had said, in three days the pain was gone.

I had no idea how deeply this incident was going to affect the rest of my life.

One day I had an out-of-this-world experience. There was an advertisement for a county fair in Denver, where one of the attractions was a ride in an airplane.

"I'd like to go up," I told Otto.

He thought about it. "All right."

The plane was a beautiful Lincoln Commander and it was a thrill just to get in it.

The pilot looked at me and said, "First time?"

"First time."

"Fasten your seatbelt," he said. "You're in for a thrill."

He was right. Flying was a surreal experience. I watched the earth swoop up and down and disappear, and I had never felt anything so exhilarating in my life.

When we landed, I said to Otto, "I want to go up again."

And I did. I was determined that someday I was going to be a pilot.

Early one morning in the spring of 1933, Otto came into my bedroom. His face was grim. "Pack your things. We're leaving."

I was puzzled. "Where are we going?"

"We're going back to Chicago."

I could not believe it. "We're leaving Denver?"

"That's right."

"But—"

He was gone.

I got dressed and went to see Natalie. "What happened?"

"Your father and Harry had a—a misunderstanding."

I looked around at the home that I thought I was going to live in for the rest of my life. "What about this house?"

"We're not buying it."

Our return to Chicago was joyless. Neither Otto nor Natalie wanted to talk about what had happened. After Denver, Chicago seemed even more unfriendly and uncaring. We moved into a small apartment and I was back to reality, a grim reminder that we had no money, and that a decent job was impossible to get. Otto was on the road again and Natalie was working as a salesclerk at a department store. My dream of going to college died. There was no money for my tuition. The apartment walls were closing in on me. Everything smelled gray.

I can't spend the rest of my life living this way, I thought. The poverty we lived in now seemed even worse after the brief, heady taste of affluence in Denver, and we were desperately short of money. Working as a delivery boy for a pharmacy was not my future.

That was when I had decided I would commit suicide, and Otto had talked me out of it by telling me I had to keep turning the pages. But the pages were not turning and I had nothing to look forward to. Otto's promise had been empty words.

When September came around, I enrolled at Senn High School. Otto was on the road again, trying to make mega-deals. Natalie was working full-time at a dress shop, but not enough money was coming in. I had to find a way to help . . .

I thought about Natalie's older brother, Sam, and the checkroom concessions he owned at several hotels in the Loop. The checkrooms were staffed with attractive, scantily-dressed young women, and hang boys. The customers were generous with their tips to the women. They had no idea that the money went to the management.

I took the elevated train downtown to the Loop to see my Uncle Sam. He was in his office at the Sherman Hotel.

He greeted me warmly. "Well, this is a nice surprise. What can I do for you, Sidney?"

"I need a job."

"Oh?"

"I was hoping that maybe I could work in the check-room at one of your hotels as a hang boy."

Sam knew our financial situation. He looked at me thoughtfully. Finally he said, "Why not? You look older than seventeen. I think the Bismarck Hotel can use you."

And he put me to work that week.

Being a hang boy was simple. The customers would give their coats and hats to the female attendant, who handed them a numbered check. She would then turn their coats and hats over to me, and I would hang them up on corresponding numbered racks. When the cus-tomer returned, the process would be reversed.

I now had a new schedule. I went to school until three, and immediately after school, I would take the El south to the Loop, get off at the station near the Bis-marck Hotel, and go to work. My hours were from five P.M. to closing, which was sometimes midnight or later, depending on whether there was a special party. My salary was three dollars a night. I turned the money over to Natalie.

Weekends were the busiest time for parties at the hotels, so I found myself working seven evenings a week. Holidays were emotionally difficult for me. Families came to the hotel for Christmas and New Year's Eve celebrations and I watched the children celebrating with their mothers and fathers, and I envied them. Natalie was busy working and Otto was gone, so Richard and I were alone, and had no one to celebrate with. At eight o'clock, while everyone else enjoyed their holiday dinners, I would hurry out to a coffee shop or a diner, have a quick bite to eat, and return to work.

The bright spot in my nightly routine was when my Aunt Frances, Natalie's effervescent younger sister, came to work at the Bismarck checkroom for a night or two. She was a small and vivacious brunette, with a quick sense of humor, and the customers adored her.

A new checkroom attendant, Joan Vitucci, came to work at the Bismarck. She was only a year older than I, and she was very pretty. I was attracted to her, and I began to fantasize about her. I would start by taking her out on dates. Even though I had no money, she would see the positive things about me. We would fall in love and get married, and we would have wonderful children.

One evening she said, "My aunt and uncle have a family lunch every Sunday. I think you would like them. If you're free this Sunday, why don't you join us?"

The fantasy was coming true.

That Sunday turned out to be a lovely experience. It was a warm, Italian family gathering of about a dozen adults and children sitting around a large dining room table, filling up on bruschetta, pasta fagioli, chicken cacciatore, and baked lasagna.

Joan's uncle was an affable, gregarious man named Louie Alterie, the head of the Chicago janitors union.

When it was time to leave, I thanked everyone and told Joan what a great time I had had. This was the real beginning of our relationship.

The following morning, Louie Alterie was machine-gunned to death as he was leaving his building where we had had lunch.

Joan disappeared from my life.

That was the end of the fantasy.

Between school during the day, the checkroom nights, and the drugstore Saturdays, I had little time for myself.

Something strange seemed to be happening at home. There was tension, but it was a different kind of tension. Natalie and Otto were whispering things to each other, and looking grim.

One morning, Otto came in to me and said, "Son, I'm going to the farm. I'm leaving today."

I was surprised. I had never been on a farm and I thought it would be fun. "I'd like to go with you, Otto."

He shook his head. "I'm sorry. I can't take you."

"But—"

"No, Sidney."

"Okay. When will you be back?"

"In three years." He walked away.

Three years? I couldn't believe it. How could he desert us for three years to live on a farm?

Natalie came into the room. I turned to her. "What's going on?"

"I'm afraid I have bad news for you, Sidney. Your father got mixed up with some evil people," she said. "He was selling vending machines to stores. What your father didn't know was that there were no vending machines. The men he worked for took the money and ran. But they were caught, and your father was found guilty, along with them. He's going to prison."

I was shocked. *So, that's the farm.* "For three years?" I did not know what to say. *What are we going to do without him for three years?*

As it turned out, I need not have worried.

Twelve months after Otto reported to Lafayette State Prison, he was on his way back home, a hero.

CHAPTER

4

We had read the story of Otto's heroism in the newspapers and had heard it over and over on the radio, but we wanted to hear it from Otto. I had no idea what prison did to a man, but somehow I had the feeling that he would come home changed; pale and burdened down. I was in for a pleasant surprise.

When Otto walked through the front door of our apartment, he was grinning and cheerful. "I'm back," he said.

There were hugs all around. "We want to hear what happened."

Otto smiled. "I'll be happy to tell it again." He sat down at the kitchen table and he began. "I was working inside the grounds of the prison with the regular cleaning crew. About fifty feet away, there was a huge reservoir that supplied the prison's water. It was surrounded by a wall that was about ten feet high. I looked up and saw a little boy come out of a building. He was probably three or four years old. The work crew had finished and I was alone.

"When I looked up again, the boy was climbing the steps of the reservoir wall, and was almost at the top. It was dangerous. I looked around for his baby-sitter or nurse or someone, but there was no one. As I watched, the little boy reached the top. He slipped and fell down into the reservoir. A guard in the tower saw what had happened, but I knew that he could never get to the boy in time.

"I got up and ran like hell to the wall. I climbed it as fast as I could. When I got to the top, I looked down and I could see the boy going under. I jumped down, into the water, and managed to grab him. I was fighting to keep the two of us afloat.

"Then, help arrived and they pulled us out. They put me in the hospital for a couple of days because I had swallowed a lot of water and I had some bruises from the jump."

We were hanging on his every word.

"As luck had it, the boy was the warden's son. The warden and his wife came to visit me in the hospital to thank me." Otto looked up at us and smiled. "And that would have been the end of it except for one thing. They found out that I couldn't swim and that's when everything got crazy. Suddenly I was a hero. It was in the newspaper and on the radio. There were phone calls and letters and telegrams coming into the prison offering me jobs and asking for leniency for me. The warden and the governor had a meeting and they decided that since my offense wasn't too serious, that it might be good public relations to pardon me." Otto held out his arms. "And here I am."

We were a family again.

It might have been a coincidence, but suddenly a scholarship that I had applied for a year earlier from

B'nai B'rith—a Jewish philanthropic organization—had been awarded to me.

It was like a miracle. I was going to be the first one in my family to go to college. A page had turned. I decided that maybe there might be a future for me somewhere after all. But even with the scholarship, we were desperately short of money.

Could I handle the checkroom job seven nights a week, Afremow's on Saturdays, and a full college schedule?

I would see.

Northwestern University is located in Evanston, Illinois, twelve miles north of Chicago. The university, a two-hundred-forty-acre campus on the shore of Lake Michigan, was spectacular. At nine o'clock on a Monday morning, I walked into the office of the registrar.

"I'm here to enter the university."

"Your name?"

"Sidney Schechtel."

The registrar picked up a heavy volume and looked through it. "Here we are. What courses would you like to take?"

"All of them."

She looked up at me. "What?"

"I mean as many as I'm allowed. While I'm here, I want to learn all I can."

"What are you mostly interested in?"

"Literature."

I watched her go through some pamphlets. She picked one up and handed it to me. "Here's a list of our courses."

I scanned the list. "This is great." I checked off the courses I wanted and then handed the list back to her.

She looked at it and said, "You're taking the maximum amount of courses?"

"That's right." I frowned. "But Latin isn't there. I really do want to take Latin."

She was looking at me. "Do you really think you can handle all this?"

I smiled. "No problem."

She wrote down "Latin."

From the registrar's office, I went to the cafeteria kitchen. "Can you use a busboy?"

"Always."

So I had another job, but it was not enough. I felt impelled to do more, as though I were making up for lost time. That afternoon, I went to the offices of the *Daily Northwestern*, the school newspaper.

"I'm Sidney Schechtel," I told the man behind the desk with a sign marked "Editor." "I'd like to work on the paper."

"Sorry," he said, "we're full up. Try us next year."

"Next year will be too late." I stood there thinking. "Do you have a show business section?"

"A show business section?"

"Yes. Celebrities are always coming to Chicago to do shows here. Don't you have someone to interview them for the paper?"

"No. We—"

"Do you know who's in town right now, dying to be interviewed? Katharine Hepburn!"

"We're not set up to—"

"And Clifton Webb."

"We've never had a—"

"Walter Pidgeon."

"I can talk to someone, but I'm afraid—"

"George M. Cohan."

He was getting interested. "Do you know these people?"

I did not hear the question. "There's no time to lose. When their shows close, they're leaving."

"All right. I'm going to take a chance on you, Schechtel."

He had no idea how excited I was. "That's the best decision you've ever made."

"We'll see. When can you start?"

"I've already started. You'll have the first interview in your next edition."

He looked at me in amazement. "Already? Who is it?"

"It's a surprise."

It was a surprise to me, too.

In what spare time I had, I interviewed many minor celebrities for the newspaper. My first interview was with Guy Kibbee, who was a minor character actor at the time. The major stars were too important to be interviewed for a school newspaper.

I was working in the checkroom and the drugstore, I was taking the maximum number of courses at school, plus Latin, I had a job as a busboy, and I was on staff at the *Daily Northwestern*. But it still wasn't enough. It's as though I were driven. I thought about what else I could do. Northwestern had a great winning football team, and there was no reason I couldn't be on it. *I'm sure the Wildcats could use me.*

The following morning, I went out to the football field where the team was practicing. Pug Rentner, who went on to a glorious career in the NFL, was the star of the team that year. I walked up to the coach, who was on the sidelines watching the action. "Can I talk to you for a minute?"

"What's on your mind?"

"I'd like to try out for the team."

He looked me over. "You would, huh? You've got a pretty good build. Where did you play?"

I didn't answer.

"High school? College?"

"No, sir."

"Grammar school?"

"No, sir."

He was staring at me. "You've *never* played football?"

"No, but I'm very quick and—"

"And you'd like to be on this team? Son, forget about it." And his attention went back to the scrimmage.

That was the end of my football aspirations.

The professors at Northwestern were wonderful and the classes were exciting. I was hungry to learn everything I could. The week after I started school, I passed a sign in the corridor that read: "Tryouts tonight. Northwestern Debating Team." I stopped and stared at it. I knew it was insane and yet I felt compelled to try out.

There is a maxim that death is the number two fear that people have and public speaking is the first. That was certainly so in my case. To me, there was nothing more terrifying than public speaking. But I was obsessed. I had to do everything. I had to keep turning the pages.

When I walked into the designated tryout room, it was filled with young men and women waiting their turn. I took a seat and listened. All the speakers sounded fantastic. They were articulate and spoke fluently, with great confidence.

Finally it was my turn. I got up and walked over to the microphone.

The man in charge said, "Your name?"

"Sidney Schechtel."

"Your subject?"

I had prepared for this. "Capitalism versus communism."

He nodded. "Go ahead."

I began to speak and I thought it was going very well. When I got halfway through my subject, I stopped. I was frozen. I had no idea what came next. There was a long, nervous pause. I mumbled something to end the speech and slunk out, cursing myself.

A student at the door said, "Aren't you a freshman?"

"That's right."

"Didn't anyone tell you?"

"Tell me what?"

"Freshmen aren't allowed on the debating team. You have to be an upperclassman."

Oh, good, I thought. *Now I have an excuse for my failure.*

The following morning the names of the winners were posted on the bulletin board. Out of curiosity, I took a look at it. One of the names was "Shekter." Someone with a name similar to mine had been chosen. At the bottom of the board was a notice that those who had been selected should report at three-thirty in the afternoon to the debate coach.

At four o'clock, I received a telephone call. "Shekter, what happened to you?"

I had no idea what he was talking about. "What? Nothing."

"Didn't you see the notice to report to the debate coach?"

Shekter. They had gotten my name wrong. "Yes, but I thought— I'm a freshman."

"I know. We've decided to make an exception in your case. We're changing the rules."

So I became the first freshman ever to be accepted on the Northwestern Varsity Debating Team.

Another page had turned.

As busy as I forced myself to be, something was still missing. I had no idea what it was. Somehow I felt unfulfilled. I had a deep sense of anomie, a feeling of anxiety and isolation. On the campus, watching the hordes of students hurrying to and from their classes, I thought, *They're all anonymous. When they die, no one will ever know that they lived on this earth.* A wave of depression swept over me. *I want people to know I've been here,* I thought. *I want people to know I've been here. I want to make a difference.*

The next day my depression was worse. I felt that I was being smothered by heavy black clouds. Finally, in desperation, I made an appointment to see the college psychologist, to find out what was wrong with me.

On the way to see him, for no reason I started to feel so cheerful that I began to sing aloud. When I reached the entrance of the building where the psychologist was located, I stopped.

I don't need to see him, I thought. *I'm happy. He'll think I'm crazy.*

It was a bad decision. If I had gone to see him, I would have learned that day what I did not find out until many years later.

My depression returned and showed no signs of abating.

Money was getting tighter. Otto was having difficulty getting a job and Natalie was clerking in a department store six days a week. I worked every night in the checkroom and at Afremow's on Saturday afternoons, but even with what Otto and Natalie earned, it was not enough. By February of 1935, we were far behind on the rent.

One night, I heard Otto and Natalie talking. Natalie said, "I don't know what we're going to do. Everybody is beginning to press us. Maybe I can get a night job."

No, I thought. My mother was already working at a full-time job and came home and made dinner for us, and cleaned the apartment. I could not let her do more.

The next morning, I quit Northwestern.

When I told Natalie what I had done, she was horrified. "You can't quit college, Sidney." Her eyes were filled with tears. "We're going to be all right."

But I knew we were not going to be all right. I started looking for another job, but 1935 was the height of the Depression and there weren't any to be found. I tried advertising agencies, newspapers, and radio stations, but no one was hiring.

On my way to another interview at a radio station, I passed a large department store called Mandel Brothers. Inside, it looked busy. Half a dozen salesmen were servicing customers. I decided I had nothing to lose, and I walked in and looked around. I started walking through the store. It was enormous. I passed the ladies' shoe department and stopped. *This would be an easy job.*

A man came up to me. "Can I help you?"

"I'd like to see the manager."

"I'm Mr. Young, the manager. What can I do for you?"

"I'm looking for a job. Do you have any openings?"

He studied me a moment. "As a matter of fact, I do. Have you had experience selling ladies' shoes?"

"Oh, yes," I assured him.

"Where did you work before?"

I recalled a store where I had bought shoes. "Thom McCann, in Denver."

"Good. Come into the office." He handed me a form. "Fill this out."

When I had finished, he picked it up and looked at it. Then he looked at me.

"First of all, Mr. Schechtel, 'McCann' is not spelled 'M-I-C-K-A-N.' And secondly, it's not located at this address."

I needed this job desperately. "They must have moved," I said quickly, "and I'm a terrible speller. You see—"

"I hope you're a better salesman than you are a liar."

I nodded, depressed, and turned to leave. "Thanks, anyway."

"Wait a minute. I'm hiring you."

I looked at him, surprised. "You are? Why?"

"My boss thinks that only people with experience can sell ladies' shoes. I think anyone can learn to do it quickly. You're going to be an experiment."

"Thank you," I said, gratefully. "I won't let you down."

I went to work, filled with optimism.

Fifteen minutes later, I was fired.

What happened was that I had committed an unforgivable sin.

My first customer was a well-dressed lady who approached me in the shoe department.

"Can I help you?"

"I want a pair of black pumps, size 7B."

I gave her my best salesman smile. "No problem."

I went into the back room where shoes were stored on large racks. There were hundreds of boxes, all labeled on the outside—5B . . . 6W . . . 6B . . . 7A . . . 8N . . . 8 . . . 9B . . . 9N. No 7B. I was getting desperate. There was an 8 Narrow. *She'll never know the difference,* I decided. I took the shoes out of the box and brought them to her.

"Here we are," I said.

I put them on her feet. She looked at them a moment.

"Is this a 7B?"

"Oh, yes, ma'am."

She studied me a moment. "You're sure?"

"Oh, yes."

"You're sure this is a 7B?"

"Positive."

"I want to see the manager."

That was the end of my career in the ladies' shoe department.

That afternoon, I was transferred to haberdashery.

CHAPTER

5

Even though I was working six days a week in haberdashery at Mandel Brothers, seven nights a week at downtown hotel checkrooms, and Saturdays at Afremow's drugstore, the money was still short. Otto got a part-time job working in a boiler room on the South Side, an operation that would now be called telemarketing, the object being to sell products to strangers over the telephone.

This particular operation was in a large bare room, with a dozen men, each with a telephone, talking simultaneously to prospects, trying to sell them oil wells, hot stocks, or anything else that would sound like an inviting investment. It was a high-pressure operation. The names and phone numbers of potential customers were obtained from master lists sold to whomever was running boiler rooms. The salesmen got a commission on the sales they made.

Otto would come home at night and talk excitedly about the boiler room. Since it was open seven days a week, I decided to drop by to see if I could earn some extra money on Sundays. Otto arranged for me to have a tryout, and the following Sunday I went to work with him. When I arrived, I stood there, in the dreary room, listening to the sales pitches.

". . . Mr. Collins, it's a lucky thing for you that I was able to reach you. My name is Jason Richards and I have some great news for you. You and your family have just won a free VIP trip to Bermuda. All you have to do is send me a check for . . ."

". . . Mr. Adams, I have some wonderful news for you. My name is Brown, Jim Brown. I know that you invest in stocks, and there's a new issue coming out that's going to have a hundred percent rise in the next six weeks. Not many people know about it, but if you want to make some real money . . ."

". . . Mrs. Doyle, this is Charlie Chase. Congratulations. You and your husband and little Amanda and Peter have been selected for a free trip to . . ."

And so it went.

It amazed me how many people actually bought the pie-in-the-sky offered by the salesmen. For some reason, doctors seemed to be the most gullible. They would buy almost anything. Most of the products that were sold were either defective, overpriced, inferior, or nonexistent.

I had my fill of the boiler room that Sunday and never returned.

My job at Mandel Brothers was boring and easy, but I was not looking for easy. I wanted a challenge, something that would give me a chance to grow. I knew that if I did well there, I would have a chance of moving up. One day I might be made head of the department. Mandel Brothers had a chain of stores around the country, so in time I could become a regional manager and even work my way up to president.

On a Monday morning, my boss, Mr. Young, came over to me. "I have some bad news for you, Schechtel."

I was staring at him. "What?"

"I'm going to have to let you go."

I tried to sound calm. "Did I do something wrong?"

"No. All the departments have orders to cut overhead. You were the last one hired, so you're going to have to be the first to go."

I felt as though someone had taken my heart and squeezed it. I needed this job desperately. He had no idea that he was not only firing a clerk in the haberdashery department, but that he was firing the future president of the company.

I knew I had to find another job as quickly as possible. Debts were piling up. We owed grocery bills, the landlord was getting nasty, and our utilities, which had already been shut off several times, were about to be shut off again.

I thought of someone who might be able to help.

Charley Fine, a longtime friend of my father, was an executive at a large manufacturing company. I asked Otto whether he thought it would be all right if I talked to Charley about getting a job.

Otto thought about it for a moment, looked at me and said, "I'll talk to him for you."

The following morning, I was walking through the huge gates of the Stewart Warner factory, the world's largest manufacturer of automobile gears. The factory was housed in a five-story building that took up an entire block on Diversey Street. A guard escorted me through the factory floor, crowded with huge, arcane machines that looked like prehistoric monsters. The noise from the machines was incredible.

Otto Karp, a short, heavyset man with a thick German accent, was waiting for me.

"So, you're going to work here," he said.

"Yes, sir."

He looked disappointed. "Follow me."

We started walking across the huge factory floor. All the machines were running at full speed.

As we approached one of the machines, Karp said, "This makes drive and driven gears for speedometers. They turn the flexible shaft that drives the speedometer. Understand?"

I had no idea what he was talking about. "Right."

He led me over to the machine next to it. "What you see coming out here are round drive gears that are pressed into the output shaft of the transmission. The long one is the driven gear that's inserted at a right angle to mesh with the drive gear."

I looked at him and wondered: *Chinese? Swahili?*

We went to the next machine. "Here they're making drive gears that press onto the front wheel hub. The driven gear is fixed to the brake backing plate to measure the drive gear. See?"

I nodded.

He walked me over to another machine. "This machine replaces worn gears. The transmission gearing has been standard for a long time. The advantage of the front wheel systems is that axle ratios can be changed, or multiple-ratio rear axles can be used without affecting the speedometer accuracy. See?"

Swahili, I decided. "Of course."

"Now I'll show you your department."

He took me over to the short order department,

where I was to take charge. The machines I had been introduced to were mammoth and were built to turn out huge orders for automobile manufacturers, a half a million gears or more at a time. The short order department consisted of three much smaller machines.

Otto Karp explained, "If someone orders five or ten gears, we can't afford to start up the big machines for that small an order. But these machines here are equipped to turn out as few as one or two gears. When a short order comes in, you will handle it and it can be filled right away."

"How do I do that?"

"First, you will be handed a purchase order. The order can be for anywhere from one to a dozen drive or driven gears. Next, you give the order to the machinist. When the gears are ready, you'll take them to the annealing department, where they'll be hardened. Your next stop is inspection and finally the wrapping department."

It sounded simple enough.

I learned that my predecessor had given the men who worked in the short order department no more than six orders a day. The rest he held back, and the men sat around half the day, doing nothing. I thought it was a waste. Within a month, I had increased the output by fifty percent. At Christmastime, I got my reward. Otto Karp handed me a check for fourteen dollars and said, "Here. You deserve it. You have a dollar raise."

Otto was traveling on the road and Natalie was working six days a week at a dress shop. Richard was going to school. My days at Stewart Warner, working in the drab surroundings of the factory, surrounded by surrealistic machinery, had become mind-numbing. My evenings were just as bad. I rode the El downtown to the Loop, walked into the hotel where I was working, and spent the next few hours receiving and returning overcoats. My life had become an ugly gray rut again and there was no way out.

Riding home on the El late one night, coming from work, an ad in *The Chicago Tribune* caught my eye:

Paul Ash Is Sponsoring an Amateur Contest
Start your career in show business

Paul Ash, a nationally known band leader, was appearing at the Chicago Theatre. The ad was catnip to me. I had no idea what the amateur contest was about, but I knew I wanted to be in it.

On Saturday, before I went to work at the drugstore, I stopped at the Chicago Theatre and asked to see Paul Ash. His manager came out of an office. "What can I do for you?"

"I'd like to enter the amateur contest," I said.

He consulted a paper. "We don't have an announcer yet. Can you handle that?"

"Oh. Yes, sir."

"Good. What's your name?"

What *was* my name? Schechtel was *not* a show business name. People were always misspelling it and mispronouncing it. I needed a name they would remember. The possibilities raced through my mind. *Gable, Cooper, Grant, Stewart, Powell . . .*

The man was staring at me. "Don't you know your name?"

"Of course I do," I said quickly. "It's Sidney Sh— Sheldon. Sidney Sheldon."

He wrote it down. "All right. Be here next Saturday,

Sheldon. Six o'clock. You'll be broadcasting from the studio on a remote from WGN."

Whatever that meant. "Right."

I hurried home to break the news to my parents and my brother, Richard. They were excited. There was one more thing I had to tell them. "I'm using a different name."

"What do you mean?"

"Well, Schechtel is not a show business name. From now on, I'm Sidney Sheldon."

They looked at one another and then shrugged. "Okay."

I had difficulty sleeping for the next few nights. I knew that this finally was the beginning. I was going to win this contest. Paul Ash would give me a contract to travel around the country with him. *Sidney Sheldon* would travel around the country with him.

When Saturday reluctantly dragged its way onto the calendar, I returned to the Chicago Theatre and was ushered into a small broadcast studio, with several other young contestants. There was a comedian, a singer, a female pianist, and an accordion player.

The director said to me, "Sheldon—"

I felt a little thrill. It was the first time anyone had spoken my new name. "Yes, sir?"

"When I point to you, you'll step up to the microphone and start the show. You'll say, 'Good evening, ladies and gentlemen. Welcome to the Paul Ash Amateur Contest. This is your announcer, Sidney Sheldon. We're going to give you an exciting show, so stay tuned!' Got that?"

"Yes, sir."

Fifteen minutes later, the director looked up at the studio clock on the wall and raised his arm. "Quiet, everyone." He began counting. He pointed to me and I was ready for show business. I had never been calmer in my life because I knew that this was the beginning of a wonderful career. And I was going to start under my new show business name.

With great composure, I stepped up to the microphone, took a deep breath, and said, in my best announcer's voice, "Good evening, ladies and gentlemen. Welcome to the Paul Ash Amateur Contest. This is your announcer—Sidney Schechtel."

CHAPTER

6

I recovered enough to introduce the other contestants. The show went well. The accordion player executed a foot-stomping tune, followed by the comedian, who did his bit like a seasoned pro. The singer sang beautifully. Nothing went wrong until the last contestant, the female pianist, was introduced. As soon as I announced her, she panicked, started to cry, and hurriedly fled from the room, leaving us with three minutes of empty air. I knew I had to fill it. I was the announcer.

I stepped back up to the microphone. "Ladies and gentlemen, we all start out as amateurs in life, but as we go on, we grow and become professionals." I got so caught up in my own words that I kept talking until finally the director signaled for me to shut up.

We went off the air. I knew that I had saved the show and they would be grateful for that. Perhaps they would offer me a job as—

The director came up to me. "What the hell's the matter with you, whatever your name is?" he yelled. "You went over by fifteen seconds."

My radio career was ended.

Paul Ash did not invite me to travel around the country with him, but there was one interesting fallout from the Paul Ash Contest. Otto, Natalie, Richard, Seymour, Eddie, Howard, and Steve all changed their last names to "Sheldon." The only remaining "Schechtel" was Uncle Harry.

Early in May, my cousin Seymour stunned us all by announcing that he was getting married.

Seymour was only nineteen, but it seemed to me that he had been an adult for most of his life.

I had met his bride-to-be, Sydney Singer, when I lived in Denver. Sydney was a young, attractive secretary who had worked in Harry's brokerage office, where Seymour met her. I found her to be warm and intelligent, with a nice sense of humor.

The wedding was simple, with just the members of the family there. When the ceremony was over, I congratulated Seymour. "She's a terrific girl," I told him. "Hang on to her."

"Don't worry. I intend to."

Six months later, they went through a bitter divorce.

"What happened?" I asked Seymour.

"She found out I was having an affair."

"And she asked for a divorce?"

"No. She forgave me."

"Then why—?"

"She caught me with someone else. That's when she divorced me."

"Do you ever see her?"

"No, she hates my guts. She told me she never wants to see me again. She went to Hollywood. She has a brother out there. She got a job as a secretary at MGM for a woman director. Dorothy Arzner."

My very brief foray into radio had given me a taste for it and I had become excited about its possibilities. Radio could well be the profession I was looking for. In every minute of my spare time, I haunted WBBM and other Chicago radio stations, looking for a job as an announcer. There were no jobs, period. I had to face the fact that I was back in the same deadly trap, with no prospects for the future.

One Sunday afternoon when everyone was out of the apartment, I sat down at our little spinet piano. I sat there, creating a melody. I decided it was not bad and I put lyrics to it. I called it "My Silent Self." I looked at it and thought *now what?* I could either let it sit inside the piano bench, or I could try to do something with it.

I decided to try to do something.

In that year, 1936, the major hotels in the country had orchestras in their ballrooms that broadcast coast to coast. At the Bismarck Hotel, the orchestra leader was an amiable young musician named Phil Levant. I had never spoken to him, but from time to time, when he passed the checkroom on his way to the ballroom, we would nod at each other.

I resolved to show my song to him. As he passed the checkroom that evening, I said, "Excuse me, Mr. Levant. I've written a song and I wonder if you would mind taking a look at it."

The expression on his face gave me an idea of how many times he had heard that request, but he was very gracious.

"Glad to," he said.

I handed him a copy of the sheet music. He glanced at it and walked away. *That's the end of that,* I thought.

An hour later, Phil Levant was back at the checkroom.

"That song of yours . . ." he said.

I was holding my breath. "Yes?"

"I like it. It's original. I think it could be a hit. Would you mind if I had an orchestration made, and we played it?"

Mind? "No," I said. "That's—that's wonderful."

He liked my song.

The following evening, while I was hanging hats and coats, from around the corner in the huge ballroom I heard "My Silent Self" being played. I was thrilled. Since the orchestra was broadcasting nationwide, people would be hearing my song all over the country. It was a heady feeling.

When I finished work late that night, I went home, exhausted, and got into a hot bath.

Just as I was relaxing, Otto hurried into the bathroom. "There's a telephone call for you."

At this hour? "Who is it?"

"He says his name is Phil Levant."

I leaped out of the tub, grabbed a towel, and hurried to the telephone.

"Mr. Levant?"

"Sheldon, there's a publisher here from Harms Music Company. They heard your song over the air, in New York. They want to publish it."

I almost dropped the phone.

"Can you come down here right away? He's waiting for you."

"I'm on my way." I dried myself off and hurriedly got dressed again. I grabbed a copy of the sheet music.

"What's going on?" Otto asked.

I explained it to him. "Can I borrow the car?"

"Certainly." He handed me the keys. "Be careful."

I hurried downstairs, got into the car, and headed for the Outer Drive, on my way to the Bismarck Hotel. My mind was racing with the excitement of having my first song published, when I heard a siren behind me and saw a flashing red light. As I pulled over to the side of the road, a policeman got off his motorcycle and came up to the car.

"What's your rush?"

"I didn't know I was speeding, Officer. I'm on my way to meet a music publisher at the Bismarck Hotel. I work there, in the checkroom. Someone wants to publish my song and I—"

"Driver's license?"

I showed him my license. He put it in his pocket. "Okay. Follow me."

I was staring at him. "Follow you where? Just give me a ticket. I'm in a big—"

"There's a new procedure," he said. "We're not giving out tickets anymore. We're taking offenders right to the station."

My heart sank. "Officer, I have to go to this meeting. If you could just give me a ticket, I'd be glad to—"

"I said follow me."

I had no choice.

He started up his motorcycle and took off ahead of me. I followed him. Instead of meeting my new publisher, I was on my way to a police station.

I reached the next corner just as the light changed from amber to red. He went through it. I stopped, waiting for it to turn green again. When I started to go, the motorcycle policeman was nowhere in sight. I went slowly to make sure that he didn't think I was trying to lose him.

And the farther I got, the more optimistic I became. He was gone. He had forgotten about me. He was looking for someone else to send to jail. I picked up speed and headed for the Bismarck.

I parked the car in the garage and hurried to the checkroom. I could not believe what I saw. The policeman was inside, waiting for me, and he was furious. "You thought you could get away from me, huh?"

I was bewildered. "I wasn't trying to get away from you. I gave you my driver's license and I told you I was coming here, and—"

"All right," he said. "You're here. Now we're going to the station."

I was desperate. "Let me call my father."

He shook his head. "I've wasted enough—"

"It will only take a second."

"Go ahead. But make it brief."

I dialed my home number.

Otto answered. "Hello."

"Otto—"

"How did it go?"

"I'm on my way to the police station." I explained the situation to him.

Otto said, "Let me talk to the officer."

I held the phone out to the policeman. "My father wants to talk to you."

He reluctantly took the phone. "Yes . . . No, I haven't time to listen. I'm taking your son to the station . . . What? . . . Oh, really? . . . That's interesting. I know what you mean . . . As a matter of fact, I do . . . I have a brother-in-law who needs a job . . . Really? Let me write that down." He took out a pen and a pad and began to write. "That's very nice of you, Mr. Sheldon. I'll send him around in the morning." He glanced at me. "And don't worry about your son."

I was listening to this conversation, open-mouthed. The officer replaced the receiver, handed me my driver's license, and said, "Don't let me catch you speeding again."

I watched him leave.

I said to the hatcheck girl, "Where's Phil Levant?"

"He's conducting the orchestra," she said, "but someone is waiting to see you in the manager's office."

In the manager's office I found a dapper, well-dressed man who appeared to be in his fifties.

As I walked in, he said, "So, this is the Boy Wonder. My name is Brent. I'm with TB Harms."

TB Harms was one of the biggest music publishers in the world. "They heard your song in New York," he told me, "and they'd like to publish it."

My heart was singing.

He hesitated. "There's just one problem."

"What's that?"

"They don't think Phil Levant is a big enough name to introduce your song. They'd like someone more important to give it a real send-off."

My heart sank. I did not know anyone more important.

"Horace Heidt is playing at the Drake Hotel," Brent said. "Maybe you could go talk to him and show him your song." Horace Heidt was one of the most popular bandleaders in the country.

"Sure."

He handed me his card. "Have him give me a call."

"I will," I promised.

I looked at my watch. It was a quarter to twelve. Horace Heidt would still be playing. I got into Otto's car and drove very slowly to the Drake Hotel. When I arrived, I made my way to the ballroom where Horace Heidt was conducting his orchestra.

As I walked in, the maître d' asked, "Do you have a reservation?"

"No. I'm here to see Mr. Heidt."

"You can wait there." He pointed to an empty table against a back wall.

I waited fifteen minutes, and when Horace Heidt stepped off the bandstand, I intercepted him. "Mr. Heidt, my name is Sidney Sheldon. I have a song here that—"

"Sorry," he said. "I don't have time to—"

"But Harms wants to—"

He started to walk away.

"Harms wants to publish it," I called after him, "but they want someone like you behind it."

He stopped and walked back to me. "Let me see it."

I handed him the sheet music.

He studied it, as if he was hearing it in his mind. "That's a nice song."

"Would you be interested?" I asked.

He looked up. "Yes. I'll want fifty percent of it."

I would have given him a hundred percent. "Great!" I handed him the card that Brent had given me.

"I'll have an orchestration made. Come back and see me tomorrow."

The following night, when I returned to the Drake Hotel, I heard my song being played by Horace Heidt and his orchestra, and it sounded even better than Phil Levant's arrangement. I sat down and waited until Heidt was free. He came over to the table where I was seated.

"Did you talk to Mr. Brent?" I asked.

"Yes. We're making a deal."

I smiled. My first song was going to be published.

The next evening, Brent came to see me at the Bismarck checkroom.

"Is everything set?" I asked.

"I'm afraid not."

"But—"

"Heidt is asking for a five-thousand-dollar advance, and we never give that much on a new song."

I was stunned. When I finished work, I drove back to the Drake Hotel to see Horace Heidt again.

"Mr. Heidt, I don't care about the advance," I told him. "I just want to get my first song published."

"We're going to get it published," he assured me. "Don't worry about it. I'm going to publish it myself. I'm leaving for New York next week. The song will get a lot of airtime."

Besides his nightly broadcast, Horace Heidt hosted a popular weekly show called *Horace Heidt and His Alemite Brigadiers.*

"My Silent Self" would be broadcast from New York, and be heard often all over the country.

During the next few weeks, I managed to listen to Horace's broadcasts, and he was right. "My Silent Self" did get a lot of airtime, both on his nightly broadcasts, and on the *Alemite* program. He used my song, but he never had it published.

I was not discouraged. If I could write one song that a major publisher wanted, I could write a dozen. And that is exactly what I did. I spent all my spare time at the piano, composing songs. I felt that twelve songs would be a good number to mail to New York. I could not afford to go to New York in person because I needed to keep my jobs, to help the family.

Natalie would listen to my songs and be beside herself with excitement.

"Darling, they're better than Irving Berlin's. Much better. When are you going to take them to New York?"

I shook my head. "Natalie, I can't go to New York. I have three jobs here. If I—"

"You have to go," she said firmly. "They're not even going to listen to songs that come in the mail. You have to go, personally."

"We can't afford it," I said. "If—"

"Darling, this is your big chance. You can't afford not to take it."

I had no idea that she was living vicariously through me.

We had a family discussion that night. Otto finally reluctantly agreed that I should go to New York. I would get a job there until my songs started selling.

We decided I would leave the following Saturday.

Natalie's parting gift was a ticket to New York on a Greyhound bus.

As Richard and I lay in our beds that night, he said to me, "Are you really going to be as big a songwriter as Irving Berlin?"

And I told him the truth. "Yes."

With all the money that would be pouring in, Natalie would never have to work again.

CHAPTER

7

I had never been inside a bus depot before my trip to New York in 1936. The Greyhound bus station had an air of excitement, with people going to and coming from cities all over the country. My bus seemed huge, with a washroom and comfortable seats. It was a four-and-a-half-day trip to New York. The long ride would have been tedious, but I was too busy dreaming about my fantastic future to mind.

When we pulled into the bus station in New York, I had thirty dollars in my pocket—money that I was sure Natalie and Otto could not spare.

I had telephoned ahead to the YMCA to reserve a room. It turned out to be small and drab, but it was only four dollars a week. Even so, I knew that the thirty dollars was not going to last very long.

I asked to see the manager of the YMCA.

"I need a job," I told him, "and I need it right away. Do you know anyone who—?"

"We have an employment service for our guests," he informed me.

"Great. Is there anything available now?"

He reached for a sheet of paper behind the desk and scanned it. "There's an opening for an usher at the RKO Jefferson Theatre on Fourteenth Street. Are you interested?"

Interested? At that moment my sole ambition in life was to be an usher at the RKO Jefferson on Fourteenth Street. "That's just what I was looking for!" I told him.

The manager wrote something on a piece of paper and handed it to me. "Take this to the theater in the morning."

I had been in New York for less than one day and I already had a job. I phoned Natalie and Otto to tell them the news.

"That's a good omen," Natalie said. "You're going to be a big success."

I spent the first afternoon and evening exploring New York. It was a magical place, a bustling city that made Chicago seem provincial and drab. Everything was larger—the buildings, the marquees, the streets, the signs, the traffic, the crowds. My career.

The RKO Jefferson Theatre on Fourteenth Street, once a vaudeville house, was an old, two-story structure with a cashier's booth in front. It was part of a chain of RKO theaters. Double features were common—patrons could see two movies back-to-back for the price of one.

I walked thirty-nine blocks from the YMCA to the theater and handed the note I had been given to the theater manager.

He looked me over and said, "Have you ever ushered before?"

"No, sir."

He shrugged. "Doesn't matter. Can you walk?"

"Yes, sir."

"And you know how to turn on a flashlight?"

"Yes, sir."

"Then you can usher. Your salary is fourteen-forty a week. You'll work six days. Your hours are from four-twenty to midnight."

"That's fine." It meant that I was free to have the whole morning and part of the afternoon to spend at the Brill Building, where the headquarters of the music business was.

"Go into the staff changing room, and see if you can find a uniform that fits you."

"Yes, sir."

I tried on an usher's uniform and the manager looked at me and said, "That's fine. Be sure to keep an eye on the balcony."

"The balcony?"

"You'll see. You'll start tomorrow."

"Yes, sir." *And tomorrow I will begin my career as a song-writer.*

The storied Brill Building was the holy of holies in the music business. Located at 1619 Broadway, at Forty-ninth Street, it was the center of Tin Pan Alley, where every important music publisher in the world was headquartered.

As I entered the building and wandered through the corridors, I heard the strains of "A Fine Romance" ... "I've Got You Under My Skin" ... "Pennies from Heaven" ... The names on the doors made my heart pound: Jerome Remick ... Robbins Music Corporation ... M. Witmark & Sons ... Shapiro Bernstein & Company ... and TB Harms—all the giants of the music industry. This was the fountainhead of musical talent. Cole Porter, Irving Berlin,

Richard Rodgers, George and Ira Gershwin, Jerome Kern . . . They all had started here.

I walked into the TB Harms office and nodded to the man behind the desk. "Good morning. I'm Sidney Schech— Sheldon."

"What can I do for you?"

"I wrote 'My Silent Self.' You people were interested in publishing it."

A look of recognition came over his face. "Oh, yes, we were."

Were? "Aren't you still?"

"Well, it's been on the air too much. Horace Heidt has been playing it a lot. Do you have anything new?"

I nodded. "Yes, I do. I can come back with some songs tomorrow morning, Mr. . . . ?"

"Tasker."

At four-twenty that afternoon, I was in my usher's uniform, escorting people down the aisle, to their seats. The manager had been right. This was a job that anyone could do. The only thing that kept it from being boring was the movies that were playing. When things were slow, I could sit at the back of the theater and watch them.

The first double bill I saw there was *A Day at the Races* with the Marx Brothers and *Mr. Deeds Goes to Town*. The coming attractions were *A Star Is Born*, with Janet Gaynor and Fredric March, and *Dodsworth* with Walter Huston.

At midnight, when my shift was over, I went back to my hotel. The room no longer looked small and dreary. I knew it was going to turn into a palace. In the morning, I would take my songs to TB Harms and the only question was which ones they would publish first—"The Ghost of My Love" . . . "I Will if I Want To" . . . "A Handful of Stars" . . . "When Love Has Gone" . . .

At eight-thirty the following morning, I was standing in front of the TB Harms Company, waiting for the doors to open. At nine o'clock, Mr. Tasker arrived.

He saw the large envelope in my hand. "I see you brought some songs."

I grinned. "Yes, sir."

We walked into his office. I handed the envelope to him and started to sit down.

He stopped me. "You don't have to wait," he said. "I'll look these over when I get a chance. Why don't you come back tomorrow?"

I gave him my best professional songwriter's nod. "Right." I would have to wait another twenty-four hours for my future to begin.

At four-twenty, I was back in my uniform at the RKO Jefferson. The manager had been right about the balcony. There was a lot of giggling going on up there. A young man and woman were seated in the last row. And as I started toward them, he moved away from her and she hastily pulled down her short dress. I walked away and did not go upstairs again. To hell with the manager. Let them have their fun.

The following morning I was at the Harms office at eight o'clock, in case Mr. Tasker came in early. He arrived at nine and opened the door.

"Good morning, Sheldon."

I tried to judge from his tone whether he had liked my songs. Was it just a casual "good morning" or did I detect a note of excitement in his voice?

We stepped inside the office.

"Did you have a chance to listen to my songs, Mr. Tasker?"

He nodded. "They're very nice."

My face lit up. I waited to hear what else he was going to say. He was silent.

"Which one did you like best?" I prodded.

"Unfortunately they're not what we're looking for just now."

That was the most depressing sentence I had ever heard in my life.

"But surely some of them—" I began.

He reached behind his desk, took out my envelope and handed it to me. "I'll always be glad to listen when you've got something new."

And that was the end of the interview. *But it's not an end,* I thought. *It's just the beginning.*

I spent the rest of the morning and part of the afternoon going around to the offices of the other publishers in the building.

"Have you ever had a song published?"

"No, sir, but I—"

"We don't take on new songwriters. Come back when you've had something published."

How was I going to get a song published if publishers wouldn't publish any of my songs until I had a song published? In the weeks that followed, when I was not at the theater, I spent my time in my room, writing.

At the theater, I loved watching the wonderful movies we showed there. I saw *The Great Ziegfeld, San Francisco, My Man Godfrey,* and *Shall We Dance,* with Fred Astaire and Ginger Rogers. They transported me to another world, a world of glamour and excitement, elegance and wealth.

My money was running out. I received a check from Natalie for twenty dollars and I sent it back. I knew that without the additional income I had been earning, and Otto not working, life would be even more difficult for them. I wondered whether I was being selfish in thinking of myself when they needed help.

When my new batch of songs was ready, I took them to the same publishers. They looked at them, and gave me the same infuriating answer: "Come back when you've had something published."

In one lobby, a wave of depression hit me. Everything seemed hopeless. I did not intend to spend my life as an usher, and no one was interested in my songs.

This is an excerpt from a letter to my parents, dated November 2, 1936:

> *I want all of you to be as happy as possible. My happiness is an elusive balloon, waiting for me to grab it, floating from side to side with the wind, across oceans, big green meadows, trees and brooks, rustic pastoral scenes and rain-swept sidewalks. First high, barely visible, far out of reach, then low, almost within reach, blown here and there by the vagaries of a playful wind, a wind one moment heartless and sadistic, the next gently compassionate. The wind of fate, and in it rests our lives.*

One morning, in the lobby of the YMCA, I saw a young man about my age, sitting on a couch, furiously writing. He was humming a melody, and seemed to be writing a lyric. I walked up to him, curious.

"Are you a songwriter?" I asked.

He looked up. "Yes."

"So am I. Sidney Sheldon."

He held out a hand. "Sidney Rosenthal."

That was the beginning of a long friendship. We spent the whole morning talking and it was as though we were soul mates.

* * *

When I went to work the following day, the theater manager called me into his office. "Our barker is sick. I want you to get into his uniform and take his place until he gets back. You'll work days. All you have to do is walk up and down in front of the theater and say, 'Immediate seating. No waiting for seats.' The job pays more."

I was thrilled—not because of the promotion, but because of the raise. I would send the extra money home.

"How much does it pay?"

"Fifteen-forty a week."

A dollar a week raise.

When I put on the uniform, I looked like a general in the Russian army. I had nothing against my job as a barker, but could not stand the boredom of saying, "Immediate seating—no waiting for seats," over and over and over. I decided to dramatize it.

I began to yell, in a stentorian voice, "An exciting double feature—*The Texas Rangers* and *The Man Who Lived Twice*. How does a man live twice, ladies and gentlemen? Come in and find out. You'll have an afternoon you will never forget. Absolutely no waiting for seats. Hurry, before we're sold out!"

The real barker never did show up and I kept the job. The only difference from before was that I now worked mornings and early afternoons. I still had time to go see all the music publishers who were uninterested in my songs. Sidney Rosenthal and I wrote a few songs together. They received a lot of praise and no contracts.

At the end of the week, I would usually find myself with only ten cents in my pocket. I had to get from the theater to the Brill Building, and I had to decide whether to have a hot dog for five cents and a Coca-Cola for five cents and walk the thirty-five blocks, or have a hot dog, no Coke, and take the subway uptown for a nickel. I got used to alternating the routine.

A few days after I started working as a barker, business at the theater began to pick up.

I was out in front of the theater, yelling, "You won't want to miss *Conquest,* with Greta Garbo and Charles Boyer. And there's another treat for you—*Nothing Sacred,* with Carole Lombard and Fredric March. These are the world's greatest lovers, who will teach you how to be great lovers. And admission is only thirty-five cents. Two lessons in love for thirty-five cents. It's the bargain of the century. Hurry, hurry, hurry, get your tickets now!"

And the customers came.

With the next films, I had even more fun. "Come and see the most fantastic double bill in the history of show business—*Night Must Fall,* with Robert Montgomery and Rosalind Russell. Keep your overcoats on because you're going to get cold chills. And with it, as an extra treat, is the new *Tarzan* picture," at which point I gave a loud *Tarzan* yell, and I watched people from a block away turning around to see what was happening, and coming back toward the theater and buying tickets. The manager was standing outside, watching me.

At the end of the following week, a stranger walked up to me.

"Where is the son of a bitch from Chicago?"

I did not like his tone. "Why?"

"The manager of the RKO theater chain told all the barkers we all have to come and watch the bastard and do what he does."

"I'll tell him when he comes back." I turned away and said, in a conversational voice, "Immediate seating inside.

No waiting for seats. Immediate seating inside. No waiting for seats."

The advantage of working days was that while I still had time to see the music publishers, my evenings were free, and at least three times a week I went to the theater to see plays, sitting in the cheapest balcony seats. I saw *Room Service . . . Abie's Irish Rose . . . Tobacco Road . . . You Can't Take It with You . . .* The variety was endless.

Sidney Rosenthal, my new friend, had found a job and one day he suggested, "Why don't we pool our money and get out of this place?"

"Great idea."

One week later, we left the YMCA and moved into the Grand Union Hotel on Thirty-second Street. We had two bedrooms and a living room, and after the little room at the YMCA, it seemed like the height of luxury.

In a letter from Natalie, she reminded me that we had a distant cousin living in New York who had a checkroom concession at the Glen Cove Casino, on Long Island. She suggested that I give him a call. His name was Clifford Wolfe. I called him and he could not have been more cordial.

"I heard you were in New York somewhere. What are you doing?"

I told him.

"How would you like to work in the checkroom for me, three nights a week?"

"I'd love it," I said. "And I have a buddy who—"

"I can use him, too."

And so three nights a week, Sidney Rosenthal and I went out to Long Island to the Glen Cove Casino and earned three dollars apiece checking hats and coats. We also scrounged as much food as we could from the buffet table.

A car carrying other employees of the casino picked us up and took us to Long Island, an hour and a half away. At the end of the evening, when we were through working, we were taken back to our hotel. The extra money I made I sent to Natalie. She invariably sent it back.

One evening, as I walked into the checkroom, Clifford Wolfe stared at me, frowning. "That suit you're wearing . . ." It was torn and shabby.

"Yes?"

"Don't you have anything nicer?"

I shook my head, embarrassed. My wardrobe would have fit into a briefcase. "I'm afraid not."

"We'll take care of that," he said.

The next night, when I arrived at Glen Cove, Clifford Wolfe handed me a blue serge suit and said, "I want you to go to my tailor and have this fitted for you."

From that time on, whenever I went to Glen Cove, I wore Clifford Wolfe's suit.

The inexplicable changes in my moods continued. I was either unreasonably elated or suicidal. In an excerpt from a letter to Natalie and Otto, dated December 26, 1936, I wrote:

At the moment I haven't much heart for this fight. Whether I am going to stick it out, I don't know. If I were more sure of my ability, it would be so much easier.

One month later, I wrote:

Well, as far as songs are concerned, it looks as if we might click. Chappell heard one of our new numbers, told us to rewrite the bridge and bring it back. They are quite particular and their liking our numbers is encouraging.

I had had two episodes of my discs tearing loose, and both times I had been in bed for three days. It was in the middle of a period of euphoria that my future opened wide. It was on one of my rounds in the Brill Building that I encountered a short, dapper man with a friendly smile. I had no idea then who he was. He happened to be in the Remick office when the manager was listening to one of my songs.

The manager shook his head. "That's not what we're looking—"

"This could be a big hit," I implored him. *"When love is gone, love is gone, the stars forget to glow, and we can hear much sadder songs than we were meant to know . . ."*

The manager shrugged.

The stranger with the friendly smile was studying me. "Let me see that," he said.

I handed him the sheet of music and he scanned it.

"That's a damned good lyric," he commented. "What's your name?"

"Sidney Sheldon."

He held out a hand. "I'm Max Rich."

I knew his name. He had two popular songs playing on the air at that moment. One was "Smile, Darn Ya, Smile" and the other was a novelty song, "The Girl in the Little Green Hat."

"Have you had anything published, Sidney?"

The same trick question. I was crestfallen. "No." I was looking at the door.

He smiled. "Let's change that. How would you like to work with me?"

I was stunned. This was exactly the opportunity I had dreamed of.

"I—I'd love it," I said. I could hardly get the words out.

"I have an office here, on the second floor. Why don't you meet me there tomorrow morning, ten o'clock, and we'll go to work."

"Great!"

"Bring all the lyrics you have."

I swallowed. "I'll be there, Mr. Rich." I was in a state of euphoria.

When I told Sidney Rosenthal what had happened, he said, "Congratulations, big-time! Max Rich can get anything published."

"I can show him some of your songs, too," I offered, "and—"

"Get yourself started first."

"Right."

That night, Sidney Rosenthal and I had a celebratory dinner, but I was too excited to eat. Everything I had longed for was about to come true. *Songs by Max Rich and Sidney Sheldon*. The names sounded good together.

I had a feeling that Max Rich was a wonderful man to work with and I knew that some of my lyrics were going to please him.

I started to call Natalie and Otto, but I thought, *I'll wait until I've started.*

As I got into bed that night, I thought, *Why would Max Rich want to write with me when he could write with anybody? I'm a nobody. He's just being kind. He's overestimated what little talent I have and he's going to be disillusioned. I'm not good enough to work with him.* Out of nowhere, the black cloud had descended. *All the publishers in the Brill Building have*

*turned me down, and they're professionals. They know talent. I
have none. I would just make a fool of myself with Max Rich.*

At ten o'clock in the morning, while Max Rich was
waiting to collaborate with me in his office at the Brill
Building, I was on a Greyhound bus, headed back to
Chicago.

CHAPTER

8

I returned to Chicago in March of 1937, a failure. Otto, Natalie, and Richard were sympathetic about my lack of success as a songwriter.

"They don't know great songs when they hear them," Natalie said.

The economic situation at home had not improved. I reluctantly went back to work at the Bismarck checkroom. I managed to get a job during the day parking cars at a restaurant on the North Side, in Rogers Park. My irrational mood swings continued. I had no control over them. I became ecstatic for no reason and depressed when things were going well.

One evening, Charley Fine, my Stewart Warner mentor, and his wife, Vera, came to the apartment for dinner. For economical reasons, we served a cheap takeout dinner I had picked up at a neighborhood Chinese restaurant, but the Fines pretended not to notice.

During the evening, Vera said, "I'm driving to Sacramento, California, next week."

California. Hollywood. It was as though a door had suddenly opened for me. I thought of all the magical hours I had spent at the RKO Jefferson Theatre, solving crimes with William Powell and Myrna Loy in *After the Thin Man,* riding with John Wayne in the covered wagon to California in *The Oregon Trail,* watching helplessly as Robert Montgomery terrorized Rosalind Russell in *Night Must Fall,* swinging through the trees with Tarzan in *Tarzan Escapes,* and having dinner with Cary Grant, Clark Gable, and Judy Garland. I took a deep breath and said, "I'd like to drive you there."

They all looked at me in surprise.

"That's very kind of you, Sidney," Vera Fine said, "but I don't want to imp—"

"It would be my pleasure," I said enthusiastically.

I turned to Natalie and Otto. "I'd like to take Vera to California."

There was an uncomfortable silence.

We picked up the conversation after the Fines had left. "You can't go away again," Otto said. "You just got back."

"But if I could get a job in Hollywood—"

"No. We'll find something for you to do here."

I knew what there was for me to do in Chicago. Checkrooms and drugstores and parking cars. I had had enough of that.

After a brief silence, Natalie said, "Otto, if that's what Sidney wants, we should give him a chance. I'll tell you what. Let's compromise." She turned to me. "If you don't find a job in three weeks, you'll come back home."

"It's a deal," I said happily.

I was sure I could easily get a job in Hollywood. The more I thought about it, the more wildly optimistic I became.

This was finally going to be my big break.

Five days later, I was packing, getting ready to drive Vera and her young daughter, Carmel, to Sacramento.

Richard was upset. "Why are you leaving again? You just got back."

How could I explain to him all the wonderful things that were about to happen?

"I know," I said, "but this is important. Don't worry. I'm going to send for you."

He was near tears. "Is that a promise?"

I put my arms around him. "That's a promise. I'm going to miss you, buddy."

It took five days to get to Sacramento, and when we arrived, I said goodbye to Vera and Carmel, and spent the night in a cheap hotel. Early the following morning I took a bus to San Francisco, where I changed to another bus, to Los Angeles.

I arrived in Los Angeles with one suitcase and fifty dollars in my pocket. I bought a copy of the *Los Angeles Times* at the bus station and turned to the want ads to look for rooms to rent.

The one that instantly appealed to me was an ad for a boardinghouse that had rooms for four-fifty a week, breakfast included. It was in the Hollywood area, a few blocks from the famed Sunset Boulevard.

It turned out to be a charming, old-fashioned house in a lovely residential area on a quiet street, at 1928 Carmen Street.

When I rang the bell, the door was opened by a small, pleasant-faced woman who appeared to be in her forties.

"Hello. Can I help you?"

"Yes. My name is Sidney Sheldon. I'm looking for a place to stay for a few days."

"I'm Grace Seidel. Come in."

I picked up my suitcase and walked into the hall. The house had obviously been converted from a sprawling family residence to a boardinghouse. There was a large living room, a dining room, a breakfast room, and a kitchen. There were twelve bedrooms, most of them occupied, and four communal bathrooms.

I said, "I understand that the rent is four-fifty a week, and that includes breakfast."

Grace Seidel contemplated my rumpled suit and my worn shirt, and said, "If you press me, I could make it four dollars a week."

I looked at her and desperately wanted to say, *I'll pay the four-fifty.* But the little money I had left was not going to last very long. I swallowed my pride and said, "I'm pressing."

She gave me a warm smile. "That's fine. I'll show you to your room."

The room was small but neat and attractively furnished, and I was very pleased with it.

I turned to Grace. "This is great," I said.

"Good. I'll give you a key to the front door. One of our rules is that you're not allowed to bring any women in here."

"No problem," I said.

"Let me introduce you to some of the other boarders."

She took me into the living room where several of the boarders were gathered. I met four writers, a prop man, three actors, a director, and a singer. As time went on, I learned that they were all wannabes, unemployed, pursuing wonderful dreams that would never come true.

Gracie had a well-mannered twelve-year-old son, Billy. His dream was to become a fireman. It was probably the only dream in the boardinghouse that would come true.

I phoned Natalie and Otto to tell them that I had arrived safely.

"Remember," Otto said, "if you don't find a job in three weeks, we want you back here."

No problem.

That night, Gracie's boarders sat around the large living room, telling their war stories.

"This is a tough business, Sheldon. Every studio has a gate and inside the gate the producers are screaming for talent. They're yelling that they desperately need actors and directors and writers. But if you're standing outside the gate, they won't even let you in. The gates are closed to outsiders."

Maybe, I thought. *But every day someone manages to get through.*

I learned that there was no Hollywood, as I had imagined it. Columbia Pictures, Paramount, and RKO were located in Hollywood, but Metro-Goldwyn-Mayer and Selznick International Studios were in Culver City. Universal Studios was in Universal City, Disney Studios was in Silverlake, Twentieth-Century-Fox was in Century City, and Republic Studios was in Studio City.

Grace had thoughtfully subscribed to *Variety,* the show business trade paper, and it was left in the living room like a Bible for all of us to look at, to see what jobs were available and which pictures were being produced. I picked it up and looked at the date. I had twenty-one days to find a job, and the clock was running. I knew that somehow I had to find a way to get through those studio gates.

The following morning, while we were having breakfast, the telephone rang. Answering the telephone was almost an Olympic event. Everyone raced to be the first to pick it up because—since none of us could afford any kind of social life—the phone call had to be about a job.

The actor who picked up the phone listened a moment, turned to Grace and said, "It's for you."

There were sighs of disappointment. Each boarder had hoped that it was a job for him. That phone was the lifeline to their futures.

I bought a tourist's guide to Los Angeles, and since Columbia Pictures was the closest to Gracie's boardinghouse, I decided to start there. The studio was on Gower Street, just off Sunset. There was no gate in front of Columbia.

I walked in the front door. An elderly guard was seated behind a desk, working on a report. He looked up as I came in.

"Can I help you?"

"Yes," I said confidently. "My name is Sidney Sheldon. I want to be a writer. Who do I see?"

He studied me a moment. "Do you have an appointment?"

"No, but—"

"Then you don't see anybody."

"There must be someone I—"

"Not without an appointment," he said firmly. He went back to his report.

Apparently the studio did not need a gate.

I spent the next two weeks making the rounds of all the studios. Unlike New York, Los Angeles was widely spread out. It was not a city for walking. Streetcars ran down the center of Santa Monica Boulevard and buses were on all the main streets. I soon became familiar with their routes and schedules.

While every studio looked different, the guards were

all the same. In fact, I began to feel that they were all the same man.

I want to be a writer. Who do I see?
Do you have an appointment?
No.
You don't see anybody.

Hollywood was a cabaret, and I was hungry. But I was outside looking in, and all the doors were locked.

I was running out of my short supply of funds, but worse than that, I was running out of time.

When I was not haunting the studios, I was in my room, working on stories on my old battered portable typewriter.

One day, Gracie made an unwelcome announcement. "I'm sorry," she said, "but from now on there will be no more breakfasts."

No one had to ask why. Most of us were behind in our rent and she could no longer afford to keep carrying us.

I woke up the next morning, starving and broke. I had no money for breakfast. I was trying to work on a story, but could not concentrate. I was too hungry. Finally, I gave up. I went into the kitchen. Gracie was there, cleaning the stove.

She saw me and turned around. "Yes, Sidney?"

I was stammering. "Gracie, I—I know the new rule about—about no breakfast, but I was wondering if—if I could just have a bite to eat this morning. I'm sure that in the next few days—"

She looked at me and said, sharply, "Why don't you go back to your room?"

I felt crushed. I walked back to my room and sat in front of my typewriter, humiliated that I had embarrassed both of us. I tried to go back to the story but it was no use.

All I could think of was that I was hungry and broke and desperate.

Fifteen minutes later there was a knock at the door. I walked over and opened it. Gracie stood there, holding a tray, and on it was a large glass of orange juice, a steaming pot of coffee, and a plate of bacon and eggs with toast. "Eat it while it's hot," she said.

That may have been the best meal I ever had. Certainly the most memorable.

When I returned to the boardinghouse one afternoon, after another futile day making the rounds of the studios, there was a letter from Otto. In it was a bus ticket to Chicago. It was the most depressing piece of paper I had ever seen. His note read: *We will expect you home next week. Love, Dad.*

I had four days left and nowhere else to go. The gods must have been laughing.

That evening, as Gracie's group and I sat around the living room, chatting, one of them said, "My sister just got a job as a reader at MGM."

"A reader? What does that mean?" I asked.

"All the studios have them," he explained. "They synopsize stories for producers, which saves them the trouble of reading a lot of trash. If the producer likes the synopsis, he'll take a look at the full book or play. Some studios have staffs of readers. Some use outside readers."

My mind was racing. I had just read Steinbeck's masterpiece, *Of Mice and Men*, and—

Thirty minutes later, I was skimming through the book and typing a synopsis of it.

By noon the next day I had made enough copies on a borrowed mimeograph machine to send to half a dozen studios. I figured that it would take a day or two to deliver them all and I should hear back about the third day.

When the third day came, the only mail I received was from my brother, Richard, asking when I was going to send for him. The fourth day brought a letter from Natalie.

The next day was Thursday, and my bus ticket was for Sunday. One more dream had died. I told Gracie that I would be leaving Sunday morning. She looked at me with sad, wise eyes. "Is there anything I can do?" she asked.

I gave her a hug. "You've been wonderful. Things haven't worked out as I hoped they would."

"Never stop dreaming," she told me.

But I had stopped.

Early the following morning, the telephone rang. One of the actors ran over to it and grabbed it. He picked up the receiver and in his best actor voice said, "Good morning. Can I help you? . . . Who? . . ."

The tone of his voice changed. "David Selznick's office?"

The room went completely silent. David Selznick was the most prestigious producer in Hollywood. He had produced *A Star Is Born, Dinner at Eight, A Tale of Two Cities, Viva Villa!, David Copperfield,* and dozens of other movies.

The actor said, "Yes, he's here."

We were literally holding our breaths. Who was *he?*

He turned to me. "It's for you, Sheldon."

I may have broken the boardinghouse record racing to the phone.

"Hello?"

A woman's high voice said, "Is this Sidney Sheldon?"

I sensed instantly that I was not speaking to David Selznick himself. "Yes."

"This is Anna, David Selznick's secretary. Mr. Selznick

has a novel that he wants synopsized. The problem is that none of our readers are available."

Is available, I thought automatically. But who was I to correct someone who was about to launch my career?

"And Mr. Selznick needs the synopsis by six o'clock this evening. It's a four-hundred-page novel. Our synopses usually run about thirty pages with a two-page summary and a one-paragraph comment. But it must be delivered by six o'clock this evening. Can you do it?"

There was no possible way I could get to the Selznick Studios, read a four-hundred-page novel, find a decent typewriter somewhere, write a thirty-page synopsis, and get it done by six o'clock.

I said, "Of course I can."

"Good. You can pick up the book at our studio in Culver City."

"I'm on my way." I replaced the receiver. *Selznick International Studios.* I looked at my watch. It was nine-thirty in the morning. Culver City was an hour and a half away. There were a few other problems. I had no transportation. I am a hunt-and-peck typist, and to have typed a thirty-page synopsis would have taken me forever, and forever did not even include time to read a four-hundred-page novel. If I arrived at the Culver City studio at eleven, I would have exactly seven hours to perform a miracle.

But I had a plan.

CHAPTER

9

It took a streetcar and two buses to get me to Culver City. On the second bus, I looked around at the passengers and wanted to tell them all that I was on my way to see David Selznick. The bus dropped me off two blocks from the Selznick International Studios.

The studio was a large, imposing Georgian structure, fronting on Washington Street. It was familiar because I recognized it from the opening credits of David Selznick's movies.

I hurried inside and said to the woman behind the desk, "I have an appointment with Mr. Selznick's secretary." At least I was going to meet David Selznick now.

"Your name?"

"Sidney Sheldon."

She reached into the desk and pulled out a thick package. "This is for you."

"Oh. I thought maybe I could see Mr. Selznick and—"

"No. Mr. Selznick is a busy man."

So I would meet David Selznick later.

Clutching the package, I left the building and started

running down the street, toward the MGM studios, six blocks away, reviewing my plan as I ran. It stemmed from a conversation with Seymour about Sydney Singer, his ex-wife.

Do you ever see her, Seymour?

No. She went to Hollywood. She got a job as a secretary at MGM for a woman director. Dorothy Arzner.

I was going to ask Sydney Singer to help me. It was a long, long, long shot, but it was all I had.

When I reached the MGM studios, I went up to the guard behind the desk in the lobby. "My name is Sidney Sheldon. I want to see Sydney Singer."

"Sydney . . . Oh—Dorothy Arzner's secretary."

I nodded knowingly. "Right."

"Is she expecting you?"

"Yes," I said confidently.

He picked up the phone and dialed an extension. "Sidney Sheldon is here to see you . . ." He repeated slowly, "Sidney Sheldon." He listened a moment. "But he said—"

I stood there, paralyzed. *Say yes. Say yes. Say yes.*

"Right." He replaced the receiver. "She'll see you. Room 230."

My heart started beating again. "Thank you."

"Take the elevator, over there."

I took the elevator and hurried down a corridor on the second floor. Sydney's office was at the end of the corridor. When I walked in, she was seated behind her desk.

"Hello, Sydney."

"Hello." There was no warmth in her voice. And I suddenly remembered the rest of the conversation with Seymour. *She hates my guts. She said she never wants to see me again.* What the hell had I gotten myself into? Would she ask me to sit down? No.

"What are you doing here?"

Oh, I just dropped in to ask you to spend your afternoon as my unpaid secretary. "It's—it's a long story."

She looked at her watch and rose. "I'm on my way to lunch."

"You can't!"

She was staring at me. "I can't go to lunch?"

I took a deep breath. "Sydney—I—I'm in trouble." I poured out the whole story, starting with the fiasco in New York, my ambition of becoming a writer, my inability to get past any of the studio guards, and the telephone call that morning from David Selznick.

She listened, and as I got to the end of the story, her lips tightened. "You took the Selznick assignment because you expected me to spend the afternoon typing for you?"

It was a bitter divorce. She hates my guts.

"I—I didn't expect it," I said. "I was just hoping that—" It was hard to breathe. I had acted stupidly. "I'm sorry I bothered you, Sydney. I had no right to ask this of you."

"No, you didn't. What are you going to do now?"

"I'm going to take this book back to Mr. Selznick. Tomorrow morning I'll leave for Chicago. Thanks anyway, Sydney. I appreciate your listening to me. Goodbye." I started for the door, in despair.

"Wait a minute."

I turned.

"This means a lot to you, doesn't it?"

I nodded. I was too upset to speak.

"Let's open that package and take a look at it."

It took a moment for her words to sink in. I said, "Sydney—"

"Shut up. Let me see the book."

"You mean you might—"

"What you've done is the most insane thing I've ever heard. But I admire your determination." She smiled for the first time. "I'm going to help you."

A feeling of relief flooded through me. I couldn't stop grinning. I watched her riffle through the book.

"It's long," she said. "How do you expect to finish this synopsis by six o'clock?"

Good question.

She handed the book back to me. I glanced at the inside cover to get a quick idea of what it was about. It was a period romance, the kind of story that Selznick seemed to enjoy making.

"How are we going to do this?" Sydney asked.

"I'm going to skim the pages," I explained, "and when I come to a story point, I'll dictate it to you."

She nodded. "Let's see how it works."

I took a chair opposite her and began turning pages. In the next fifteen minutes, I had a fairly clear sense of the story. I began skimming through the book, dictating when I came to something that seemed pertinent to the plot. She typed as I talked.

To this day, I don't know what made Sydney agree to help me. Was it because I had blundered into an impossible situation, or because I looked desperate? I will never know. But I do know that she sat at her desk all that afternoon, typing the pages as I thumbed through the book.

The clock was racing. We were only halfway through the novel when Sydney said, "It's four o'clock."

I started reading faster and talking faster.

By the time I finished dictating the thirty-page synopsis, the two-page summary, and the one-page comment, it was exactly ten minutes to six.

As Sydney handed me the last page, I said gratefully, "If there is anything I can ever do for you—"

She smiled. "A lunch will be fine."

I kissed her on the cheek, stuffed the pages into the envelope with the book, and raced out of the office. I ran all the way back to the Selznick International Studios, and arrived there at one minute to six.

I said to the same woman behind the desk, "My name is Sheldon. I want to see Mr. Selznick's secretary."

"She's been waiting for you," she said.

As I hurried down the corridor, I knew that this was just the beginning. I had read that Selznick had started as a reader at MGM, so we had something in common that we could chat about.

Selznick will put me on the staff. I'll have an office here. Wait until Natalie and Otto hear that I'm working for him.

I reached his secretary's office. When I walked in, she looked at her watch. "I was getting worried about you," she said.

"No problem," I told her, nonchalantly. I handed her the package and watched her glance through the pages.

"This is beautifully done." She handed me an envelope. "There's ten dollars in there."

"Thank you. I'm ready to do the next synopsis whenever—"

"I'm sorry," she said, "our regular reader will be back tomorrow. Mr. Selznick doesn't usually use outside readers. As a matter of fact, you were called by mistake."

I swallowed. "Mistake?"

"Yes. You're not on our regular list of readers."

So I was never going to be a part of David Selznick's team. We were not going to have a cozy chat about his days as a reader. This frantic day had been the beginning and the end. At that moment, I should have been deeply depressed. Oddly enough, I felt happy. Why? I had no idea.

When I reached Gracie's, the boys were waiting for me.

"Did you see Selznick?"

"What's he like?"

"Are you going to work there?"

"It's been an interesting afternoon," I said. "Very interesting." And I went into my room and closed the door.

I saw the bus ticket on the table next to my bed. It was the symbol of failure. It meant going back to the checkrooms and the drugstore and parking cars and the life I thought I had escaped from. I had reached a dead end. I picked up the bus ticket and it was all I could do to keep from tearing it in half. How could I turn this failure into a success? *There has to be a way. There has to be a way.*

And then it came to me. I called home. Natalie answered the phone. "Hello, darling. We can't wait to see you. Are you all right?"

"I'm fine. I have some good news. I just did a synopsis for David Selznick."

"Really? That's wonderful! Was he nice?"

"Yes. Couldn't have been nicer. And this is only the beginning. The gates here have opened, Natalie. Everything is going to be great. I just need a few more days."

She did not hesitate. "All right, darling. Let us know when you're coming home."

I'm not coming home.

The following morning, I went to the bus station and cashed in the ticket Otto had sent me. I spent the rest of the day writing letters to the literary departments of all the major studios.

The letters read, in part:

At his personal request, I have just finished a synopsis of a novel for David O. Selznick, and I'm now free to do other synopses . . .

The telephone calls began coming in two days later. Twentieth-Century-Fox called first, then Paramount. Fox needed a book synopsized and Paramount wanted me to synopsize a play. Each synopsis paid five or ten dollars, depending on the length.

Since each studio had its own staff of readers, the only time they called in outside readers was when they were overburdened. I could do only one novel a day. It took me that long to get to a studio to pick it up, return to Gracie's boardinghouse, read the book, type a synopsis, and take it back to the studio. I averaged two or three calls a week. I didn't have Sydney in my life anymore.

To augment my meager income, I telephoned a man I had never met. Vera Fine had mentioned him on the drive to California. His name was Gordon Mitchell. He was head of the Technical Branch of the Academy of Motion Picture Arts and Sciences.

I called and mentioned Vera Fine's name, and told him I was looking for a job. He was very cordial. "As a matter of fact, I have something here that you can do."

I was thrilled. I would be working for the esteemed Academy.

The following day, I met him in his office.

"It's perfect timing," he said. "You'll be working evenings here, watching films in our projection room."

"Great," I said. "What's the job?"

"Watching films in our projection room."

I was staring at him. He went on to explain.

"The Academy is testing different film preservatives. We've coated different sections of the film with different chemicals. Your job is to sit in the projection room and keep a record of the number of times each film is run." He added, apologetically, "I'm afraid it only pays three dollars a day."

"I'll take it."

The first movie I saw over and over was *The Man Who Lived Twice,* and I was soon able to quote every line. I spent my evenings watching the same films and my days waiting for the telephone to ring.

On the fateful date of December 12, 1938, I received a call from Universal Studios. I had just done a few synopses for them.

"Sidney Sheldon?"

"Yes."

"Could you come in to the studio this morning?"

Another three dollars.

"Yes."

"Go to Mr. Townsend's office."

Al Townsend was the story editor at Universal. When I arrived at the studio, I was ushered into his office.

"I've read the synopses you've done for us. They're very good."

"Thank you."

"We need a staff reader here. Would you like the job?"

I wondered if he would be offended if I kissed him. "Yes, sir," I said.

"It pays seventeen dollars a week. We work six days a week. Your hours will be from nine to six. You'll start Monday."

I called Sydney at her office to break the news to her and invite her to dinner.

An unfamiliar voice answered the phone. "Yes?"

"I would like to speak to Sydney Singer."

"She's not here."

"When will she be back?"

"She's not coming back."

"What—? Who is this?"

"This is Dorothy Arzner."

"Oh. Do you have her forwarding address, Miss Arzner?"

"She didn't leave one."

I never saw Sydney again, but I have never forgotten the debt I owe her.

Universal was a studio that made B pictures. It had been founded by Carl "Papa" Laemmle in 1912, and it was noted for its thriftiness. A few years earlier the studio had called the agent of a top western star and said they wanted to hire him to work on a low-budget movie.

The agent laughed. "You can't afford him. He makes a thousand dollars a day."

"That's all right," the studio executive assured him. "We'll pay him."

The movie was about a masked bandit. The first day of production the director shot endless close-ups of the star in various locations, and at the end of the day they told him that he was finished. What they did after that was to substitute a minor actor who wore a mask throughout the picture.

On Monday morning, when I walked through the gates onto a studio lot for the first time, I was filled with a sense of wonder. I walked past the facades of western towns and Victorian houses, San Francisco streets and New York streets, and felt the magic.

Al Townsend explained my duties to me. My job was to read the dozens and dozens of screenplays that had been written for silent movies and to try to weed out the ones that might be worth making into talkies. Nearly all of the screenplays were hopeless. I remember one memorable line describing a villain:

He had a bag of gold in his eyes.

During Papa Laemmle's regime, Universal was an easygoing, shirt-sleeved kind of studio. There was no feeling of pressure. It was like a large family.

I was now receiving a weekly paycheck and I was able to pay Gracie regularly. I reported to the studio six days a week and never got over the thrill of walking onto the studio lot where dreams were created every day. I knew that this was just the beginning. I had come to Universal as a reader, but I would start working again on original stories and sell them to the studio. I wrote to Natalie and Otto to tell them how well things were going. I had a permanent job in Hollywood.

One month later, Papa Laemmle sold Universal and along with everyone else, I was fired.

I did not dare tell Natalie or Otto what had happened because they would insist that I return to Chicago. I knew that my future was here. I would have to find another job—*any job*—until I could get back into a studio.

I looked through the want ads. One item caught my eye:

Hotel switchboard operator wanted.
No experience necessary. $20 a week. Brant Hotel.

The Brant Hotel was a chic hotel off Hollywood Boulevard. When I arrived there, the lobby was deserted except for the hotel manager.

"I'm here about the switchboard operator job," I said.

He studied me a moment. "Our telephone operator

just quit. We need someone right away. Have you ever run a switchboard?"

"No, sir."

"There's really not much to it."

He took me behind a desk, where there was a large, complicated-looking switchboard.

"Sit down," he said.

I sat down. The switchboard consisted of two rows of vertical plugs and about thirty holes to plug them into, each hole connected to a numbered room.

"You see these plugs?"

"Yes, sir."

"They're in twos, one above the other. The lower one is called the sister plug. When the board lights up, you put the front plug into that hole. The caller will tell you the room he wants and then you take the sister plug and plug it into that room number, and you move this button to ring the room. That's all there is to it."

I nodded. "That's easy."

"I'll give you a week's trial. You'll work nights."

"No problem," I said.

"How soon can you start?"

"I've started."

The manager had been right. Running a switchboard was easy. It became almost automatic. When a light flashed, I would put in a plug from the first row. "Mr. Klemann, please."

I would look at the roster of guests. Mr. Klemann was in Room 231. I put the sister plug into the hole for Room 231 and pushed the button that rang the room. It was as simple as that.

I had a feeling that operating a switchboard was just a beginning. I could move up to night manager, and then perhaps general manager, and since the hotel was part of a chain, there was no telling how high I could go, and I would write a screenplay about the hotel business with the knowledge of an insider, sell it to a studio, and be back where I wanted to be.

Two nights after I had started, at three o'clock in the morning, one of the guests rang the switchboard. "I want you to get a number for me in New York."

He gave me the number.

I pulled out the room plug and dialed the New York number.

After half a dozen rings, a woman answered. "Hello."

"I have a call for you," I said. "Just a moment, please."

I picked up the key that plugged into the guest rooms and stared at the switchboard. I had no idea which guest had placed the call. I looked at the holes in the switchboard, hoping for inspiration. I knew generally what area of the board the caller was in. I began ringing all the rooms in that section, hoping to find the right one. I awakened a dozen guests.

"I have the New York call for you."

"I don't know anyone in New York."

"I have the New York call for you."

"Are you out of your mind? It's three o'clock in the morning!"

"I have the New York call for you."

"Not me, you idiot!"

When the hotel manager arrived in the morning, I said, "A funny thing happened last night. I—"

"I heard, and I don't think it's funny. You're fired."

I obviously was not destined to manage a hotel chain. It was time to move on.

* * *

There was an ad for a part-time driving instructor and I took the job. Most of the students were scary. Red lights meant nothing to them and they all seemed confused about the difference between the brake and the accelerator. They were nervous, blind, or bent on suicide. Every time I went to work, I felt I was putting my life on the line.

I kept my sanity by doing outside reading for various studios, when their own readers were busy. One of the studios I had written synopses for was Twentieth-Century-Fox. The story editor was James Fisher, a bright young New Yorker.

Late one afternoon, he telephoned me. "Are you free tomorrow?"

"Yes." *Another three dollars.*

"I'll see you at ten o'clock."

"Right." Maybe it would be a big book. Ten dollars. My funds were running low again.

When I got to his office, Fisher was waiting for me. "How would you like a staff job here?" he asked.

I could hardly get the words out. "I—I'd love it."

"You're hired. Twenty-three dollars a week."

I was back in show business.

10

Working at Twentieth-Century-Fox studios was radically different from working at Universal Studios. Where Universal was laid-back and casual, Fox was a no-nonsense, efficiently run studio. The prime reason for that was Darryl F. Zanuck, the head of production. Unlike most other studio heads, Zanuck was a hands-on executive. He was a brilliant showman, involved in every phase of every movie the studio made, and he knew exactly what he wanted. He also had a sense of who he was. Once, at a studio production meeting, he turned to his assistant and said, "Don't say yes until I'm finished talking."

Darryl Zanuck had a great respect for writers. He once said, "Success in movies boils down to three things: story, story, story. Just don't ever let the writers know how important they are."

There were twelve staff readers at Fox, ranging in age from thirty-five to sixty. A majority of them were relatives of studio executives, put on the payroll as a kind of sinecure.

Julian Johnson, one of the Fox studio's top executives, called me into his office one morning. Johnson was an imposing figure, tall and heavyset. He had once been married to Texas Guinan, the famous nightclub queen.

"Sidney, from now on, you'll work only on synopses for Mr. Zanuck. When he's interested in a new book or play, I want you to handle it."

"Great."

"Every synopsis will be a rush job—"

"No problem."

In fact, I was delighted. From that moment on, I got to read the best of all the new novels and plays that were submitted to the studio.

Since Zanuck was in a hurry to beat every other studio to new material, I often worked past midnight. I was enjoying my job, but I was impatient to become a writer. The studio had started a junior writer division and I told Julian Johnson I would like to be in it. He was sympathetic, but not encouraging. "You're doing work for Zanuck," he said. "That's more important."

My little office was in an old, creaky wooden building at the back of the lot. At night the lot was deserted, and sometimes I was uneasy working there alone, surrounded by darkness. One night I was doing a rush job on a book that Zanuck was excited about. It was a ghost story that was quite scary.

I was just typing the line, "He opened the closet door and as the grinning corpse inside started to fall on top of him . . ." when the closet door of my office flew open, books began flying through the air, and the room began to shake. I broke all speed records getting out of there.

It was my most memorable earthquake.

In early September, a stranger walked into my office and introduced himself.

"My name is Alan Jackson. I'm a reader at Columbia."

"Glad to meet you." We shook hands. "What can I do for you?"

"We want to form a readers guild and we need your help."

"How?"

"You can get the readers here to agree that we should have a guild, and join us. When we get the readers at all the other studios, we can form a committee and negotiate a deal with the studios. Right now we have no power. We're underpaid and overworked. Will you help us?"

I did not consider myself underpaid or overworked, but I knew that the majority of readers were. "I'll do everything I can."

"Great."

"There may be a problem," I warned him.

"What's that?"

"Almost everyone here at Fox is related to an executive at the studio. I don't think they'd be willing to get involved, but we'll see."

To my amazement, every reader at the studio agreed to join the readers guild when we formed one.

When I told Alan Jackson the news, he said, "That's great. We have all the other studio readers signed up. We're forming a negotiating committee. By the way, you're on it."

Our negotiation took place in a conference room at Metro-Goldwyn-Mayer Studios. Our committee consisted of six readers from various studios. Sitting opposite us, at the large table, were four studio executives. Six lambs and four lions.

Eddie Mannix, a tough Irishman who was one of the top executives at Metro-Goldwyn-Mayer, started the meeting by growling, "What's your problem?"

One of our group spoke up. "Mr. Mannix, we're not getting a living wage. I make sixteen dollars a week and I can't afford to—"

Eddie Mannix leaped to his feet and screamed, "I'm not going to listen to this shit!" and he stormed out of the room.

The six of us sat there, petrified. The meeting was over.

One of the other executives shook his head and said, "I'll see if I can get him to come back."

A few minutes later, he returned with a furious Mannix. We sat there, watching him, cowed.

"What the hell do you want?" he demanded.

We began our negotiations.

Two hours later, there was an official Readers Guild, to be recognized by all the studios. Their committee had agreed to a base pay of twenty-one dollars and fifty cents a week for staff readers and a twenty percent increase for outside readers. I was elected vice president of the guild.

It was not until years later, when I met him again, that I realized what a brilliant act Eddie Mannix had put on.

I called Otto and Natalie to tell them what had happened. They were thrilled. I later learned that after my phone call, Otto had gone around telling his friends that I had single-handedly saved all the studios in Hollywood from a ruinous strike.

One of the new boarders at Gracie's was a shy young man named Ben Roberts. He was my age, short, with a dark complexion, thin hair, and a smiling face. He had a dry, laconic sense of humor. We soon became friends.

Ben was a writer, but his only credit was on a Leon Errol short. We started talking about collaborating. Every evening, Ben and I would go to the corner drugstore and have a sandwich for dinner, or drop in at a cheap Chinese restaurant. Collaborating with Ben was easy. He was very talented, and in a few weeks, we had completed an original story. We mailed it out to all the studios and eagerly waited for the offers to pour in.

They never came.

Ben and I went to work on another story with the same result. We decided the studios obviously did not recognize talent when they came across it.

A third story went un-bought and we were becoming discouraged.

One day, I said, "I have an idea for a mystery story. We'll call it *Dangerous Holiday*." I told Ben the idea and he liked it. We wrote a treatment and mailed copies to the studios. Again, there was no response.

A week after we had sent out the story, I arrived at the boardinghouse, and Ben was waiting for me, filled with excitement.

"I gave our story to a producer I know, Ted Richmond. He's at PRC."

That was one of the smallest studios, Producers Releasing Corporation.

"He loved *Dangerous Holiday*," Ben said. "He's offered us five hundred dollars for it. That includes us writing the screenplay. I told him I would talk to you and let him know."

I was thrilled. Of course we were going to take it. The most important credit in Hollywood was always the first one. It reminded me of my experience in New York.

Have you had any songs published?

No.

Come back when you've had something published.

Now it was, "Do you have any screen credits?"

"No."

"Come back when you have a screen credit."

Well, now we had one. *Dangerous Holiday.*

A few months earlier, I had met Ray Crossett, who was in charge of the literary department at the Leland Hayward Agency, one of the top talent agencies in Hollywood. For some reason, Crossett had faith in me and had promised that one day he would represent me.

I telephoned Ray to tell him the good news about Ted Richmond.

"Ben and I just sold our first story," I said. *"Dangerous Holiday."*

"To whom?"

"PRC."

"What's a PRC?"

That set me back. Ray Crossett, one of the top agents in the business, had never even heard of PRC.

"It's a studio called Producers Releasing Corporation. A producer there named Ted Richmond offered us five hundred dollars, including the screenplay we have to write."

"Did you make a deal?"

"Well, we said we'd let him know, but—"

"I'll call you back," Ray said, and he hung up.

Two hours later, Ray was on the phone. "I just sold your story to Paramount. They'll pay you a thousand dollars and you don't have to write the screenplay."

My first reaction was shock, but I knew what had happened. Every studio had a synopsis of every story submitted to it. When Ray called Paramount and told them *Dangerous Holiday* was being bought by another studio, they rose to the bait.

"Ray," I said, "that's—that's great—but we can't accept it."

"What are you talking about? It's twice the money and a major studio."

"I can't do it. I feel obligated to Ted Richmond and—"

"Look. Call him and tell him what happened. I'm sure he'll understand."

"I'll try," I said.

But I was sure that Ted Richmond would not understand.

I called his office. His secretary said, "Mr. Richmond is in the cutting room. He can't be disturbed."

"Will you have him call me? It's very important."

"I'll give him the message."

One hour later I called again.

"I need to talk to Mr. Richmond. It's urgent."

"I'm sorry. He can't be disturbed. I gave him your message."

I tried three times that afternoon and finally gave up.

I called Ray Crossett. "Richmond won't return my calls. Go ahead and make the deal with Paramount."

"I made it four hours ago."

When Ben came in, I brought him up-to-date.

He was excited. "That's fantastic," he said. "Paramount is an important studio. But what do we tell Ted Richmond?"

Good question. *What were we going to tell Ted Richmond?*

That evening, I called Ted's home and he answered the telephone.

Because I felt guilty, I went on the offensive. "I called you a half a dozen times today. Why didn't you call me back?"

"I'm sorry. I was in the cutting room and—"

"Well, you should have called. Because of you, Ben and I almost lost a deal."

"What are you talking about?"

"Paramount just bought *Dangerous Holiday*. They

made an offer, and when we couldn't reach you, we finally sold it to them."

"But I've already put it on our schedule and we—"

"Don't worry about that," I said reassuringly. "You're in luck. Ben and I have a story for you that's much more exciting than *Dangerous Holiday*. It's called *South of Panama*. It's a drama, with a love story, suspense, and a lot of action. It's one of the best things we've ever written."

There was a moment of silence. "All right," he said. "Meet me and Alex at the Pig & Whistle at eight o'clock tomorrow morning."

Alex was the executive head of PRC.

"I'll be there," I said. I replaced the receiver and turned to Ben. "We'll skip dinner. We've got to come up with a plot that has a love story, suspense, and a lot of action. We have until seven o'clock tomorrow morning."

Ben and I worked all night, tossing ideas back and forth, finding a plot, adding and deleting characters. It was getting more and more exhausting. We finished *South of Panama* at five in the morning.

"We did it!" Ben said. "You show it to them this morning."

I agreed. I set my alarm for seven o'clock. I would get two hours sleep before the meeting.

When the alarm clock awakened me, I got up and groggily read our story. It was terrible. I hated the plot, the characters, and the dialogue. But I still had to go to the meeting and face Alex and Ted.

At eight o'clock I slunk into the Pig & Whistle. Ted and Alex were seated at a booth, waiting for me. I had brought two copies of the story.

"I can't wait to read it," Alex said.

Ted nodded. "Neither can I."

I sat down and handed them each a copy. They

started reading. I couldn't bear to look at them. They were turning pages. *No* comment. More pages. Silence.

It's what we deserve, I thought. *How can anyone write a story under that kind of pressure?*

They both finished at the same time. Alex looked up at me. "It's brilliant."

"Wonderful," Ted chimed in. "You're right. This is better than *Dangerous Holiday.*"

I could not believe what I was hearing.

"We'll give you five hundred dollars," Alex said, "and you and Ben will write the screenplay for that."

I took a deep, deep breath. "It's a deal."

Ben and I had performed a miracle. We had sold two stories in a period of twenty-four hours.

That night, Ben and I went to Musso & Frank's, one of Hollywood's classic restaurants, to celebrate. It was the first time we had been able to afford it. It was one day past my twenty-fourth birthday.

South of Panama was made by the Producers Releasing Corporation and starred Roger Pryor and Virginia Vale. Paramount made *Dangerous Holiday* and renamed it *Fly-By-Night.* It starred Richard Carlson and Nancy Kelly.

Ben and I were on a roll. The first thing I did was quit my reader's job at Fox. Mr. Zanuck would have to get along without me. Shortly after I left Fox, Ben and I sold another story, called *Borrowed Hero*, to Monogram, a small studio that made B movies, and *Dangerous Lady* and *Gambling Daughters* to PRC. For each story and screenplay we received five hundred dollars, which Ben and I shared. It would be hyperbole to suggest that these were memorable movies, but at least we were now recognized screenwriters.

Leonard Fields, a producer at Republic Studios—the

top of the B studio list—bought a story of ours called *Mr. District Attorney in the Carter Case.* For the story and the screenplay, Ben and I received the munificent sum of six hundred dollars.

The picture proved to be successful and Leonard Fields called me in. "We'd like to put you and Ben under contract."

"Great!"

"Five hundred a week."

"For each of us?"

"For the team."

Ben and I worked on screenplays at Republic for a year, until our contract was up. At Christmas, Leonard Fields sent for us.

"You boys are doing a terrific job. We're going to re-sign you."

"That's great news, Leonard. The only thing is that Ben and I would like six hundred dollars a week."

Leonard Fields nodded. "I'll call you."

We never heard from Leonard Fields again.

I talked to Ray Crossett, and I asked him why he could not get us a job at a major studio.

"I'm afraid your credits are not very impressive. I'd have a better chance if you'd never written any of those pictures."

So Ben and I continued to write and sell B pictures. It was a living.

I went home to Chicago for Thanksgiving, and it was wonderful to see Richard and my parents. Otto insisted on having the neighbors in, so that they could meet his son, who controlled Hollywood.

CHAPTER

11

It was wonderful to be home. Richard had grown up. He had graduated grammar school and was ready for high school. The only thing that marred my trip home was that Natalie and Otto were still fighting. And this time it was Richard who was caught in the middle.

I spoke to Natalie and Otto about it, but the bitterness ran too deep for them to stop fighting. They were simply wrong for each other.

I decided it was time for Richard to come to Hollywood. Ben and I were selling enough stories for me to support myself and my brother.

I said to Richard, "How would you like to go to Hollywood High?"

He was staring at me. "Do you mean it?"

"You bet I do."

There was a silence and then a yell that I thought was going to break my eardrums.

One week later, Richard moved into Gracie's boardinghouse and I introduced him to everyone. I had never seen him so happy. I realized how much we had missed each other.

Three months after Richard and I left Chicago, Natalie and Otto got a divorce. I had mixed feelings about it, but I decided it was the best thing for everyone.

Early one morning, I received a phone call.

"Sidney?"

"Yes."

"Hi, pal, this is Bob Russell."

Not only was I not his pal, but I had never heard of Bob Russell. *Probably a salesman.* "I'm sorry," I said, "but I haven't time to—"

"You should have done some songs with Max Rich."

I was startled for a moment. Who could have known—? But then I realized who it was. "Sidney Rosenthal!"

"Bob Russell," he corrected. "I'm coming out to Hollywood to see you."

"Great!"

One week later, Bob Russell arrived and moved into the last available room in Gracie's boardinghouse. It was wonderful to see him. He was still as enthusiastic as ever.

"Are you still writing songs?" I asked.

"You bet I am. You shouldn't have given it up," he chided me.

Richard, who was gregarious, had already made friends at Hollywood High. Sometimes he brought them to Gracie's boardinghouse and other times he was invited to their homes.

One night, when we were invited to a dinner party, I was taking a shower, and as I reached for the soap, the herniated disc in my back slipped out, and I fell to the floor in agony. I was in bed for the next three days. I decided that, like it or not, it was something I would have to live with for the rest of my life.

Natalie called me one evening. "I have some news for you, darling. I'm getting married."

I was thrilled for her. I hoped this time she would be treated as she deserved to be treated. "Who is it? Do I know him?"

"His name is Martin Leeb. He's a toy manufacturer. And he's a doll."

"That sounds wonderful," I said enthusiastically. "When am I going to meet him?"

"We'll come out there and visit you."

When I told Richard the news, he was as excited as I was.

The next call, the following week, was from Otto. "Sidney, I just want to tell you I'm getting married."

"Oh?" I was caught off guard. "Anyone I know?"

"No. Her name is Ann Curtis. She's a very nice woman."

"Well, I'm pleased for you, Otto. I hope you'll be happy."

"I know I'm going to be."

I wondered.

With Bob Russell there, it was like old home week.

He had brought with him the latest song he had written. "It's a torch song," Bob said. "See what you think of it."

I played it on the piano and said, "It's beautiful." I had an idea. "There's a singer opening at a club on the east side Saturday. I'll bet she could use this. Do you mind if I show it to her?"

"Be my guest."

The following day I went to the club where the singer was rehearsing and showed her the song.

"I like it," she said. "I'll give you fifty dollars."

"I'll take it."

When I gave the money to Bob, he grinned. "Thank you. Now I'm a professional."

Hollywood had its temperamental mini-storms every day, but in Europe, there was a real storm brewing. It had started in 1939, when Germany and the Soviet Union invaded Poland. Britain, France, and Australia had declared war on Germany. In 1940, Italy had joined with Germany, and now a dozen European countries were at war. America had declared its neutrality. But not for long.

On December 7, 1941, Pearl Harbor was attacked by the Japanese, and the following day, President Franklin D. Roosevelt declared war on Japan.

An hour after Roosevelt had declared war, Louis B. Mayer, the head of Metro-Goldwyn-Mayer, who was appointed by the MGM president, Nicholas Schenk, called a meeting of his top producers and directors. When they were assembled, Mayer said solemnly, "You all heard what happened at Pearl Harbor yesterday. Well, we're not going to stand for it. We're going to fight back." He looked around the room. "I know that I can count on every one of you to join me in standing behind our great president—Nicholas M. Schenk."

Ben and Bob and I were all of draft age and we knew we were going to be inducted soon.

Ben said, "There's a training film unit at Fort Dix in New Jersey. I'm going to enlist and see if I can get into that."

He volunteered the next day and the Army was happy to get him. One week later he was on his way east.

"What are you going to do?" I asked Bob.

"I don't know yet. I have asthma. They won't take me in the Army. I'm going back to New York and see what I can do to help. What are you going to do?"

"I'm going to join the Air Corps."

On October 26, 1942, I applied for the Army Air Corps.

In order to have my application accepted, it was necessary to get three letters of recommendation from prominent people. I did not know any prominent people. I started writing letters to members of Congress, telling them that I was determined to serve my country and that I needed their help. It took me two months to finally collect my three letters.

The next step was to make an appointment at the Federal Building in downtown Los Angeles, to take a written examination. There were approximately two hundred applicants in the room. The test, which covered logic, vocabulary, mathematics, and general knowledge, lasted four hours.

The mathematics section baffled me. Because I had changed schools so often, I had never really learned some of the basics of math. I missed most of the questions in that section and was sure I would be rejected.

Three days later, I received a notice to report for an Air Corps physical examination. To my surprise, I had passed the written test. I later learned that only thirty applicants in the group had been accepted.

I was sent to an armory uptown for my physical examination, sure that I would pass with flying colors.

When the examination was finished, the doctor asked, "Any physical problems I should know about?"

"No, sir." And as I said it, I thought about my herniated disc and I wondered if that was important. "I—"

"What?"

I knew I was on dangerous ground. "I do have a problem, sir, but it's very minor. I have a herniated disc that slips out once in a while, but—"

He was writing on my application, "herniated disc." I watched him pick up a rubber stamp with the word DISQUALIFIED in red letters.

"Wait a minute!" I said.

He looked up at me. "Yes?"

I was not going to let anything stop me. "That disc doesn't go out anymore. It's cured. I can't even remember the last time I had a problem. I only mentioned it because it was something I used to have." I didn't even know what I was saying, but I knew that if he red-stamped my application, I was through. I kept talking until finally he put the rubber stamp down. "All right. If you're sure—"

In my sincerest voice, "I'm positive, sir."

"Very well."

I was in! All that remained was the eye test, and that would be no problem.

I was sent to another office, where I was handed two index cards, each one containing the name of an optometrist who could approve my application.

"Take this card to either doctor," I was told. "When you've passed your eye examination, have him sign it. Then bring it back here."

I went back to Gracie's and told Richard how well everything was going. It looked like I was going to be in the Air Corps.

Richard was devastated that I might be leaving. "I'll be here all alone."

"Gracie will take care of you," I assured him. "And Mother and Marty will be out here soon. Anyway, the war can't last very long."

Sidney the prophet.

The following morning I went to see Dr. Fred Severn, whose name was on the first card. His reception room was crowded with men waiting to take their eye tests. I sat in his waiting room for an hour. Finally I was ushered into Dr. Severn's office.

"Be seated." He looked at the card I handed him and nodded. "A pilot, huh?"

"Yes, sir."

"Well, let's see if you have the twenty/twenty vision they require."

He led me into a smaller room with a large eye chart on the wall. Dr. Severn darkened the room.

"Read it from the top."

It was easy—until I got to the last two lines. I could not read a single letter. *But surely getting that close was enough.*

The lights came on.

The doctor was writing something on the card.

I had made it!

"Just give this to the receptionist," he said.

"Thank you, Doctor."

As I walked out the door, I looked at the card. My name was on the card and at the bottom he had written, "Physically disqualified. Defective visual acuity." Signed, "Dr. Fred Severn."

I could not believe it. I could not accept that. Nothing was going to stop me from getting into the Air Corps.

I started to walk out with the card.

The receptionist said, "Sir, may I have your card?"

I kept walking, pretending not to hear.

"Sir—"

I was out the door.

I still had one doctor left to go to. But how could I make sure that I would pass his test?

One hour later, I was in the office of my regular optometrist, Dr. Samuel Peters. I told him what had happened.

"For twenty/twenty vision," he explained, "you need to read all the lines."

"Is there any way you can help me?"

He thought for a moment. "There is."

He reached into one of the drawers and pulled out a pair of glasses with lenses that looked like glass bottle tops.

"What's that?"

"That's what's going to get you into the Air Corps."

"How?"

"Before you go in for your next eye test, wear them for a while. They will inhibit your vision so that your eyes will be straining to see, so when you walk in for the test, your vision will be better than ever."

"Great," I said. I shook his hand, thanked him, and left.

I had made an appointment with the second doctor, Dr. Edward Gale, for ten o'clock the following day.

I walked into the lobby of the building his office was in and sat down on a bench. I put on the thick glasses, and waited for them to do their magic.

Thirty minutes before my appointment, I took the glasses off and walked into Dr. Gale's reception area.

"Mr. Sheldon," the nurse said. "The doctor is waiting to give you your test."

I smiled smugly. "Thank you."

I walked into the inner office and handed the card to

Dr. Gale. He looked at it and said, "Air Corps, huh? Sit down."

The doctor darkened the room and a lighted eye chart appeared.

"Go ahead. Start at the top."

There was one little problem. I could not see one single letter on the chart.

He was waiting. "You can start now."

On the first line there was something that could have been a big A, but I wasn't sure. I took a chance. "A."

"Yes. Go on."

There was nowhere to go. I was almost blind. "I can't—"

He was staring at me. "What's the next line?"

"I—I can't read it."

"Is this a joke?" He was angry. "You can't read any of those lines?"

"No, I—"

"And you want to fly in the Air Corps? Forget it!" He picked up my card and started to write.

My last chance had just gone down the drain. I was panicky. I started babbling. "Wait," I said, "don't write anything yet."

He looked up at me, surprised.

"Doctor, you don't understand. I haven't slept all week. I've been taking care of my mother. My eyes are tired. I haven't been well. My favorite uncle just died. It's been horrible. You have to give me another chance."

He was listening. But when he spoke, he said, "I'm afraid there's no way you can—"

"Just one more chance."

He could hear the desperation in my voice. He shook his head. "Well, we'll try again tomorrow, but you're wasting—"

"Oh, thank you," I said quickly. "I'll be here."

I rushed back to my optometrist's office.

"Thanks a lot," I said bitterly. I told Dr. Peters what had happened.

"How long did you wear the glasses?" he asked.

"Twenty, thirty minutes."

"You were only supposed to wear them for ten minutes."

Now he tells me. "This is important to me," I told him. "I have to do something."

He sat back in his chair for a moment, thinking. "Did he darken the room when you read the chart?"

"Yes."

"Good."

He walked into a closet and came out holding an eye chart.

"Oh, that's great," I said. "I'll memorize it and—"

"No. Different charts have different letters."

"Then what's the point of my—?"

"Here's what you do. Practice on this chart. You squint the letters in. That will sharpen your vision. Keep working on it until you can read the two bottom lines. In the dark, he won't see what you're doing."

I was skeptical. "Are you sure that—"

"That's up to you. Good luck."

I spent the whole evening squinting in the letters of the eye chart. It seemed to be working, but I wasn't sure how I would do with Dr. Gale.

At ten o'clock the next morning, I was back at Dr. Gale's office. When he saw me, he said, "I don't know why we're bothering. After yesterday—"

"Just let me try."

He sighed. "Very well."

We went back into the same room. He turned out the

lights. "All right. Go ahead." I sat in the chair and started squinting in the letters of the chart. Dr. Peters had been right. I could see the letters very clearly. I read everything, including the last line. The lights came on.

Dr. Gale was staring at me in astonishment. "I can't believe it. I've never seen anything like this," he said. He went on. "You missed a few letters in the last two lines. You have twenty/twenty-two vision. Let's see what the Air Corps has to say." He signed the card and handed it to me.

The next morning I reported to an Army officer at the Federal Building. He looked at the card and said, "Twenty/twenty-two. That's not bad, but we can't train you to do combat flying. For that you need twenty/twenty vision."

I was shocked. "You mean I can't—"

"I'll tell you what you can do. Have you ever heard of War Training Service?"

"No, sir."

"It's a new branch of the Army Air Corps. It used to be called the Civil Air Patrol. In the War Training Service, they'll train you to fly ferry planes to Europe or to be a flight instructor. But no combat flying. Would you like to be in that?"

"Yes, sir." I was going to be an Air Corps pilot after all.

"Since you're not going to be in the regular Air Corps, you have to supply your own uniform. You'll get a cadet's pay and a place to live. Is that satisfactory?"

"Yes, sir."

"Your flight training will be at Richfield, Utah. You'll report there a week from Monday."

I had never been so excited.

* * *

Natalie came to town with her husband and Richard and I finally got to meet Marty. He was short, gray-haired, and heavyset, with a friendly face. I liked him immediately. We all had dinner together, and I brought Natalie and Marty up-to-date on what was happening.

"So you're going to need a uniform," Marty said. "Let's go shopping."

"You don't have to—"

"I want to."

Since there was no regulation regarding our uniforms, Marty took me to an Army-Navy store and bought me beautifully tailored officer's uniforms, and a leather flying jacket. I bought a white scarf to wear around my neck, so I could look as much like a flying ace as possible.

I was ready to help America win the war.

CHAPTER

12

Richfield, Utah, was a small town with a population of sixty-five hundred, surrounded by the Monroe Mountains. There was a pleasant hotel on the main street. Following instructions, we cadets checked into our rooms and then returned to the lobby. There were fourteen of us. We had been in the lobby for thirty minutes when a tall, craggy-faced man in uniform walked in. He looked us over.

"Has everyone checked in?"

There was a chorus of "Yes, sir."

"Good. I'm Captain Anderson, your chief instructor. This hotel is fifteen minutes from the airport. A bus will pick you up at six o'clock every morning. Get a good night's sleep. You're going to need it."

And he left.

The following morning we were picked up by an Army bus and driven to the airfield. It was much smaller than I had expected.

Captain Anderson was waiting for us. "Follow me," he said.

He walked over to a nearby building and we followed him inside. The building had been turned into a school, with rooms converted to classrooms.

When we were seated, Captain Anderson said, "You're about to embark on a six-month flying course." He paused. "But because there's a war on, we're going to do it in three months. You're going to have classes in map reading, aerodynamics, weather, navigation, cross-country flight planning, and engine theory. You're going to learn the Morse Code and how to pack your own parachutes. Each class will have a different instructor. Any questions?"

"No, sir."

Our first class was in aerodynamics. The class lasted for an hour. When it came to an end our instructor said, "I'm going to pass out your textbooks on aerodynamics. I want you to answer the questions in each chapter from one to twenty. That's your homework. Come in with your answers tomorrow. Dismissed."

I riffled through the textbook. There were long questions after every chapter. I would probably be up late.

Our next class was navigation. An hour later, when the class was over, our instructor said, "Take your textbooks and work on pages one to one-fifty. Answer all the questions."

We looked at one another. This was getting to be a heavy load.

The third class was engine theory. It was very technical and I made voluminous notes. When we were finally ready to leave, the instructor said, "Your homework is to read the text and answer the questions from page one to page one hundred twenty."

It was all I could do not to laugh. There was no way to cope with this mountain of homework and we were not through with our classes yet. The last class was parachute packing—a complicated and tedious task to learn, especially after a long day.

We were beginning to understand what Captain Anderson had meant when he said, *It's a six-month course, but you're going to do it in three months.* I think every cadet was up until four or five in the morning, trying to complete the homework.

Every day the routine was the same. We would finish our classes and go out to the field to become acquainted with our planes. I would be flying Piper Cubs, propeller planes with the instructor and the pupil side by side.

All of us had come here because we wanted to learn to fly, but the homework finally became so onerous, keeping us up till three or four o'clock every morning, that we kept hoping our flights would be delayed so that we could finish the homework.

I had been assigned to Captain Anderson. He watched as I packed my parachute for my first flight and put it on. We got into the plane.

"Observe everything I do," he said.

I watched as Captain Anderson skillfully took off. "You have to remember two important things. Number one is swivel. Keep your head turning all the time, looking around to see if there are any other planes near you. The second lesson is to coordinate your speed with your altitude, so that you're never in danger of crashing."

As we rose higher and higher, I realized that the airfield was completely surrounded by mountains. When we had climbed to seventy-five hundred feet, Captain Anderson said, "Now we're going to do some spins," and the plane began to circle down in quick spins. That was when I learned I had a problem. I got airsick.

Captain Anderson looked at me in disgust. I was flushed with embarrassment.

The following day, we did stalls and cloverleafs and I was sick again.

When we landed, Captain Anderson said, "Did you have breakfast this morning?"

"Yes, sir."

"From now on you will not eat anything until lunchtime."

That meant nothing to eat from dinner the previous night until one-thirty the next afternoon.

The first time Captain Anderson had me take the controls, all feelings of airsickness left me. From then on, when I was piloting the plane, I felt wonderful, concentrating on what I was doing.

Every week I called Richard at Gracie's, and Natalie and Marty, to let them know I was all right. Everything seemed to be fine there and I assured them that I was going to be the flying ace of World War II.

One day Richard called. "I have some news for you, Sidney. I just enlisted."

For a moment my heart stopped. He was too young to—and then I realized he was no longer a little boy. I said, "Richard, I'm proud of you."

One week later, he was on his way to boot camp.

Regularly, during our training, Captain Anderson would turn off the ignition without warning.

"Your engine just died, Sheldon. Make an emergency landing."

I looked down. There was no place to land. But I could tell by his expression that that was not what he wanted to hear. I gradually lost altitude, until I could see a suitable place for a landing.

As I started to land, Captain Anderson switched on the ignition. "Good. Take it up."

On the day Captain Anderson said, "You're ready to solo, Sheldon," I was filled with excitement.

"Be sure to coordinate your altitude and speed."

I nodded, strapped on my parachute, and got into the plane, alone for the first time. The other flight groups were watching. I started taxiing down the field and moments later I was in the air. It was a fantastic feeling. A feeling of freedom. A feeling of breaking the bonds of earth and soaring into a new world. A feeling of not getting airsick.

I reached my pattern altitude of sixty-one hundred feet and went through my routine maneuvers.

I had been instructed to stay up in the air for twenty minutes. I glanced at my watch. It was time to show them all what a perfect landing looked like. I pushed the stick forward and began my descent. I could see the men down below, waiting for me on the field.

The rules for landing are fixed. The speeds at set altitudes had been drilled into us. As I got closer to the ground, I looked at the altimeter and suddenly realized that I had forgotten what speed I was supposed to be at. In fact, everything I had learned about flying had instantly gone out of my head. I had no idea what I was doing.

In a panic, I pulled the stick back to gain altitude and keep from crashing. I frantically tried to remember the formula for altitude and speed, but my mind was a blank. If I made a mistake in landing, I would crash and die. I flew around, shaken, trying to figure out what to do. I thought of bailing out, but I knew that the Air Corps could not spare any planes. But I could not stay up here forever. I had to land sometime.

I started my descent again, vainly trying to remember what my airspeed was supposed to be as I approached the runway. Down to a thousand feet, speed sixty miles an hour . . . Three hundred feet, speed fifty miles an hour . . . Was I going too fast? I circled the field three times, getting closer and closer to the ground. *Fifty miles an hour. Too fast? Too slow?* I took a deep breath and went for it.

The plane hit the ground, bounced up, hit the ground again, bounced up again, and finally settled, as I pulled back the stick and hit the brakes. I got out of the plane, trembling.

Captain Anderson, who had been on his way to town, had stopped when he saw what was happening and sped back to the airfield. He came rushing up to me.

"What the hell do you think you were doing?" he demanded.

I was sweating profusely. "I—I don't know. Next time I'll be—"

"Not next time. Now!"

I was confused. "Now?"

"That's right. Get back in that plane and take it up again."

I thought he was joking.

"I'm waiting."

So he meant it. I knew the saying "If you fall off a horse, you've got to get right back on." Captain Anderson apparently felt that the same thing also applied to planes. He was sending me to my death. I looked into his eyes and decided not to argue. I got back in the plane and sat there to control my breathing. If I died, it was going to be his fault.

Everyone was watching as I taxied down the runway.

I was in the air again. I tried to relax and concentrate on remembering everything I had been taught about speed, altitude, and flight angles. Suddenly, blessedly, my mind started to clear. I stayed up for another fifteen minutes and this time I was ready. I made an almost perfect landing.

As I stepped out of the plane, Captain Anderson growled, "That's better. You'll do it again tomorrow."

The rest of my flight training went without incident except for one memorable day near the end of the course.

That morning, as I was about to take off, Captain Anderson said, "We have a report that there's a bad storm heading this way, Sheldon. Keep an eye out for it. When you see it coming, land immediately."

"Yes, sir."

I took off, reached my altitude, and began circling around the mountains, going through my spins and stalls. *There's a bad storm heading this way . . . When you see it coming, land immediately . . .*

What if I were caught in it and couldn't see a place to land? I visualized the headlines: "*Pilot Trapped in Storm.*"

The news would be on the radio and television. The world would be holding its breath to see whether the young cadet made it safely or not. The landing field below me would be swarming with ambulances and firefighting equipment. I was completely caught up in my daydream, enjoying my bravery in the face of this great disaster, when it suddenly grew dark. The reason it grew dark was that my plane was in the middle of the storm. I was flying blind, surrounded by ominous black clouds. I could not see the airfield or anything around me. All I knew for certain was that on every side of me were un-forgiving mountain peaks and I could crash into one of them at any second. I had lost all sense of direction. Was the airfield ahead of me? Behind me? To the side of me?

The wind began to bounce the plane around. The headlines I had been daydreaming about were becoming real. In an effort to avoid the mountains surrounding me, I started to fly in very small circles, going lower and lower, bouncing around, trying to stay in the same safe area. When I got down to thirty feet, I could see the airfield. The whole crew was down there, watching.

When I landed the plane, my instructor came up to me, furious.

"What's the matter with you? I told you to watch out for the storm."

"Sorry. Yes, sir. It crept up on me."

I got my wings exactly three months after I had ar-rived in Richfield.

Captain Anderson called us all together. "You're ready for training in multiple engine planes, BT-19s and DAT-6s. Unfortunately, at the moment, the advanced flight schools are all full. So you're going to be on standby. There could be openings at any minute. You don't have to stay here while you're waiting, but leave a phone number with the sergeant where you can be reached, day or night.

"The minute we have openings for an advanced flight school, we'll be in touch with you. Good luck."

And the thought that came into my mind was Ben Roberts. I decided that while I waited for a flight school to open up, I would go to New York. I made a reservation at a hotel in Manhattan and gave the telephone number to the sergeant. I had a feeling that the minute I arrived in New York, there would be a message ordering me to return.

I said goodbye to my fellow fliers, and that afternoon I was on a plane to New York, to see Ben.

CHAPTER

13

It was a smooth, pleasant flight. I sat in a large commercial plane filled with passengers, wearing my Air Corps uniform with shiny wings and getting continually airsick while all the passengers stared at me. I'm convinced that if I had been allowed to fly combat, the war would have been shorter. But we would have lost.

We arrived in New York, at the land of the Brill Building and the RKO Jefferson and Max Rich, and the memories that flooded in seemed to belong to another world, another time.

Ben Roberts was at the airport to greet me with a big hug. On the way to the hotel, Ben brought me up-to-date on his activities.

"I'm stationed at Fort Dix," he said, "writing war training films. You can't believe what they're like. In one film we spend ten minutes showing recruits how to raise the hood of a car. It's like writing for five-year-olds. How long are you going to be in New York?"

I shook my head. "It could be an hour, it could be a week. I think it's going to be closer to an hour." I explained my situation to him. "I'm waiting for a call to report back to the Air Corps, and it could come at any minute."

We reached the hotel where I had reservations, and I went to the desk. "I'm expecting a very important long-distance phone call," I told the clerk. "*Very* important. Please make sure I get it immediately."

Ben and I made a date for dinner the following night.

The next morning, I telephoned my agent, Louis Schur, in California. I told him that I was in New York and had free time until the secondary flying school opened up.

"Why don't you go to the office," he suggested, "and see my partner, Jules Zeigler? He might have something for you to do while you're here."

Jules Zeigler, head of the New York office, turned out to be a swarthy man in his forties, with a quick, nervous energy.

"Louie told me you'd be coming," he said. "Are you looking for a project to do?"

"Well, I—"

"I have something interesting. Have you ever heard of Jan Kiepura?"

"No. Is that some holiday?"

"Jan Kiepura is a big opera star in Europe. So is his wife, Marta Eggerth. They've made a lot of movies over there. They want to do a show on Broadway, *The Merry Widow*."

The Merry Widow, a famous operetta by Franz Lehár, was the story of a prince from a small kingdom who courts a wealthy widow to keep her money in his country. It was always playing somewhere around the world.

"They want someone to update the book. Are you interested in meeting them?"

What was the point? I was not going to be in New York long enough to write a letter, let alone a Broadway show.

"I don't think that I can—"

"Well, at least go meet with them."

I met Jan Kiepura and Marta Eggerth in their suite at the Astor Hotel. When Kiepura opened the door for me, he looked at my uniform and said, puzzled, "Are you the writer?"

"Yes."

"Come in."

Jan was a powerfully built man in his forties, with a heavy Hungarian accent. Marta was slim and attractive, with wavy shoulder-length hair, and a welcoming smile.

"Sit down," Kiepura said.

I sat.

"We want to do *The Merry Widow,* but we want it to be modernized. Jules says you're a good writer. What have you written?"

"*Fly-By-Night, South of Panama . . .*" I named some of the B pictures that Ben and I had done.

They looked at each other blankly. Jan Kiepura said, "We will let you know."

That's that. It's over. And it's just as well.

Thirty minutes later, I was back in Jules Zeigler's office.

"They just called," Zeigler said. "They want you to write the show."

The black cloud descended over me. There was no way I could do it. Broadway was the Mecca every writer aspired to. What did I know about writing a Broadway show? Absolutely nothing. I would make a fool of myself and destroy the production. Anyway, I expected to receive the phone call to report back to the Air Corps at any second.

Jules Zeigler was watching me. "Are you all right?"

I did not have the courage to tell him I was not going to do the show. "Sure."

"They want you to start right away."

"Right."

I went back to my hotel room. I would have to tell them that there was no way I could do it. But as I thought about it, I realized that there was a way. *Ben Roberts.* Ben could write the show with me. And when I got called back to the Air Corps in the middle of the project, Ben could finish it.

I called him at Fort Dix.

"What's new?" he said.

"I'll tell you what's new. You and I are going to write a new book for *The Merry Widow.*"

There was a pause. "I didn't know you drank."

"I'm serious. I've talked to the stars of the show. They want us."

He was speechless.

The following day, I went to the theater where *The Merry Widow* was going to open. The show was being produced by the New Opera Company, headed by Yolanda Mero-Irion, a short, buxom, middle-aged woman with a high, shrill voice.

It was a first-class production. The choreography was being done by the legendary George Balanchine, who was one of the century's foremost choreographers. Balanchine was of medium height with the well-developed body of a dancer. He had a friendly smile and a faint Russian accent.

The director was the brilliant Felix Brentano, and the conductor was Robert Stolz, who was a wonderful composer in his own right. The prima ballerina was Milada Mladova, a stunning young European dancer.

I had a meeting with Balanchine, Stolz, and Brentano, and we discussed the libretto.

"It must be as modern as possible," the director said, "but we must not lose its period flavor."

"Entertaining and amusing," Balanchine said.

"Lighthearted," Robert Stolz commented.

Right. Modern, but keeping the period flavor, entertaining and amusing, lighthearted. "No problem."

Ben and I had figured out a way to collaborate. Since he was stationed at Fort Dix in New Jersey all day, working on training films, he would come into New York at night, where we would have dinner and work together until one or two in the morning.

My fears about writing a Broadway play had evaporated. Working with Ben made everything seem easy. He was incredibly creative and he gave me a confidence I lacked.

When we finished writing the first act, I took it to our producer, Yolanda Mero-Irion. I watched eagerly while she read the pages.

She looked up at me. "This is terrible. Dreadful," she spat out.

I was stunned. "But we did everything that—"

"You've written a flop for me! A flop! You hear me?" Her tone was vicious.

"I'm sorry. Tell me what you don't like and Ben and I will rewrite it and—"

She got up, glared at me, and walked out.

I was back to my first opinion. What made me ever think I was capable of writing a Broadway show?

As I sat there, contemplating the disaster that was

about to happen, George Balanchine and Felix Brentano came into the office.

"I hear you have a first act."

I nodded glumly. "Yes."

"Let's look at it."

I was tempted not to show it to them. "Sure."

They started reading it and I wished I were somewhere else, anywhere.

I heard a chuckle. It was Felix Brentano. And then a laugh. It was George Balanchine. They were both grinning as they read it.

They liked it!

When they finished, Felix Brentano said to me, "This is wonderful, Sidney. Exactly what we were hoping for."

George Balanchine said, "If the second act is as good as this . . ."

I couldn't wait to give the news to Ben.

At the hotel, I stayed close to the telephone, expecting the call from the Army Air Corps at any moment, and when I was out of the hotel, I always left instructions as to where I could be reached.

For singles, New York can be a lonely town. I had had some casual conversations with our prima ballerina, Milada Mladova, and we had gotten along well. One Sunday, when there was no rehearsal, I invited her to dinner and she accepted.

I wanted to impress her, so I took her to Sardi's, the favorite restaurant of show people. I was still in uniform.

During dinner, Milada and I discussed the show and she told me how excited she was to be in it.

And finally dinner was over. I asked for the check. It came to thirty-five dollars. Very reasonable. Except that I did not have thirty-five dollars. I stared at the check for a long time. Credit cards were not yet in existence.

"Is anything wrong?" Milada asked.

"No," I said, hastily. I made a decision. "I'll be right back."

I got up and walked over to the entrance, where Vincent Sardi, the owner, was standing.

"Mr. Sardi . . ."

"Yes?"

This was going to be difficult. Vincent Sardi had not built up his business by catering to deadbeats.

"It's about my check," I said nervously.

He was studying me. *He knows a deadbeat when he sees one.*

"Is there something wrong with it?"

"No. It's fine. I—I just don't have—I don't have—you know—the money." I wondered if Milada was watching. I quickly went on. "Mr. Sardi, I wrote the play that's opening at the Majestic Theatre, across the street. But it hasn't opened yet. And at the moment, I—I don't have enough to—I wonder if you could trust me until the play opens."

He nodded. "Of course. It's no problem. And I want you to know you are welcome to come here at any time."

My spirits lifted. "Thank you so much."

"Not at all." He shook my hand. There was a fifty-dollar bill in it.

Our producer, Yolanda, hated everything that Ben and I wrote. I had the feeling she hated it even before she read it.

"The show's going to be a flop," she kept saying. "It's going to be a flop."

I desperately hoped that she was not psychic.

George Balanchine, on the other hand, along with

Felix Brentano and Robert Stolz, loved what Ben and I were writing.

During rehearsals, Yolanda leaped around the stage like an overgrown grasshopper, barking orders at everyone. The professionals were too busy to be bothered.

One day, during a break mid-rehearsal, Balanchine came to me and said, "I would like to talk to you."

"Certainly. Is anything wrong, George?"

"No. A friend of mine, Vinton Freedley, is producing a new play. He's looking for a writer. I told him about you and he would like to meet you."

"Thanks," I said gratefully. "I'd love to meet him."

Balanchine looked at his watch. "As a matter of fact, you have an appointment to see him at one o'clock."

Two Broadway plays on at the same time? Unbelievable.

Vinton Freedley was one of the most important producers on Broadway. Among his credits were *Funny Face, Girl Crazy,* and at least half a dozen more hits. Freedley was an efficient, down-to-business producer who got right to the point.

"George tells me you're good."

"I try."

"I'm doing a show called *Jackpot.* It's about a girl who raffles herself off to raise money for the war effort and the winning ticket is won by three soldiers."

"It sounds like fun," I said.

"I already have a writer, Guy Bolton, but he's English and I think he needs an American to work with him. Would you like the job?"

"I certainly would." Then I added, "By the way, I have a collaborator, Ben Roberts. He would work with me."

Freedley nodded. "That's fine. The score is being written by Vernon Duke and Howard Dietz."

Two top Broadway names.

"How soon can you start?" Vinton Freedley asked.

"Right away." I tried to sound confident, but at the back of my mind was the thought that *the call* could come in at any second and I would have to report back for advanced flight training.

Freedley was talking. "We've begun casting already. So far, we have Allan Jones and Nanette Fabray. Let me show you the set."

I was surprised that the set had been built before the play was written. Freedley walked me over to the Alvin Theatre and we went inside.

On the stage was a huge white southern house with a picket fence.

I looked at Freedley, confused. "You said this show was about American soldiers who win a girl in a—"

"This is the set from my last show," Freedley explained. "The show flopped, so we're going to use the set for this one. It will save a lot of money."

I wondered how we were going to work a gothic southern mansion into a modern war story.

"Let's go back to the office. I want you to meet Guy."

Guy Bolton turned out to be a charming Englishman in his fifties who had written several plays with P. G. Wodehouse, the British icon.

I had been afraid that he would resent another writer being brought in on his play, but he said, "I'm delighted that we're going to work together."

And I knew we would get along.

When I returned to my hotel, I asked the hotel clerk if there had been any messages, and I held my breath while he looked.

"Nothing, Mr. Sheldon."

Great. No advanced flying school has opened up yet.

I hurried to my room and telephoned Ben at Fort Dix.

"You and I are writing a musical for Vinton Freedley," I said.

There was a long silence. "They took us off *The Merry Widow?*"

"No. We're doing *The Merry Widow and* the Freedley play."

"My God. How did you arrange that?"

"I didn't. George Balanchine did. We're working with an English writer named Guy Bolton."

CHAPTER

14

I was busy and happy, but I kept waiting for that momentous phone call.

For the next three weeks I spent my mornings working on *The Merry Widow*, my afternoons working on *Jackpot*, and my evenings working with Ben on both shows. I was getting exhausted. I decided I needed some relaxation.

On a Sunday, I went to the USO, a New York entertainment center for soldiers on leave. There was music, beautiful young women, dancing, and food. It was like an oasis from the war.

An attractive blond hostess came up to me. "Would you like to dance, soldier?"

Indeed, I would.

Just as we began to dance, I felt a hand tap my shoulder.

I said, "Hey, we just started. No cutting—" I turned around. There were two large MPs standing there.

"You're under arrest, soldier. Let's go."

Under arrest? "What's the trouble?"

"Impersonating an officer."

"What are you talking about?"

"You're wearing an officer's uniform. Where's your officer's insignia?"

"I don't have any. I'm not an officer."

"That's why you're under arrest. Come along." They took hold of both my arms.

"Wait a minute. You're making a big mistake. I'm allowed to wear this."

"Who gave you permission, your mother?"

They started to pull me off the dance floor.

I was in a panic. "You don't understand. I'm in a special branch of the Air Corps and—"

"Right."

I kept talking while they were shoving me toward the door. "I'm serious. Have you ever heard of a division of the Army called War Training Service?"

"No."

We were outside. There was an official car parked at the curb.

"Get in."

I dug in my heels. "I won't go. You've got to make a phone call. I'm telling you that I'm in the Army Air Corps, in a branch called War Training Service, and we can wear anything we damn please."

The two MPs were looking at each other. "I think you're nuts," one of them said, "but I'll make the call. Who do I call?"

I gave him the number. He turned to his buddy.

"You hang on to him. We're going to throw in 'resisting arrest.' I'll be back."

Twenty minutes later the MP returned, a bewildered look on his face.

"What happened?" the other MP asked.

"I talked to a general and got chewed out for not knowing about an outfit called War Training Service."

"You mean it's legitimate?"

"I don't know if it's legitimate, but it's real. It's a branch of the Army Air Corps."

The other MP released my arm. "I'm sorry," he said. "I guess we made a mistake."

I nodded. "It's all right."

I went back inside. My girl was dancing with someone else.

Guy Bolton was a pleasure to work with. He had written many successful plays and was very knowledgeable about the theater. He spoke in English idioms and it was our job to convert them to American phrases. I remembered the line of George Bernard Shaw: "The Americans and the English are divided by a common language."

Guy had rented a beautiful home on Long Island and on weekends Ben and I worked with him there. He was very social and had an interesting group of friends.

At a dinner party there one evening, I was seated next to one of the most beautiful young women I had ever seen.

"Guy tells me that you're writing a Broadway musical with him," she said.

"Yes."

"That's interesting."

"What do you do?" I asked.

"I'm an actress."

"I'm sorry. I didn't get your name."

"Wendy Barrie."

Wendy was British and she had made half a dozen pictures in England. Her godfather was J. M. Barrie, and he had used Wendy's name in *Peter Pan*. I found her fascinating, but she seemed to be preoccupied.

When dinner was over I asked, "Are you all right?"

She shook her head. "Let's go for a walk."

We went outside and started walking down a moonlit gravel path. Because of the wartime blackout there were no electric lights and the only illumination came from a full moon. As we walked, Wendy began to cry.

I stopped. "What's the matter?"

"Nothing . . . Everything . . . I don't know what to do."

"What's happening?"

"It's my—my boyfriend. He—he beats me." She could barely get the words out.

I was filled with indignation. "Why would you let him?" I said. "Nobody should be allowed to behave like that. Why don't you leave him?"

"I—I—don't know. It's—it's difficult."

She began sobbing. I put my arm around her.

"Wendy, listen to me. If he's beating you now, you can be sure it will only get worse. Leave him while you can."

"I know you're right," she said. She took a deep breath. "I'm going to."

"Good for you."

"I feel better. Thank you."

"My pleasure. Do you live in New York?"

"Yes."

"Are you doing anything tomorrow night?"

She looked at me and said, "No."

"Let's have dinner."

"I'd love to."

The following night, Wendy Barrie and I had dinner at Sardi's and we enjoyed each other's company. We were together for the next two weeks.

One Friday morning, I got a telephone call.

"Sidney?"

"Yes."

"Do you enjoy your life?"

"Very much. Why?"

"If you do, stop seeing Wendy Barrie."

"What are you talking about?"

"Do you know who's paying her rent?"

"No. We never—she never told me."

"Bugsy Siegel."

The hit man for the mob.

I never saw Wendy Barrie again.

I met our two *Jackpot* stars, Allan Jones and Nanette Fabray. Allan Jones was movie star handsome, just under six feet, with a powerful physique and a wry smile. He had a wonderful singing voice and was a recording icon. Nanette Fabray was a real charmer. She was in her early twenties, had a great body, an upbeat personality, and was a natural comedienne—perfect for the part.

I had a good feeling about the show.

After rehearsal one day, Roy Hargrave, the director of *Jackpot*, said, "You boys are doing a great job on the script."

I thought of Yolanda Mero-Irion. *A disaster.* "Thank you, Roy."

"I have a friend who's producing a musical and he's looking for a writer. I told him about you. Would you like to meet him?"

Impossible. Ben and I were already writing two shows, and I was going to be called back to the Air Corps any minute.

"Love to," I said.

"His name is Richard Kollmar. He's married to Dorothy Kilgallen."

I read Dorothy Kilgallen's popular newspaper column. She and Kollmar were a power couple on the Broadway scene.

"I'm going to call and make an appointment for you with Dick."

Roy Hargrave made a telephone call and when he finished, he said, "Ten o'clock tomorrow morning."

Richard Kollmar had produced, directed, and acted in hit Broadway musicals, and he was only in his early thirties. He was slim, enthusiastic, and welcoming.

"Roy told me that you're a really good writer," he said. "I'm doing a fantasy musical. It's going to be a big production with great sets and costumes. It's about a soap opera writer who falls asleep and dreams that she is Scheherazade and that she must continuously tell stories to the sultan or die."

"Sounds interesting. Who's playing Scheherazade?"

"Vera Zorina."

The world-famous ballet dancer who had become a Broadway star, and who was, incidentally, married to George Balanchine.

"Ronald Graham is playing opposite her. Would you like to write the show with Dorothy?"

"I'd love it," I said. "By the way, I have a collaborator."

He nodded. "Ben Roberts. How soon can you start?"

"Right away."

Ben and I could get some sleep after the war.

I called Ben as soon as I got back to the hotel.

"We're writing a musical for Richard Kollmar called *Dream with Music*."

"Wait a minute," he said. "Why did the other shows drop us?"

"They didn't. We're still doing those."

"We're writing *three* Broadway shows at once?"

"Doesn't everyone?"

I was still wearing my uniform, waiting for the call to report for advanced flight training. But now I was so busy writing all three shows that I hoped the call would be delayed. I needed only two or three more months.

The gods must have been laughing.

Two hours after I met with Richard Kollmar and accepted the assignment, the Phone Call came.

"Sidney Sheldon?"

"Yes."

"This is Major Baker. You have orders to report tomorrow morning at 0900 to Captain Burns at Army headquarters in the Bronx."

My heart sank. The timing could not have been worse. We were deserting three shows. Ben was available only at night, and I would be overseas somewhere.

Captain Burns was a tall, bald man, wearing a neatly pressed uniform. He looked up as I walked into his office.

"Sheldon?"

"Yes, sir."

"Sit down."

I took a seat. He studied me a moment. "You finished primary flight training?"

"Yes, sir."

He glanced at a paper on his desk. "And you're scheduled to go to a secondary flight school?"

"Yes, sir."

"Those plans have been changed."

I was puzzled. "Changed?"

"The war has taken a new turn. We're on the offensive now. We're going after the bastards. What we need are fighter pilots. You're not qualified because of your eyesight. We have orders to disband the entire War Training Service unit."

It took me a moment to digest it. "What does that—?"

"All the volunteers in WTS are being given a choice. You can report to an infantry unit as a private in the Army or we can turn your name back to your draft board."

Hobson's choice. But I needed the time. It would probably take the draft board at least a month to process my papers before they sent me overseas and I could use that time working on the shows.

"I prefer the draft board, sir."

He made a note. "Fine. You'll hear from them."

I did not doubt it. The question was when? How much time would I have to work with Ben and Guy and Dorothy to get the shows in shape? I knew we could do a great deal in one month, working seven days a week. *If the Army gave me one month . . .*

When I returned to my hotel, I immediately called Ben. "We'll be working very late tonight."

"What's happened?"

"I'll tell you when you get here."

"Late" turned out to be three A.M., when Ben finally stumbled out of our hotel room and returned to Fort Dix.

Ben had been as dismayed by the news as I was. I tried to reassure him. "Don't worry. Draft boards move slowly."

During the next three days, I worked feverishly, going from theater to theater, working against the time that the call would come from the draft board.

On the fourth day, when I returned to my hotel, the hotel clerk handed me a letter. It began: *Greetings.*

My heart sank. I was to report to the draft board in the Bronx the following day. My career as a playwright was over before it had begun. I was deserting three shows that had been counting on me, and I would be going overseas to face possible death. And suddenly I was filled with an overwhelming sense of elation.

I knew my emotions were completely out of control. I had no idea what was the matter with me. I looked at the idiotically happy face in the mirror and I began to cry.

The next morning at nine o'clock, I reported for my physical examination at Army draft headquarters. It was the same examination I had had in California. It was over in thirty minutes and I was asked to report to the doctor's office.

He was studying a sheet of paper. "Your medical report shows that you have a herniated disc."

"Yes, sir. But they knew that when I had my first examination and they—"

He interrupted me. "They had no business accepting you. If you suffered an attack during a combat engagement, you could endanger not only yourself, but everyone around you. That is not acceptable."

"Sir—"

"I'm marking you 4F."

I was speechless.

"I'll notify your draft board in California. You're dismissed."

I sat there for a long moment, stunned, trying to comprehend what had just happened. Then I got up to leave.

As I walked toward the door, he said, "And take off that uniform."

I was a civilian again.

It was with a feeling of unreality that I went into a clothing store that afternoon and bought two suits, some shorts, shirts, and ties. I was ready to go back to work being a playwright.

* * *

On August 4, 1943, *The Merry Widow* opened at the Majestic Theatre, and it turned out to be one of the most successful revivals ever to play on Broadway. The reviews were raves.

The *New York Times:* "A worthy revival."

The *Herald Tribune:* "Gives the town something to be proud of and happy over."

The *Mirror:* "Beautiful, opulent, tasteful and tuneful."

The *Journal-American:* "A lovely, relaxing, charming, laughing love story."

Walter Winchell: "August had a first night boom. *The Merry Widow* was revived into a sellout."

Howard Barnes: "The new season has been gladdened by a delicious revival. *The Merry Widow* has been brought to the Majestic with taste, melodic eloquence and pageantry."

Frank Sullivan: "I'm happy to report that *The Merry Widow* book has been dusted off and reupholstered very deftly by the Messrs. Sidney Sheldon and Ben Roberts."

One down, two to go.

The show ran on Broadway for nearly a year and toured for another two years. On opening night, after the show, the whole company went to Sardi's to celebrate. Vincent Sardi was standing near the door.

I walked up to him and said, "I can pay you back now, Mr. Sardi."

He smiled. "You've already paid me back. I saw the show tonight."

CHAPTER

15

Dorothy Kilgallen was a bright, creative woman with a nice sense of humor. She was a joy to collaborate with.

Having first found fame as a crime reporter, Dorothy went on to become a powerful Broadway and Hollywood columnist. She later returned to her top-notch investigative reporting and was crucial in helping to secure a new trial for Dr. Sam Shepard, whose murder case was the basis for the popular TV series *The Fugitive.*

While Dorothy and Ben worked on *Dream with Music,* Guy Bolton and I finished the libretto of *Jackpot.* Vinton Freedley decided to send the show on tour before its Broadway opening, and it turned out to be a long and profitable run. Along with Allan Jones and Nanette Fabray, the show now starred Jerry Lester and Betty Garrett.

On January 13, 1944, at the Alvin Theatre, *Jackpot* opened on Broadway. Most of the critics loved it.

The *Herald Tribune:* "*Jackpot* dances along at a smart pace, an elegant production."

The *Mirror:* "*Jackpot* has pleasing-to-the-ear songs and

a bang up cast. Nanette Fabray is a delight. Jerry Lester and Benny Baker are top-flight laugh provokers."

The *New York Post:* "Another hit from the Freedley factory."

Ben and I had another triumph. We went to Sardi's to celebrate. It was a month before my twenty-seventh birthday.

We all knew that our biggest hit was coming up.

It was obvious to everyone from the beginning that *Dream with Music* was destined to be a gigantic success. Unlike Vinton Freedley, Richard Kollmar was sparing no expense to create one of the most elaborate productions Broadway would ever see. Stewart Chaney designed the intricate sets, Miles White created the beautiful period costumes. George Balanchine was the choreographer. The production contained a flying carpet on which Ronald Graham, our leading man, would make his entrance. A treadmill circled the entire stage, and the sets included a Baghdad palace, a bazaar, and a colorful game preserve with dancing animals.

Ben and I stayed on the same working schedule. I wrote with Dorothy Kilgallen during the day, in her beautiful penthouse apartment, and Ben and I worked at night in my hotel room, when he could get away from Fort Dix.

One evening when Ben and I were writing, I dropped a pen and as I bent down to pick it up, my disc slipped out, and I fell to the floor in agony, unable to move. Ben called for an ambulance and I spent the next three days in a hospital. Bad timing. We had a lot of work to do.

When I got out of the hospital, we started again, and finished the libretto.

* * *

Dorothy, Ben, and I sat in the theater watching the rehearsals, which were breathtaking. On the stage was a dazzling array of colorful costumes, beautiful backgrounds, and the exquisite dancing of Vera Zorina.

The romantic scenes between Vera Zorina and Ronald Graham, our leading man, played well. Richard Kollmar watched the dress rehearsal and said, "We're ready."

Natalie and Marty had come to New York for opening night. We all sat near the front of the theater, in the house seats. The theater had filled quickly. Through some mysterious alchemy, theatergoers always know when they are about to see the opening of a hit show. There is an excited, knowing buzz in the audience. Ben and I looked across at each other and smiled. Three hits in a row.

The orchestra began the overture, filling the theater with the bright, melodic music of Clay Warnick and Edward Eager. The show had begun.

Stewart Chaney had arranged for an enormous silk pink bow to be sewn on the outside of the house curtain.

The overture was over and the house curtain began to rise. We could feel the anticipation of the audience. The curtain was halfway up, when the beautiful pink bow caught on a beam, loudly ripped off, and slammed into the orchestra pit. The audience gasped. What none of us knew at that moment was that that was going to be the best thing to happen that evening.

Dream with Music consisted of two acts and thirteen scenes, and the first scene opened with a dozen beautifully costumed African-American showgirls, nude from the waist up, gaily walking on the huge treadmill. But moments after the scene began, the treadmill started to speed up, and the girls began tumbling to the stage floor, one by one. The audience looked on, unbelievingly.

That was just the beginning. Things were about to get worse.

Vera Zorina, one of the most acclaimed ballerinas in the world, who had danced at the rehearsal perfectly, began her ballet, and halfway through it, in the middle of a jeté, she slipped and fell, sprawled out on the stage floor. The audience was watching in horror. Ben and I were sinking in our seats. But the fates had not finished with us.

Two scenes later, Vera Zorina and Ronald Graham, in gorgeous period costumes, came out and walked to center stage, to play their love scene, in soft moonlight, with beautiful forest scenery behind them. They began speaking the tender words that Dorothy and Ben and I had written. The scene was going well and the audience was listening intently.

Suddenly, every light in the theater blacked out. The audience and the actors were plunged into total darkness. Zorina and Graham stood on the stage, not sure what to do. They began haltingly trying to continue with the dialogue, and then stopped in confusion, wondering whether to go ahead, or wait for the lights to come back on.

At that moment, out from the wings came the stage manager in rolled-up shirtsleeves, carrying a flashlight. He ran to the center of the stage and held the flashlight over the heads of the two lovers. It was so incongruous to see the contrast of the two beautifully costumed stars with the man in shirtsleeves holding a flashlight over their heads that the audience began to giggle. The actors bravely started to go on with the love scene. And suddenly every light in the theater blazed on.

That night was probably the most disastrous opening in the history of Broadway. There was no celebration at Sardi's. Natalie, Marty, Ben, and I went to a quiet restaurant, stoically waiting for the reviews.

A few of the critics tried to be kind.

"What conscientious fuse wouldn't blow itself out over the responsibility of lighting *Dream with Music . . .*"

"Energetic and eager. An extravaganza . . ."

"The season has produced no musical comedy prettier to look at than *Dream with Music . . .*"

But the major critics were hostile.

"She lived but the show died . . ."

"It's enough to make the judicious weep . . ."

"Pretty but awfully dull . . ."

"An immense, beautiful, ultra-expensive bore . . ."

Natalie looked at the reviews and declared, "They're mixed."

The show closed after four weeks. But during its brief run, Ben Roberts and I had three plays on Broadway.

Shortly after the closing of *Dream with Music*, I received a strange telephone call. A man with a thick, Hungarian accent said, "My name is Ladislaus Bush-Fekete. George Haley suggested I call you."

George Haley was a writer I knew in Hollywood. "What can I do for you, Mr. Bush-Fekete?"

"I would like to talk to you. Could we have lunch?"

"Yes."

When I hung up the phone, I called George Haley. "What is a Ladislaus Bush-Fekete?" I asked.

He laughed. "He's a famous Hungarian playwright in Europe. He's had a lot of hits over there."

"What does he want with me?"

"He has an idea for a play. He came to me but I'm

busy, so I thought of you. He needs someone to work with who speaks good English. Anyway, it can't hurt you to meet with him."

We had lunch at my hotel. Ladislaus Bush-Fekete was an affable man who was about five foot four and must have weighed three hundred pounds. With him was a pleasant, matronly-looking brunette.

"This is my wife, Marika."

We shook hands. As we sat down, Bush-Fekete said, "We are playwrights. We have done many things in Europe."

"I know. I talked to George Haley."

"Marika and I have a fantastic idea for a play, and we would be very happy if you would write it with us."

"What's the idea?" I asked cautiously.

"It's about a soldier who comes back from the war to a little hometown, to a fiancé. The problem is the soldier has fallen in love with someone at the front."

It did not sound very exciting to me. "I'm sorry," I said, "but I don't think—"

"The twist is that the soldier who comes back to the little hometown is a woman."

"Oh." The more I thought about that, the more the idea appealed to me.

"She has to choose between her fiancé and the soldier she met."

"Are you interested?" Marika asked.

"I'm interested. But I have a partner I work with."

Ladislaus Bush-Fekete said, "That's fine, but his share will come out of your share."

I nodded. "That's all right."

I called Ben that evening and told him what was happening.

"I'm afraid you'll have to do without me," he said. "My

CO is teed off that I've taken so much time away from the post. From now on, I'm trapped here."

"Damn! I'll miss you."

"Me, too, buddy. Good luck."

Laci, as he asked me to call him, and Marika and I went to work. Marika's accent was not too bad, but Laci was difficult to understand. We called the play *Star in the Window.*

We finished the play in four months and my agent showed it to a producing team, Choate & Elkins, and they were eager to produce it. The director was Joseph Calleia. We began casting. Peggy Conklin, an excellent Broadway actress, was set as the female lead. We tested a lot of men, but we were having trouble finding the male lead. One day an agent sent over a young actor.

"Would you mind reading?" I asked him.

"Of course not."

I handed him five pages of the script. He and Peggy Conklin began to read the scene. They had read about two minutes when I said to the actor, "Thank you very much."

His chin went out and he said angrily, "Right."

He shoved the pages back at me and started to walk off the stage.

"Wait a minute," I called. "You've got the part."

He stopped, confused. "What?"

"That's right."

He had caught the essence of the character instantly and I knew he would be perfect for the role.

"What's your name?" I asked.

"Kirk Douglas."

* * *

The rehearsals went well and Peggy Conklin and Kirk Douglas turned out to be a perfect combination. When the rehearsals were finished, we took the play out of town. Washington, D.C., was our first stop, and the reviews fully justified our optimism.

"*Star in the Window* shines bright."

"Peggy Conklin plays the lieutenant with a great deal of spirit and vitality."

"Kirk Douglas is delightful as Sergeant Steve, always assured of himself and never missing a beat in his line of patter."

"The audience last night found *Star in the Window* gay and amusing and gave it an enthusiastic round of applause that kept the curtain going up."

I was delighted. After the debacle of *Dream with Music,* it would be wonderful to have another hit on Broadway. Before the New York opening, the producers had decided to change the title of the play to *Alice in Arms.*

The play opened on Broadway January 31, 1945. Everything went smoothly. After the opening night curtain came down, we all went to Sardi's to celebrate the reviews. The *New York Times* was the first one we saw: "A plague on the house. The dialogue is so wooden it could splinter."

Daily News: "A mistake."

Herald Tribune: "Shopworn."

PM: "Harmless but halting."

And these were the most positive reviews.

I locked myself in my hotel room for the next three days, refusing to answer the telephone. I kept going over the reviews in my mind, again and again. *The dialogue is so wooden it could splinter . . . shopworn . . . a mistake . . .*

The critics were right. I was not good enough to write

for Broadway. My successes had been the result of dumb luck.

Whatever was going to happen, I knew that I could not spend the rest of my life in a hotel room feeling sorry for myself. I decided to return to Hollywood. I would write an original treatment, try to sell it, and write the screenplay. The problem was that I had no story ideas. In the past they had come easily to me, but now my mind was too distressed to concentrate. I had never tried to force an idea before, but I was desperate to come up with a project.

Early the next morning, I put a straight-back chair in the middle of my hotel room and sat down with a thick yellow pad and a pen, determined not to get up from the chair until I had a premise I liked. I discarded idea after idea until two hours later, when I came up with something that I thought could work.

I wrote a thirty-page outline and called it *Suddenly It's Spring*. I was ready for Hollywood.

On my way to Los Angeles, I stopped in Chicago to visit Natalie and Marty.

Natalie greeted me at the door with a hug and a kiss. "My writer."

I had not told her about the reviews for *Alice in Arms*, but somehow she knew about them. She put her finger right on the problem with the play.

"They never should have changed the title."

I spent the next few days in Chicago, visiting my aunts Fran, Emma, and Pauline, who had come in from Denver. It was wonderful to be with them and to see their pride in me. One would have thought that *Dream with Music* and *Alice in Arms* were the biggest hits on Broadway.

Finally, it was time to say my farewells, and I was on a plane back to Hollywood.

* * *

It seemed as if I had been away forever, but it had been only two years. So much had happened in that period of time. I had learned to fly and had been discharged from the Air Corps. I had written two Broadway hits and two Broadway flops.

With the war still raging, living space was scarce, but I had been lucky. One of the actresses in *Jackpot* kept a small apartment in Beverly Hills and she had agreed to rent it to me. The apartment was on Palm Drive and when I got there and started to put the key in the lock, the door was opened by a young, vibrant man. He looked at the key in my hand.

"Hello."

"Hello."

"Can I help you?"

"Who are you?"

"My name is Bill Orr."

"Sidney Sheldon."

His face lit up. "Ah, Helen told me you'd be coming here."

He opened the door wider and I stepped inside. It was a lovely little well-furnished apartment, with a bedroom, a small living room, a den, and a kitchenette.

"I hate to put you out," I said, "but I—"

"Don't worry. I was ready to leave anyway."

I found out why when I read the next morning's *Los Angeles Times*. Bill Orr was about to marry Jack Warner's daughter and would later become head of Warner Television.

My next stop was the boardinghouse on Carmen Street to visit Gracie. Nothing had changed except for the faces. There were new wannabes filling the rooms—

tomorrow's stars and directors and cameramen, all waiting for the Phone Call.

Gracie had not changed at all. She still bustled around, mothering all her nestlings, dispensing soothing advice and commiserating with those who had given up and were leaving.

I got a big hug and an "I hear you're famous now." I was not sure whether I was famous or infamous.

"I'm working on it," I said.

We spent a couple of hours talking about old times, and finally I told her I had to go. I was seeing my agent.

I had signed with the William Morris Agency, one of the top agencies in Hollywood, and was being handled by Sam Weisbord, a short, dynamic agent with a constant tan, which I later learned was replenished from time to time in Hawaii. Sammy had started as an office boy at William Morris, and years later would work his way up to president.

Sammy introduced me to some of the other agents and to Johnny Hyde, who was the vice president of the agency.

"I've been hearing about you," Hyde said. "We're going to do some interesting things together."

At that moment, his secretary walked in.

"This is Dona Holloway."

She was lovely, tall and slim, with intelligent gray eyes and a warm smile. She held out her hand. "Hello, Mr. Sheldon. I'm glad you're going to be with us."

I was going to like this agency.

I said to Sammy and Johnny Hyde, "I wrote an original story that I brought with me."

"Fine," Sammy said. "How would you like to go to work right away?"

"I'd like that."

"One of our clients, Eddie Cantor, has a picture deal at RKO. The problem is he hasn't been able to come up with a script that the studio will approve. The deal runs out in three months and if we don't have a script that the studio okays by then, it's off. He'd like you to create something. A thousand dollars a week."

And I had only been back in Hollywood one day.

"Great."

"He wants to see you this afternoon."

I had no idea what I was in for.

CHAPTER

16

Eddie Cantor had starred in half a dozen movies and was arguably one of the most popular comedians in the country. He had appeared on Broadway for Florenz Ziegfeld, and *Whoopee!* and *Roman Scandals* had made him a star in the movies. He had his own radio show and it was a huge success.

I met Eddie in his large, sprawling house on Roxbury, in Beverly Hills. He was a short, dynamic man who never stopped moving. As he talked, he paced. As he listened, he paced. I almost had the feeling that while we were sitting at lunch, Eddie was mentally pacing.

"I don't know if they explained it to you, Sidney, but here's the situation: RKO has turned down three scripts that my boys prepared." "His boys" were his radio writers. "I'm running out of time. I need a script the studio will approve in the next three months or the deal is off. Do you think you can come up with a blockbuster story for me?"

"I'd like to try."

"Good. You're going to have to work your ass off to

get the script in on time. But when you finish the first draft and the studio approves it, then you'll have all the time in the world to polish the dialogue, tighten it up, do whatever you want with it. It will be all yours."

"That sounds fair," I said.

"Meanwhile, we're under a deadline. We're going to have to work eight days a week."

I thought about the pressure of the Broadway shows I had done. "I'm used to that."

The telephone rang and he picked it up. "This is Eddie Cantor."

And to this day, I have never heard a man say his own name with such pride.

We went to work. We discussed the framework of an idea I had, to star Eddie and Joan Davis. He liked it, and I began to write. I usually worked at his house, starting early in the morning and leaving about seven o'clock in the evening, including Saturdays and Sundays.

The evenings were mine and I relaxed. I met a very attractive girl who seemed to like me and we began to have dinners together. The problem was that she could see me only every other evening.

I was curious. "What do you do on the evenings I don't see you?" I asked.

"I'm seeing someone else, Sidney. I like you both very much, but I have to make up my mind."

Who's the other man?

"His name is José Iturbi. He wants to marry me."

José Iturbi was a famous pianist-conductor who gave concerts all over the world, and he had guest-starred in musicals at MGM, Paramount, and Fox. There was no way I could compete with a famous man like Iturbi.

She said to me, "José told me that you're a Coca-Cola."

I blinked. "I'm a *what?*"

"A Coca-Cola. He said there are millions of you and only one of him."

I never saw her again.

Three days before Eddie Cantor's contract with RKO would have expired, I delivered my screenplay. Sammy Weisbord sent it to RKO, and the following day it was approved. Now I could take my time and polish the dialogue and tighten the script. There were a lot of things I wanted to do with it that I had not been able to do because of the time pressure.

Sammy Weisbord called me. "Sidney, I'm afraid you're off the picture."

I wasn't sure I had heard him correctly. "What?"

"Cantor is bringing in his radio writers to do the polish."

I thought of all the long days and weekends I had worked. *You're going to have to work your ass off to get the script in on time. But when you finish the first draft and the studio approves it, then you'll have all the time in the world to polish the dialogue, tighten it up, do whatever you want with it. It will be all yours . . .*

Welcome to Hollywood.

On September 2, 1945, the Japanese formally surrendered. Richard was on his way home. I could not wait to see him.

On Christmas Eve, Richard's ship finally docked in San Francisco. We had dinner his first night in Los Angeles. He looked thinner and physically fit. I was eager to hear all that had happened to him. I knew where he had been. New Guinea, Morotai, Leyte, Luzon . . .

"What was it like?"

My brother looked at me a long time. "Let's never discuss this again."

"Fair enough. Do you know what you're going to do now?"

"Marty Leeb offered me a job. I'm going to take it. I'll get to spend more time with Mom."

I was delighted. I knew he and Marty would get along well.

Sam Weisbord called the next day. "You have two offers for *Suddenly It's Spring.*"

"That's great," I said excitedly. "Who are they from?"

"One is from Walter Wanger." He had produced many prestigious movies, including *Stagecoach, Foreign Correspondent,* and *The Long Voyage Home.*

"And the other one?"

"David Selznick."

My heart stopped for a moment. *"David Selznick?"*

"He loves your treatment. Dore Schary is going to coproduce for him. Wanger is offering forty thousand dollars. Selznick is offering thirty-five thousand dollars and each offer includes your writing the screenplay."

I wasn't concerned about the money. The idea of working with Selznick was thrilling. Besides, hadn't he started me in the business? It would be good to get together with my fellow reader again.

"Take the Selznick offer."

The following morning I met with David Selznick and Dore Schary. Selznick was a tall, imposing figure, seated behind a huge desk in an ornate, beautifully furnished

office. Dore Schary was dark and trim with a visible intel-
ligence. We shook hands.

Selznick said, "Sit down, Sheldon, I'm glad to meet
you."

I thought maybe I could see Mr. Selznick—
No, Mr. Selznick is a busy man.

"I liked your story. It's excellent. I hope your screenplay turns out as good as your original treatment."

Dore said, "I'm sure it will be."

Selznick studied me a moment. "I heard you had another offer from Wanger. I'm glad you came to me. I
talked to your agent. We'll pay you thirty-five thousand
for the original and the screenplay."

I flashed back to Selznick's secretary handing me an
envelope. *There's ten dollars in there.*

I started to work that morning. I was given an office at
the RKO studios, where we were going to make *Suddenly
It's Spring.* RKO was an important studio. They were cur-
rently shooting *It's a Wonderful Life, The Farmer's Daughter,*
and *Dick Tracy.* In the commissary I saw James Stewart,
Robert Mitchum, and Loretta Young, and because I had
seen them so often in movies, I felt as though they were
old friends. But I didn't have enough courage to speak to
any of them.

I was enjoying writing the screenplay. The story involved a playboy, a young girl, and her sister, a judge. The
man I had had in mind when I wrote the treatment was
Cary Grant, but he was always so busy that I was sure it
would be impossible to get him.

I thought the screenplay was coming along well.
Knowing Selznick's penchant for hiring writer after
writer on the same project, I was flattered that he had not

tried to replace me. And then one day, I came across a memo from Selznick to Dore Schary:

Why don't we fire Sheldon and bring another writer in?

To Dore's credit, he had never mentioned that to me, and apparently found a way around Selznick's request.

My moods were still fluctuating. I would go from periods of elation to periods of despondence, with no transition. At the Brown Derby restaurant one evening, a friend was seated with a young woman. He waved me over.

"Sidney, I want you to meet Jane Harding."

Jane was from New York. She was amusing and intelligent, with a restless vitality. I was taken with her immediately. We started dating, and within two months, we were married.

There was no time for a honeymoon. The studio was starting to cast *Suddenly It's Spring* and Dore urged me to get my rewrites finished quickly.

Regretfully, in less than a month, Jane and I realized we had made a mistake. Our interests and personalities were totally opposite. We spent the next nine months trying in vain to make the marriage work. When we finally decided it was impossible, we agreed to a divorce. The pain was devastating. The day we got the divorce, I went out and got drunk for the first time in my life.

If things were disastrous at home, they were going very well at the studio. I had finished the script.

David Selznick called me to his office. "We sent your script to Cary Grant."

"Oh? What—what did he say?"

Selznick paused dramatically. "He's crazy about it. He's going to do it."

I was thrilled. "That's fantastic!"

"We've also signed Shirley Temple and Myrna Loy."

It was a perfect cast.

"Irving Reis is going to be the director, and Cary Grant wants to meet you."

Cary Grant was always everybody's first choice for a comedy. There was no second choice. If you could not get Cary, you dropped down several levels.

I liked Cary immediately. Besides being incredibly handsome, he was intelligent, with a quick, inquiring mind. Unlike some of the stars I worked with later, Cary had absolutely no sense of vanity about himself.

Cary was born Archibald Alexander Leach into a lower-middle-class family, in Bristol, England. He had started in the circus as a stilt walker in Coney Island and broke into vaudeville as a bit player.

When Archie Leach was nine, his mother was sent to a mental institution. They told Cary that his mother had gone to a seaside resort. He did not see her again until he was in his late twenties.

Cary Grant was a legend—suave and sophisticated and smooth.

"Everyone wants to be Cary Grant," he once said. "Even I want to be Cary Grant."

When I met Shirley Temple, she was an eighteen-year-old grown-up, and she was a delight. As a child, she had been the biggest star in the motion picture world, her pictures grossing hundreds of millions of dollars. In spite of her fame, she had turned into a normal, attractive young woman.

The cast was rounded out by Myrna Loy, a skilled actress. Myrna had starred in The Thin Man series, *The Best Years of Our Lives, Arrowsmith,* and dozens of other movies.

I was thrilled with the cast. We were almost ready to make the movie.

Cary and I were having lunch in the studio commissary a week before *Suddenly It's Spring* was to start. He said, "We're having a problem finding a second male lead. We've tested half a dozen people and no one is right. You know who would be perfect for the role?"

I was curious. "Who?"

"You. Would you be interested in testing with me?"

I looked at him in surprise. Did I want to be an actor? I had never thought about it. But why not? I could be a writer/movie star. Noel Coward and a few others had done it.

"Are you interested, Sidney?"

"Yes." I knew how simple acting was. I had written the original story, the screenplay, and the test scene, so I knew every word. All I had to do was say the lines. Anyone could do that.

Cary got up and telephoned Dore Schary, and when Cary and I finished lunch, we walked back to the set. The test scene was with just Cary and me. It was a simple scene, with only a dozen or so lines.

As I looked at Cary, I wondered what stardom was going to be like for me, because I knew that co-starring in a movie with Cary Grant was going to change my life. I would be getting offers and proposals to star in other movies. I would be internationally famous. From now on, I would have no privacy and no leisure. My life would belong to the public. But I was prepared to make the sacrifice.

We had reached the soundstage. Irving Reis said, "Quiet on the set, everybody."

Everyone was suddenly still, watching us.

Irving Reis said, "Camera." He turned to us. "Action."

Cary gave me my cue. I stared at him for a long, long moment while he waited for me to speak. I looked up at what seemed to be millions of people staring down from the catwalk, and suddenly I was back at school, with my play, standing on the stage, laughing hysterically. I panicked and, without a word, I turned and fled from the soundstage.

That was the end of my acting career. Now that the burden of stardom was no longer weighing me down, I could go back to work on my screenplay.

Dore hired Rudy Vallee to replace me and *Suddenly It's Spring* began shooting. Everyone seemed pleased with the way it was going.

One day David Selznick called me into his office. "I want you to do something for me."

"Certainly, David."

"It's National Brotherhood Week. Every year a different studio makes a short film about bringing all religions together."

I knew about it. When the short film was over, the lights would come on in the theaters and ushers would walk up and down the aisles, collecting money for the charity.

"We're doing it this year. I want you to write it."

"No problem."

"We have half a dozen stars lined up. You'll write about two minutes for each one."

"I'll get to work on it."

The next day I brought in a two-page script I had written for Van Johnson, who was to be photographed first. Selznick read it. "Good. Take it to Van. He's in a bunga-low on the back lot."

I carried the two pages over to Van Johnson's bungalow. When he saw me, he opened the door, and I introduced myself. At that time Van Johnson was one of the biggest stars at MGM.

"Here are your pages," I said. "We're ready to shoot as soon as you are."

"Thank you." He added, ruefully, "I had a terrible dream last night."

"What was that?"

"I dreamt that this big star coming over from Metro-Goldwyn-Mayer learned his lines, and then they kept changing them, and he panicked. The dream woke me up."

I laughed. "Don't worry. These are your lines."

He smiled and glanced down at the pages. "I'll be ready in a few minutes."

I went back to Selznick's office.

"It's all set," I said.

"I have an idea," Selznick replied. "I want you to change Van's lines."

"David, I just left him. He was nervous. He had a nightmare about his lines being changed."

"To hell with him. Here's what I want." And he gave me a new direction for the scene. I hurried back to my of-fice, rewrote it, and showed it to Selznick.

"Good," he said. "That's it."

I hurried back to Van Johnson's bungalow. He opened the door.

"I'm ready."

"Van, there's been a slight change. Mr. Selznick

thought this would be better." I handed him the new pages. He turned pale.

"Sidney, I wasn't joking about my dream. I really—"

"Van, it's only two pages. It's a cinch."

He took a deep breath. "All right."

I went back to David Selznick's office.

"I have another idea," he said. "It would be better if we took this angle with Van . . ."

I was horrified. "David, he's already panicky. We can't keep changing his lines."

"He's an actor, isn't he? Let him learn them."

He told me what he wanted. Reluctantly, I went back to my office and rewrote the scene.

The hardest part was facing Van Johnson again.

I walked up to his bungalow. He started to say something, then looked at my face. "You didn't . . ."

"Van, it's only two pages. This is the last time."

"God damn it. What are you doing to me?"

I finally got him calmed down. "Come over to the set when you're ready," I told him.

I did not go back to David Selznick's office. The rest of Van's segment went smoothly.

Richard telephoned the next day.

"Bro?"

It was great to hear his voice. "How are you doing, Richard?"

"Whatever I've been doing, I have to do for two now. I'm getting married."

I was thrilled. "That's great news! Do I know her?"

"Yes. Joan Stearns." Joan and Richard had gone to school together in Chicago.

"When is the wedding?"

"In three weeks."

"Damn! I have to be out of the country, shooting a segment for this project I'm doing for National Brotherhood Week."

"You'll meet her when you come back. We'll come for a visit."

As promised, Richard and his lovely, upbeat wife arrived in Los Angeles a month later. It was obvious that they were very much in love. We spent a delightful week together, until it was time for them to return to Chicago.

The next morning, when I arrived at my office, my secretary said, "Mr. Selznick would like to see you."

He was waiting for me. "Sidney, I have some news for you."

"What's that?"

"I'm changing the name of the picture. We're not going to call it *Suddenly It's Spring*."

I was listening. "What are you going to call it?"

"The Bachelor and the Bobby-Soxer."

I looked at him a moment, thinking he was joking. He was serious.

"David, no one is going to pay money to see a picture called *The Bachelor and the Bobby-Soxer*."

Fortunately, it turned out that I was wrong.

CHAPTER

17

The Bachelor and the Bobby-Soxer opened at the six-thousand-seat Radio City Music Hall, the largest movie theater in the world. It played there seven weeks and was the top grosser in the history of the theater. In England, it was the biggest grosser after *Gone With the Wind*.

The reviews delighted me:

"I beg you, please don't miss *The Bachelor and the Bobby-Soxer* . . ."

"One of the best comedies to hit this town in more than a year . . ."

"A blessed concoction of fun, whimsy and heart . . ."

"A first-rate comedy. You'll laugh out loud . . ."

"Sidney Sheldon has created the most agreeable film fare . . ."

The cast was praised, the director was praised. The reviews were unanimous. The movie won the Box Office Blue Ribbon Award and I was nominated for an Oscar. I knew that nothing could stop me now. Careers in Hollywood were like elevators constantly going up and down. The trick was not to leave the elevator when it was down.

The elevator for me was definitely up. I was on top of the world.

I had written an original treatment about a troubled marriage, called *Orchids for Virginia*. Eddie Dmytryk, a director at RKO, liked it.

"I'm going to ask the studio to buy it for me. I want you to do the screenplay. I'll get you thirty-five thousand dollars."

"Great." I was more than pleased because I needed the money.

One week later, Dore Schary was made the executive producer in charge of production at RKO. He called me into his office and I knew he wanted to congratulate me on *Orchids for Virginia*. I was going to ask him how soon I could start the screenplay.

"Eddie Dmytryk wants to direct your story," Dore said.

I smiled. "Yes. That's terrific."

"I'm not going to let the studio buy it."

It took a moment for it to sink in. "What? Why?"

"I'm not going to make a picture about a man who's unfaithful to his wife and plans to murder her."

"But Dore—"

"That's it. We're giving the story back to you."

I was devastated. "Okay."

I would have to find another project to work on.

I had no idea that Dore's rejection of my script was going to change my life.

My agent, Sammy Weisbord, called. "I just made a deal for you at MGM with a two-week guarantee. They want you to write *Pride and Prejudice*."

I had not read the book in years. All I remembered about it was that it was a Jane Austen, pre-Victorian, English society classic about five daughters looking for husbands.

The idea of working at MGM was exciting. It was the Tiffany of all Hollywood studios. The roster of their movies included classics like *Gone With the Wind, Meet Me in St. Louis, The Wizard of Oz, The Philadelphia Story, The Great Ziegfeld,* and dozens of other great films.

I was twenty-nine years old when I walked onto the MGM lot for the first time. I was awed. MGM was a city in itself. It had its own supply of electricity, food, and water. Every conceivable need was met on site.

The studio, like the other six major studios, produced an average of one film a week. There were 150 writers under contract at MGM, and they included famous novelists and playwrights.

On my first day there, I had lunch at the huge commissary. I was invited to sit at the writers' table, where a dozen writers had gathered. They were a friendly group and there was a lot of advice offered.

"Don't worry if some of your scripts aren't made. The rule of thumb here is if you get a script made every three years, you're okay . . ."

"Try to get on a picture with Arthur Freed. He's the big producer here . . ."

"When your contract is about to run out, make sure you get on an assignment so they'll pick you up . . ."

I did not explain that my contract consisted of a two-week guarantee.

I had been given a small office and a secretary.

"We're going to do *Pride and Prejudice*," I told her. "Can you get a copy of the book for me? I'd like to read it again."

"Certainly."

She dialed a studio number and said, "Mr. Sheldon would like a copy of *Pride and Prejudice*."

The book was delivered in thirty minutes.

That was my introduction to the studio system. Every studio had a library, a research department, a casting department, a set department, a cinematography department, and a business department. It was almost biblical. All you had to do was ask and it was given to you.

The following morning, Sammy Weisbord came into my office. "How are you doing?" he asked.

"I'm just getting started," I told him.

"Arthur Freed would like to see you."

I was surprised. "Why?"

"Let him tell you. He's waiting for you."

I had heard stories about Arthur Freed. He had started as an insurance salesman and had become a successful songwriter, with songs such as "The Broadway Melody," "Good Morning," "On a Sunday Afternoon," and "Singin' in the Rain."

He had gotten friendly with Louis B. Mayer, who made him a producer.

It was said of Freed that he always had to be first to know things. One of the writers told me the following story:

A friend invited Freed to the opening of a play. "I've seen it," Freed said.

Another time someone asked him if he'd like to go to the premiere of a movie. "I've seen it," Freed said.

A friend asked him if he'd like to go to a baseball game that night. "I've seen it," Freed said.

Sammy and I walked down the hall and took the elevator up to the third floor, where Arthur Freed's office was. Freed sat behind his desk in a huge office. He was a stocky man in his fifties, with thin gray hair.

"Sit down, Sheldon."

I sat.

"I have a problem. I have a script here that I can't seem to cast. Everyone's turning it down. It's a musical and it's well written, but the plot is wrong. It's too heavy. It needs a light touch. Do you think you can help it?"

"Well, I'm working on *Pride and Prejudice,* but—"

"Not anymore," Freed said. "You're working on this."

"What's the name of it?"

"*Easter Parade.* You'll be working with Irving Berlin."

That was a magical moment. It was my third day at MGM and I was going to work with the legendary Irving Berlin.

"I'd love to do it," I said.

"Judy Garland and Gene Kelly are going to star in it."

I tried to look nonchalant. "Oh?"

"I want to get it into production as soon as possible."

"Yes, sir."

"Look over the screenplay and see what you think you can do with it. You'll have a meeting here tomorrow with Irving."

I floated out of Freed's office. Weisbord watched me and smiled.

"Come through with this," he said, "and you're fixed for life."

I was glowing. "I know."

The elevator was definitely up.

The original screenplay of *Easter Parade* had been written by the husband and wife team of Albert Hackett and Frances Goodrich. They were brilliant writers who later wrote the smash Broadway play *The Diary of Anne Frank.*

But Freed was right. What the screenplay needed was humor and a light touch. The story the Hacketts had written was too serious for a musical. I sat down to create a new story line.

The following morning, I was summoned to Arthur Freed's office. With him was a short man with a cherubic face and bright, inquisitive eyes.

"This is Irving Berlin."

In the flesh. The genius who had written "Alexander's Ragtime Band," "God Bless America," "There's No Business Like Show Business," "Puttin' on the Ritz," and "Top Hat." Someone once asked Jerome Kern what he thought Irving Berlin's place would be in American music.

Kern said simply, "Irving Berlin *is* American music."

"I'm Sidney Sheldon," I said, pretending not to be completely awestruck.

Mr. Berlin held out his hand. "I'm happy to meet you. I understand we're going to work together." He spoke in a high-pitched voice.

"Yes, sir." I did not mention my New York experience where I had almost replaced him as the top songwriter in America because we were going to work together, and I did not want to make him nervous.

When we started to work on *Easter Parade*, Irving Berlin was sixty years old, with the enthusiasm of a teenager.

He had been born Israel Baline in Russia and had come to the United States when he was five. He started his career as a singing waiter at the Chinatown Cafe in New York. He had never learned to play the piano on a regular piano. He used only the black keys, and he had an instrument that changed keys at the push of a lever.

Irving Berlin had questions and comments as I talked about the possible directions the screenplay could go, but oddly enough, Arthur Freed seemed to take no interest in what we were doing. He was completely silent. It was not until later that I found out why.

I said, "Mr. Berlin, I want to tell you—"

He stopped me. "Irving."

"Thank you. I want to tell you how excited I am to be working with you."

He smiled. "We're going to have a good time."

The writing was going well. I remembered what Sam Weisbord had said. *Come through with this, and you're fixed for life.*

Several times a week, while I was writing the script, Irving Berlin would bounce into my office.

"Tell me what you think of this," he would say enthusiastically. And in that shrill voice of his, he would begin singing a song he had just written. The only problem was that he could not carry a tune, and I had no idea what the song sounded like. He could not play the piano, and he could not sing. All he had was his genius.

I had lunch every day at the writers' table in the commissary and one of the writers would usually invite me to visit his set after lunch. The pictures shooting on the lot were *The Best Years of Our Lives,* with Myrna Loy and Fredric March; *Saratoga Trunk,* with Gary Cooper and Ingrid Bergman; and *The Secret Life of Walter Mitty,* with Danny Kaye and Virginia Mayo.

I went on the soundstages and watched the stars going through their scenes just a few feet away from me. These were the stars I had watched from the back aisle of the RKO Jefferson Theatre, when I was an usher. Now, every week I saw the biggest stars in Hollywood making their movies, and it was a wondrous time for me.

* * *

I was finishing the script of *Easter Parade* when Sammy Weisbord came into my office.

"I have good news, Sidney. I got a call from MGM. They want to negotiate a long-term contract with you."

"That's wonderful," I exclaimed. That was the dream of every Hollywood writer.

"We haven't worked out all the details yet. There are still a lot of things we're discussing." He smiled. "But don't worry. It will happen."

I was elated. I turned in my screenplay to Arthur Freed and waited to hear his reaction. Silence. *He hates it, I decided.*

Another day went by. I reread the script. *The New York critic is right about my lack of talent. The dialogue is so wooden it could splinter.*

No wonder Arthur Freed doesn't want to talk to me.

One week after I had given the script to Arthur Freed, his secretary finally called.

"Mr. Freed would like you to be in his office tomorrow morning at ten o'clock to meet Judy Garland and Gene Kelly."

I felt a sudden sense of panic. I simply could not meet them. They would find out what a fraud I was, just as Arthur Freed had. They would all hate my screenplay. I knew I could not go to that meeting. It was déjà vu. Max Rich saying, *Meet me at my office, ten o'clock tomorrow morning, and we'll go to work,* and Irving Reis saying, "Camera . . . Action," and my running away from the screen test with Cary Grant. I knew I had to run away again.

I got little sleep that night. I had vivid dreams of Arthur Freed screaming at me about the terrible script I had written.

In the morning, I made a decision. I would go to the meeting, but I would not say anything. I would listen to their derogatory criticisms and when they were through, I would quit. I spent the hour prior to the meeting packing up my office, getting ready to leave the studio.

At ten o'clock, I walked into Arthur Freed's office. Freed was seated behind his desk.

He nodded. "Interesting screenplay."

Whatever that meant. Was that a euphemism for "You're fired"? Why did he not come out and say what he really thought?

At that moment, Judy Garland walked in and my spirits lifted. It was like seeing an old friend. She was Betsy Booth, the girlfriend of Mickey Rooney's character in the Andy Hardy series. She was Dorothy in *The Wizard of Oz*. She was Esther Smith in *Meet Me in St. Louis*. When I was an usher, I had seen her movies over and over.

Judy Garland, née Frances Gumm, had been with MGM since she was in her teens. *The Wizard of Oz* had made her a star when she was just fifteen. She had become so popular that the studio put her in movie after movie, giving her no chance to rest. She made nineteen movies in nine years.

To keep up her energy, she began taking barbiturates and became addicted, taking uppers in the daytime and sleeping pills at night. She had tried to commit suicide and, unbeknownst to me, had just come from the Menninger Clinic when I met her.

Her first words were, "Hello, Sidney. I loved your screenplay."

For a moment, I was stunned. Then I began to grin like an idiot. "Thank you."

"It was good, wasn't it?" Arthur Freed said. It was the first comment I had heard him make about my screenplay.

The door opened and Gene Kelly came in. By now I

began to relax. Gene Kelly was another familiar face. I had seen him in *Thousands Cheer, Cover Girl,* and *Anchors Aweigh.* He felt like an old friend.

He greeted Judy and Arthur, and then turned to me. "Author author," he said, "you did a damn fine job."

"He did, didn't he?" Arthur Freed said.

I was filled with a sudden sense of euphoria. All that worrying for nothing.

"Any suggestions you have—" I began.

"It's just right for me," Judy said.

Gene Kelly added, "Me, too. It's perfect."

Arthur Freed smiled. "It looks like it's going to be a short meeting. We're all set to go. We start shooting Monday."

After the meeting, I went back to my office and started unpacking.

My secretary was watching, puzzled. "May I ask what's going on?"

"I changed my mind."

On Friday, Arthur Freed called me into his office.

"We have a problem," he said.

I stopped breathing. "Something wrong with the script?"

"No, it's Gene Kelly. He broke his ankle playing volleyball over the weekend."

I swallowed. "So, we're going to postpone the picture?"

"I sent your script to Fred Astaire. He retired last year but if he likes your script, he'll do it."

I shook my head. "Fred Astaire is forty-eight years old. Judy is twenty-five. The audience is going to be rooting for them *not* to get together. That will never work."

He said, tolerantly, "Let's see what Fred has to say."

Fred Astaire said yes. I met him in Arthur Freed's office the next day and he said, "Thank you for a wonderful script. It's going to be exciting to make."

Looking at him, my misgivings about the casting disappeared. He looked young and alert and energetic. He had the reputation of being a perfectionist. On a picture he did with Ginger Rogers, he kept rehearsing a new routine with her until her feet were bleeding.

I was on the soundstage on Monday, the first day of shooting *Easter Parade*. Fred Astaire was at the far end of the stage where they were setting up the first shot. I was at the other end of the stage, telling a story to Judy. In the middle of it, the assistant director hurried over. "We're ready for you, Miss Garland."

I started to get up.

"No," Judy said, "finish the story."

"All right." I started talking faster because I knew how expensive it was to keep a shooting company waiting. I looked over at the other end of the stage where they were set up and waiting, and I said, "Judy, I'll finish the story later. It's really not important—"

"No," she insisted. "Finish it now." She seemed upset.

"Judy, don't you want to do this scene?"

She shook her head. "No."

"Why not?"

She hesitated a moment, then blurted out, "I have to kiss Mr. Astaire in this scene, and I've never met him."

Everyone had just assumed that these two superstars knew each other. I felt then a deep sense of how vulnerable Judy Garland was.

"Come on," I said. I took her hand and led her over to the other end of the stage where they were all impatient to get started.

"Fred," I said, "this is Judy Garland."

He smiled. "It certainly is. I'm a big fan of yours."

"And I'm a fan of yours." Judy smiled.

Chuck Walters, the director, said, "Take your places."

Easter Parade began shooting.

One day, I dropped in at the rehearsal hall, where Fred was working alone on a new dance number. Tapping and turning his way around the stage, he did not see me. I crept up on him and when he stopped for a moment, I tapped him on the shoulder. He turned.

I said patiently, "No, Fred. Like *this*." And I did a little bad soft shoe.

He grinned. "Very good. I used to dance that way."

Not likely.

Shortly before shooting began, Arthur Freed had hired Jules Munshin, a New York actor, for comedy relief. I had written a small part for him as a maître d'. The day before Munshin was to shoot his scene, my disc slipped out again. I was at home, in bed, suffering in agony.

The phone rang. It was Jules Munshin.

"Sidney, I have to see you."

"Not now. I'll be out of bed in three days and—"

"No. I have to see you today. Right away."

The pain was so bad, I could hardly speak. "Jules, this is not a good time. I really don't feel well. I—"

"Your secretary gave me your address. I'll be there in fifteen minutes."

I took another pain pill and gritted my teeth.

Fifteen minutes later, Jules Munshin arrived at my bedside. "You look great," he said, cheerfully.

I was glaring at him.

"The studio brought me out from New York, and I

have only one little scene that I could have phoned in. I need you to do something with that scene."

There was a small problem. I was in such pain that I could barely remember his name.

"I shoot my scene tomorrow," he reminded me.

I closed my eyes and thought about the scene I had written for him. In it, he was an arrogant maître d' who prided himself on the way he mixed a salad, with the exaggerated gestures of a snobbish gourmet.

"The scene is nothing," Munshin said.

I suddenly knew how to make it something. "Jules, the answer is very simple."

"What?"

"There *is* no salad. You're going to do it in pantomime."

It turned out to be one of the funniest scenes in the picture.

Easter Parade won the Box Office Blue Ribbon Award and the WGA Screen Award for Best Written American Musical of 1948, an award I shared with Frances Goodrich and Albert Hackett.

Easter Parade also turned out to be one of the most successful musicals MGM ever made. It has played on television every Easter for the last fifty-seven years.

CHAPTER

18

In September of 1947, there began one of the most disgraceful episodes in American history. A thunderbolt was about to strike Hollywood with a vengeance.

America's alliance with Russia had ended and a Red Scare swept the U.S. An ambitious senator named Joseph McCarthy sensed an opportunity to make himself important. One day, he announced that there were communists in the Army.

"How many?" he was asked.

"Hundreds."

McCarthy's answer created a furor and he was on the covers of magazines and on the front pages of newspapers everywhere.

His next announcement was that he had discovered communists in the Navy and defense industries, and each time he gave an interview to the press, the numbers kept changing—always growing.

An investigative committee was formed by J. Parnell Thomas and a small group of congressmen. It was called HUAC—the House Un-American Activities Committee.

The committee first targeted a group of Hollywood screenwriters, accusing them of being members of the Communist Party and inserting communist propaganda into their screenplays. Witnesses were subpoenaed to appear for hearings before the committee, in Washington.

As McCarthy's fame increased, he became more reckless. Innocent people who were being accused of being communists lost their jobs, with no chance to defend themselves. Defense industries and other businesses were investigated by the committee, but Hollywood had the highest profile, and the committee took advantage of it.

The writers, producers, and directors called to testify had three choices: They could admit they were communists and name names; they could deny they were communists; or they could refuse to testify and face imprisonment. The committee was ruthless. They insisted that if any of the people brought before them admitted they were communists, they must then name fellow communists.

Ten accused writers who refused to answer the committee's questions were sent to jail. In addition, 324 people were blacklisted in the industry, and hundreds of innocent lives were destroyed.

In Hollywood, the studio heads held a secret meeting to decide how to put the best face on what was happening. They made an announcement that they would not employ anyone who was in the Communist Party. This was the beginning of a ten-year blacklist.

Dore Schary, who was running RKO studios, boldly declared that he would quit before firing a writer accused of being a communist. Shortly after that, when the committee named a writer working at RKO, Schary fired him. The members of the Screenwriters Guild were outraged.

Schary asked for a chance to explain his position to the writers. The guild auditorium was packed.

"I want to remind all of you," Schary said, "that I'm a writer, too. That's how I got started. I know a lot of you expected me to resign as head of RKO when they forced me to fire one of my writers. The reason I didn't was that I felt that staying on as head of the studio, I can do more to protect you."

And that was when he lost his audience. His self-serving speech brought boos and hisses, and the meeting abruptly ended.

One morning in the midst of all of this, Marvin Schenck, a studio executive who was a relative of Nicholas Schenck, called me into his office. No one was sure exactly what Marvin Schenck's job was, but there was a rumor that he was getting paid three thousand dollars a week to look out his window and raise the alarm if he saw a glacier moving toward the studio.

Marvin was in his late forties, a small balding man, with the charisma of an undertaker.

"Sit down, Sidney."

I sat.

He looked at me and said, accusingly, "Did you vote for Albert Maltz at the Writers Guild meeting last night?"

We had had a meeting the night before to elect a new board of directors. It was a closed meeting, but I was so startled by the question that I didn't think to ask him how he knew how I had voted.

"Yes, I did," I said.

"Why did you vote for Maltz?"

"I just read a novel of his, *The Journey of Simon Mc-Keever*. It's a beautifully written book and we need good writers like him on the guild's board."

"Who told you to vote for him?"

I was getting angry. "No one told me to vote for him. I told you why I voted for him."

"Someone must have told you to vote for him."

My voice was raised. "Marvin—I just told you I voted for him because he's a damned good writer."

He studied a sheet of paper in front of him and then looked up. "Have you been going around the studio the last few weeks, raising money for the children of the Hollywood Ten?"

That was when I lost it. What he was saying was true. I had started with my own contribution and then had gone around the studio raising more money to take care of the children whose fathers had been jailed.

I don't lose my temper often, but when I do, it erupts.

"I'm guilty, Marvin. I shouldn't have done that. Let the damned kids starve. If their fathers are in prison, the kids don't deserve to eat. Let them all die!" I was screaming.

"Calm down," he said. "Calm down. I want you to go home and try to remember who told you to vote for Albert Maltz. I'll see you in the morning."

I stormed out of the office. I felt violated. The indignity of what was happening was lacerating.

I got no sleep that night. I tossed and turned and finally came to a decision. At nine o'clock in the morning, I went back into Marvin Schenck's office.

"I quit," I said. "You can tear up my contract. I don't want to work at this studio anymore." I started toward the door.

"Wait a minute. Don't be hasty. I talked to New York this morning. They said if you'll sign a statement that you're not a communist and have never been a member of the Communist Party, this whole thing will be forgotten." He handed me a piece of paper. "Will you sign this?"

I looked at it and started to calm down. "Yes," I said, "because I'm not a communist and I've never been a communist."

It was a humiliating experience, but nothing compared to what so many innocent people went through during that time.

I will never forget the dozens of talented friends of mine who would never work in Hollywood again.

In February of 1948, the Academy Award nominations were announced. I was one of five nominees, for writing the original screenplay of *The Bachelor and the Bobby-Soxer.* I started to receive congratulations from my fellow workers, my agent, and friends, but I knew something they did not know: I had no chance of winning the Oscar.

The pictures I was up against were extremely popular. They included Chaplin's *Monsieur Verdoux, A Double Life, Body and Soul,* and the powerful foreign picture *Shoeshine.* Just being a nominee was honor enough. I wondered which one of them would win.

I got a call from Dona Holloway, congratulating me on my nomination. Dona and I had become good friends. We often went to the theater together, or a concert, and she was always interesting company.

The morning of the Oscars, Dona telephoned. She had recently left William Morris and had gone to Columbia Studios as Harry Cohn's personal assistant, and I felt that Cohn was lucky to have her.

"Getting ready to go to the Oscars?" Dona asked.

"I'm not going."

She sounded shocked. "What are you talking about?"

"Dona, I don't have a chance of winning. Why should I sit there and be embarrassed?"

"If everyone felt the way you do," she said, "there wouldn't be anyone there to receive an Oscar. You have to go. What do you say?"

I thought about it. *Why not be a good sport and applaud the winner?* "Will you go with me?"

"You bet I will. I want to see you up on that stage."

The Twentieth Annual Academy Awards were held at the Shrine Auditorium. The awards were not televised then, but they were carried by two hundred ABC radio stations and the Armed Forces Radio Network. The auditorium was packed. Dona and I took our seats.

"Are you nervous?" Dona asked.

The answer was no. This was not my evening. This evening belonged to one of the other writers who would get an Oscar. I was a spectator. I had no reason to be nervous.

The ceremonies began. The winners began stepping up to the stage to receive their Oscars and I sat back, relaxed, enjoying it.

Finally, they came to the award for best original screenplay. George Murphy, an actor who had starred in many movie musicals, announced, "The nominees are . . . Abraham Polonsky, for *Body and Soul* . . . Ruth Gordon and Garson Kanin, *A Double Life* . . . Sidney Sheldon, *The Bachelor and the Bobby-Soxer* . . . Charles Chaplin, *Monsieur Verdoux* . . . and Sergio Amidei, Adolfo Franci, Cesare Giulio Viola, and Cesare Zavattini for *Shoeshine*.

George Murphy opened the envelope. "And the winner is . . . Sidney Sheldon, for *The Bachelor and the Bobby-Soxer!*"

I sat frozen in my seat. Any nominee with half a brain

would have prepared a just-in-case speech. I had prepared nothing. *Nothing.*

George Murphy called my name again, "Sidney Sheldon."

Dona was prodding me. "Get up there!"

I got up in a daze and stumbled toward the stage, while the audience applauded. I walked up the steps and George Murphy shook my hand.

"Congratulations!"

"Thanks," I managed.

George Murphy said, "Mr. Sheldon, in the interests of science and posterity, would you mind telling us where you got this original idea?"

How could I not have prepared something? Anything?

I was staring at him. "Er—well—when I was back in New York, they had a lot of—you know—bobby-soxers around, and watching them gave me the idea that there might be a picture in it. So, I—I put it together."

I could not believe the asininity of what I was saying. I felt like a complete fool. I finally pulled myself together long enough to thank the cast and Irving Reis. I thought about Dore Schary and whether I should mention his name. He had behaved disgracefully and I was angry with him. On the other hand, he had co-produced the movie.

". . . and Dore Schary," I added. I accepted my Oscar and stumbled off the stage.

When I got back to my seat, Dona said, "That's so wonderful. How do you feel?"

How *did* I feel? I felt more depressed than I had ever felt in my life. I felt as though I had stolen something from people who deserved it more than I did. I felt like a phony.

The awards went on, but from that moment, what was happening on the stage became a blur. Ronald Colman was holding an Oscar and talking about *A Double Life.* Loretta Young was thanking everyone for *The Farmer's Daughter.* Everything seemed to go on forever. I could not wait to get out of there. On what should have been the happiest night of my life, I was suicidal. *I have to see a psychiatrist,* I thought. *Something is wrong with me.*

The psychiatrist's name was Dr. Judd Marmer. He had been recommended to me by friends who had consulted him. I knew that he had many patients in show business.

Dr. Marmer was a large, earnest man, with silver-gray hair and probing, blue eyes.

"Mr. Sheldon, what can I do for you?"

I thought of how I had run away from the meeting with the psychologist at Northwestern University.

"I don't know," I said honestly.

"Why did you come to see me?"

"I have a problem and I don't know what it is. I have a job I like at MGM. I'm making a lot of money. I won an Oscar a few days ago and—" I shrugged. "I'm just not happy. I'm depressed. I fought hard to get there, and I succeeded and . . . there's no 'there.'"

"I see. Do you get depressed often?"

"Sometimes," I said, "but everyone does. I'm probably wasting your time."

"I have plenty of time. Tell me about some of the things that have depressed you in the past."

I thought about all the times when I should have felt happy, and instead felt miserable, and all the times when I should have been depressed and was happy.

"Well, when I was in New York, a songwriter named Max Rich . . ." I talked and he listened.

"Have you ever felt suicidal?"

The sleeping pills from Afremow's drugstore . . . You can't stop me, because if you stop me now I'll do it tomorrow . . .

"Yes."

"Do you feel a loss of self-esteem?"

"Yes."

"Do you have a feeling of worthlessness?"

"Yes."

"Do you feel that you don't deserve your success?"

He was reading my mind. "Yes."

"Do you have feelings of inadequacy and guilt?"

"Yes."

"Excuse me." He leaned forward and pressed a button on the intercom. "Miss Cooper, tell my next patient that there will be a delay."

I felt a cold chill.

Dr. Marmer turned to look at me. "Mr. Sheldon, you're suffering from manic depression."

I hated the sound of it. "What exactly does that mean?"

"It's a brain deviation that involves episodes of serious mania and depression, where moods swing from euphoria to despair. It feels as though there's a thin screen between you and the world. So, in a sense, you're an outsider looking in."

My mouth was dry. "How serious is it?" I asked.

"Manic-depressive illness can have a devastating effect on people. At least two million Americans suffer from it, one in ten families. For some reason, it seems to strike artistic people. Vincent Van Gogh had it, Herman Melville, Edgar Allan Poe, Virginia Woolf, to name a few."

That made me feel no better. That was *their* problem.

"How long will it take to cure it?" I asked.

There was a long pause. "There is no cure."

I started to panic. *"What?"*

"The best we can do is to try to control it with drugs."
He hesitated. "The problem is that sometimes there are
bad side effects. Approximately one in five people who
are manic-depressive eventually commit suicide. Twenty
to fifty percent attempt suicide at least once. It's a major
contributing factor in thirty thousand suicides a year."

I sat there, listening, feeling suddenly sick.

"There will be times when, with no warning, you will
lose control of your words and your actions."

I was finding it hard to breathe.

Dr. Marmer continued. "There are various forms of
the disorder. Some people can go weeks, months, or
years with no extreme ups and downs. They have periods
of normal moods. That type is classified as 'euthymia.' I
believe that's the form you have. Unfortunately, as I said,
there is no cure."

Now at least what was happening to me had a name.
He gave me a prescription and I left his office, shaken.
And then I thought, *He doesn't know what he's talking about.
I'm fine. I'm fine.*

CHAPTER

19

Myths and rumors surround Oscar. If you win him, you'll never want again. If you win him, you'll never work again.

A week after I received my Oscar, Sam Weisbord stopped by my office.

"Congratulations, again. Where are you going to keep it?"

"I want to be modest about it. What would you think about the roof of my house with half a dozen spotlights on it?"

He laughed. "Spectacular!"

"I have to tell you, Sammy, winning it was a complete shock to me."

"I know," he said, dryly. "I heard your speech." He sat down and added casually, "By the way, I've just come from Benny Thau's office." Thau was Metro's deal-maker. "You have a seven-year contract here. They gave us everything we asked for."

I couldn't believe it. "That's wonderful." *The power of the Oscar.*

"One of the things they caved in on was your request to take three months a year off anytime you want to."

"Great." I wanted to be free to do other things.

I had moved into a small carriage house in Westwood. The house consisted of a small bedroom, a small den, a small living room, a small kitchen, and two small bathrooms. There was a garage attached that was bigger than the house. Tony Curtis and the beautiful Janet Leigh, both extremely talented actors, lived in an apartment a few doors away. They had a car, but no place to park it.

At a dinner party one night, Tony said, "We're having a problem parking on the street. I wonder if we could rent your garage."

"You can't rent it," I said, "but you can use it," and from then on their car was parked in my garage.

My house was much too small to give parties in, but I didn't know that, so I gave a lot of parties. I had been lucky enough to find a terrific Filipino cook, who also bartended and cleaned the house. Since I started at MGM, I had met a lot of interesting people. Ira Gershwin came to dinner with his wife, Lee. Kirk Douglas, Sid Caesar, and Steve Allen also came, along with their significant others. It was a long and wonderful guest list. More than once, Jules Stein, head of MCA, the most powerful talent agency in Hollywood, came to dinner with his wife, Doris. We often sat on the floor because there were not enough chairs, but no one seemed to mind.

One of the most interesting men I met was Robert Schiffer, head of makeup at Disney Studios. He was English and had flown with the Royal Air Force during World War II. He owned a yacht and had traveled all over the world.

In 1946, Schiffer was working on a Rita Hayworth

movie. Rita was about to start another one for Harry Cohn. Instead, she and Schiffer decided to run away to Mexico. The picture was held up while they had a romantic vacation. Harry Cohn was going crazy because he could not find them.

Every Saturday afternoon, I had a gin game at my house. There were half a dozen regulars. Jerry Davis, a writer-producer, was one of them, along with the director Stanley Donen, Bob Schiffer, and several others. Elizabeth Taylor, then in her early twenties, was going with Stanley, and every Saturday she would come to prepare lunch for us while we played gin.

Elizabeth was petite and sensual, with incredible violet eyes and a hint of the magic that was going to make her a legend. It was hard to believe that this beauty was in my kitchen making sandwiches every Saturday.

Cyd Charisse was under contract to MGM. She was sexy and talented. She had joined the Ballet Russe when she was thirteen, and was a superb dancer. I had taken her out a few times. We had a date for a Saturday night when she called to cancel it.

"Is there a problem?" I asked.

Cyd was evasive. "I'll tell you more about it Monday."

She did not have to tell me. It was in all the headlines. Over the weekend she had married the popular singer Tony Martin.

Cyd called me. "I guess you heard the news."

"I did. I hope you and Tony will be very happy."

I tried to forget Cyd by burying myself in my work. I was ready for another assignment.

Kenneth McKenna, head of the MGM story department, summoned me to his office. McKenna was in his mid-fifties, a ramrod-straight, gray-haired martinet who ran his department like a fief.

No greeting. "I have an assignment for you. *Show Boat.*"

It was a fantastic assignment. *Show Boat* was one of the great musicals. It had a brilliant score and a wonderful libretto. I loved it. But I had a problem.

"Kenneth," I said, "I've just done two adaptations. I'd like to work on some original material."

He got up from his chair. "You'll work on whatever I tell you to work on. You're under contract to this studio. You'll scrub floors if I tell you to."

I never did write *Show Boat.* I was much too busy scrubbing floors for the next few weeks.

I had planned a trip to Europe during my three months off that year, and I was very excited about it. I had booked passage on the *Liberté,* a French ship that I heard was fantastic.

I called Natalie and Marty, and Richard and Joan, to say goodbye, then flew to New York to board the ship.

Among the passengers was Charles MacArthur, whom I had met before. He was a brilliant playwright who, with Ben Hecht, had written *The Front Page, Jumbo,* and *Twentieth Century.* With him was his wife, America's preeminent actress, Helen Hayes.

When Charles had first seen her at a party, he was instantly smitten. He had picked up a bowl of peanuts, offered them to her, and said, "I wish these were diamonds."

They were married shortly thereafter. The following year, on Helen's birthday, Charles handed her a small bowl of diamonds and said, "I wish these were peanuts."

Other passengers included: Rosalind Russell and her

husband, producer Fred Brisson, and Elsa Maxwell, the famous party giver.

The first day out to sea, Charles came to me and said, "Elsa Maxwell heard about you winning an Oscar. She wants to invite you to her dinner party tonight. I told her that you did not socialize."

"Charlie! I'd love to go to her dinner party."

He smiled. "You have to play hard to get. I'll tell her you're thinking about it."

Later that afternoon, Elsa Maxwell herself came up to me and said, "Mr. Sheldon, I'm giving a small dinner party tonight. I would love to have you join us."

"I'll be there."

Dinner was delightful and the guests seemed to enjoy themselves. At the end of the meal, as I got up to leave, a steward said, "Excuse me, Mr. Sheldon. That will be three dollars for the table."

I shook my head. "I'm a guest of Miss Maxwell."

"Yes, sir. That will be three dollars."

I was furious.

Charlie tried to calm me down.

"I don't mind the idea of it," I said, "it's the money I object to."

Charlie laughed. "Sidney, her skill lies in bringing people together. She never pays for anything."

When I got to London, I checked into the storied Savoy Hotel. Though the war was over, England was still feeling the effects of it. Rationing was in effect and there was a shortage of everything.

When the room service waiter came to see me in the morning, I said, "I'll have grapefruit, scrambled eggs, bacon, and toast."

He looked pained. "I'm terribly sorry, sir. None of

that is available. You have a choice of mushrooms or kippers."

"Oh." I chose the mushrooms.

The next morning, I ordered the kippers.

When I went to a restaurant that night, there was almost nothing edible on the menu.

The following morning I was surprised by a call from Tony Martin. "You didn't tell us you were in town."

"I've been busy."

"I want you to come to my show tonight."

I had no intention of meeting the man who had married the lady I was very fond of. "I can't—I—"

"I'm leaving a ticket for you at the box office." He added, "Come backstage after the show," and hung up.

I had no interest in seeing his show. I would go backstage, tell him how brilliant he was, and leave.

I went to see his performance that evening anyway and he was amazing. The audience loved him. I went backstage to his dressing room to congratulate him and Cyd was there. I got a big hug, and Cyd introduced me to Tony.

"You're going to have supper with us tonight," Tony said.

I shook my head. "Thanks, but I'll—"

"Let's go."

Tony Martin turned out to be one of the nicest men I had ever met.

Supper was at an exclusive, private club. What I did not know was that the private clubs in London were immune to rationing.

The waiter said, "We have lovely steaks tonight."

We all ordered steaks.

The waiter said to me, "Would you like an egg on your steak, sir?"

And that was the first egg I had since arriving in London.

I spent every night after that with Cyd and Tony, having a marvelous time on their honeymoon.

One night, Tony said to me, "We're leaving for Paris in the morning. Get packed. You're coming with us."

I did not argue.

We flew to Paris, and it was fabulous. Tony hired a limousine to take us to the usual tourist spots—the Arc de Triomphe, the Louvre, Napoleon's Tomb—and we ate delectable meals.

On Sunday morning, Tony had arranged for a limousine to take us to Longchamps to see the races. Unfortunately we had all gotten food poisoning the night before and we were in terrible shape.

Tony phoned. "Cyd and I feel awful. We're not going to be able to go to the track."

"Neither am I, Tony. I feel—"

"There's a limousine downstairs, waiting for you. Take it."

"Tony—"

"Take it. Put a bet on a horse for us."

I went to Longchamps alone, semiconscious. There was a long line at the betting window. When I finally got to the head of it, the man behind the counter said, "*Oui?*"

I spoke no French. I shoved some money across the counter and held up one finger, "Number *une*," and I touched my nose. He said something unintelligible and shoved the money back at me.

I tried again. "Number *une*." I held up my finger and touched my nose. "On the nose, to win."

He shoved the money back again. The people in line

behind me were getting impatient. A man stepped out of the line and came up to me.

"What's the problem?" he asked in English.

"I'm trying to bet this money on number one to win." The man spoke in French to the cashier, then turned to me.

"Number one has been scratched," he said. "Pick another horse."

I chose number two, got a handful of tickets, and stumbled out to watch the race.

Number two won, and Tony and Cyd and I split the money.

That trip was something I never forgot and I resolved to go to Europe every year.

That August, Dore Schary resigned as head of RKO after accepting an offer from Louis B. Mayer to become head of production at MGM. My old boss was now my new boss.

I was assigned to write the screenplay for *Nancy Goes to Rio*, which was to star Ann Sothern, Jane Powell, Barry Sullivan, Carmen Miranda, and Louis Calhern.

The picture was being produced by Joe Pasternak, a middle-aged Hungarian producer with a heavy accent. Before he came to MGM, he produced small pictures at Universal, a studio on the verge of bankruptcy. A young actress named Deanna Durbin was released from her contract at MGM and went to Universal. Joe Pasternak was assigned by Universal to do a picture with Deanna called *Three Smart Girls*.

To the studio's amazement, the picture exploded at the box office. Overnight, Deanna Durbin became a major star and Universal was saved. Shortly after that, Joe Pasternak accepted an offer at MGM as a producer.

One day, Dore Schary called a meeting of the producers on the lot.

When they were all seated in his office, Dore said, "We have a problem. I just bought a play called *Tea and Sympathy*. It's a big Broadway hit, but the censorship office won't let us make it because it involves a homosexual. We have to come up with another angle. I want to hear your suggestions."

There was a thoughtful silence. Then one of the producers said, "Instead of a homosexual, we could make him an alcoholic."

Another producer said, "He could be on drugs."

"He could be a cripple."

A dozen different ideas were floated around the room, none of them satisfactory.

After a silence, Joe Pasternak spoke up. "It's very simple," he said. "You keep the play exactly as it is. He is a homosexual." And then he added, triumphantly, "But in the end, it's all a dream."

That was the end of the meeting.

One of the bonuses of working on *Nancy Goes to Rio* was meeting Louis Calhern. Calhern had started out in the theater and was a brilliant actor. He had a regal appearance, tall and hawk-nosed, with a stentorian voice. He had been briefly married to three actresses and was on his fourth. He had a wonderful sense of humor and was a delight to be with. He had just starred in *The Magnificent Yankee*, the story of Justice Oliver Wendell Holmes.

When Louis would come to my house for dinner, as he walked through the front door, he would bellow, "Where the hell is the food?"

I received a telegram from him one day that read:

"Understand that my wife has been hoodwinked into making an engagement for you with me on Saturday night, the fourth. I will meet you in the theater after the lights are out. Please do not expect to be seen in public with me. Calhern."

An agent introduced me to a beautiful young Swedish actress whom I'll call Ingrid, who had come to the United States to make a test at Universal. She was enchanting and we began a romance.

A few weeks later on a Sunday morning, while I was asleep, the doorbell began to ring. I looked at the bedside clock. It was four A.M. The ringing became more frantic. I reluctantly got up, put on a robe, went to the door and opened it. A stranger, holding a gun, shoved me aside and came into the room.

My heart began to pound. "If this is a holdup," I said, "take whatever—"

"You son of a bitch! I'm going to kill you."

It was not a holdup.

At moments like that a writer is supposed to think: *This is great material.* But what *I* thought was: *I'm going to die.*

"I don't know you," I said.

"No, but you know my wife," he shouted. "You've been sleeping with her."

I knew he had made a mistake. I never had affairs with married women. "Look," I said, "I don't know what you're talking about. I don't know who your wife is."

"Ingrid." He raised the gun.

"I—" It was no mistake. "Wait a minute! Ingrid never told me she was married."

"The bitch married me so she could get a visa to come to this country."

"Hold it," I said. "This is all news to me. She doesn't wear a wedding ring, and she never mentioned a husband, so there's no way I could have known. Sit down and let's talk about it."

He hesitated a moment and sank into a chair. We were both sweating profusely.

"I'm not like this," he said, "but I—I love her, and she used me."

"I don't blame you for being upset. I think we can both use a drink." I fixed stiff drinks for both of us.

Five minutes later, he was telling me his life story. He was a writer and he had met Ingrid in Europe. He was now unable to get work in Hollywood.

I said, "You need a job? Let me take care of it. I'll talk to Kenneth McKenna, at Metro."

His face lit up. "Would you? I'd sure appreciate it."

Five minutes later, he and his gun were gone.

I turned out the lights, went back to bed breathing hard, and had finally fallen asleep when I heard a banging at the front door.

He's back, I thought. *He's changed his mind. He's decided to kill me.*

I got out of bed, went to the door and opened it. Ingrid was standing there. She had been beaten up badly. Her face was bruised, she had two black eyes, and her lip was bleeding. I pulled her inside the house.

She could hardly talk. "I have to tell you—"

"You don't have to tell me. Your husband was here. Get in bed. I'm going to call a doctor."

I managed to wake up my doctor, and an hour later he was at the house, tending to Ingrid. She had a broken rib and deep bruises all over her body.

When the doctor left, Ingrid said, "I don't know what to do. I have a screen test at Universal this morning."

I shook my head. "Not anymore. You can't go in looking like that. I'll call and cancel the test." And I did.

Ingrid left that evening and disappeared.

In 1948, Cy Feuer and Ernie Martin, a new producing team, came to the studio to see me.

"We're doing a Broadway play called *Where's Charley?* It's based on the classic, *Charley's Aunt*. We want you to write it. We've cleared your name with the Brandon Thomas Estate. Frank Loesser is going to write the score. Ray Bolger will star."

Frank Loesser had written several popular songs, but he had never done a Broadway show. I knew the plot of *Charley's Aunt* and I liked it. I thought it could be a big hit.

"I'd like to meet with Frank."

"We'll set it up."

Frank Loesser was a dynamo. He was in his late thirties, talented and ambitious. He had written the wartime hit "Praise the Lord and Pass the Ammunition," and several other popular movie songs, including "The Moon of Manakoora," "On a Slow Boat to China," "The Boys in the Back Room," and "Kiss the Boys Goodbye."

"I have some great ideas," Frank said. "We can make this a big hit."

"I think so, too."

"I'll work on the libretto with you."

"That will be wonderful, Frank," I said, "and I'll work on the score with you."

He grinned. "Never mind."

I went to see Dore Schary. "I'm going to take my three months off," I said, "to do a Broadway show."

"What show?"

"*Where's Charley?* It's a remake of *Charley's Aunt*."

Dore shook his head. "Broadway's risky."

I laughed. "I know. I've been there, Dore."

"I don't think you should do it."

"Well, I've already committed and—"

"I'll make a deal with you. How would you like to write the screenplay of *Annie Get Your Gun?*"

"What?"

"If you forget about that play, I'll assign you to write *Annie.*"

Annie Get Your Gun was the biggest hit on Broadway. It had been playing for three years and had four road companies out.

In 1945, Herbert and Dorothy Fields had gone to Richard Rodgers and Oscar Hammerstein and suggested they do a show about Annie Oakley. Dorothy Fields would write the lyrics and Jerome Kern agreed to do the score.

Three days after Kern arrived in New York, he suffered a stroke, and a few days later he died. Rodgers and Hammerstein decided Irving Berlin should write the score. The show contained half a dozen hits, including the standard, "There's No Business Like Show Business." MGM had paid six hundred thousand dollars for the rights to *Annie Get Your Gun*, the highest price up to then for a musical.

"What do you say?" Dore asked.

I thought about it. I was certain that *Where's Charley?* was going to be a hit, but I was excited about the chance to work with Irving Berlin again. It was impossible to say no to Dore's offer.

"I'll do it," I said.

That afternoon, I called Feuer and Martin and Frank Loesser, and told them of my decision.

"I know you're going to have a big hit," I said.

And I was right.

CHAPTER

20

It was exciting to work with Irving Berlin again. He had
lost none of his energy. He danced into my office,
grinned and said, "This is going to be better than the
play. Let's go talk to Arthur."

Arthur Freed was in his office, seated behind his desk.
He looked up as we entered.

"This is going to be a big one," Freed said. "The studio is behind it a hundred percent."

I asked, "Do you have any casting in mind, Arthur?"

"Judy Garland is going to play Annie, and a talented
young actor and singer named Howard Keel is going to
play Frank. Louie Calhern is Buffalo Bill. George Sidney
is set to direct."

I was going to work with Judy again. And spend time
with Lou Calhern.

Arthur Freed said to me, "We're going to fly you to
New York and Chicago to see the play."

Ethel Merman was playing *Annie* in New York and
Mary Martin was playing *Annie* in Chicago.

"When do you want me to leave?"

"Your plane leaves at nine o'clock tomorrow morning."

Annie Get Your Gun was marvelous entertainment. The book by Herbert and Dorothy Fields was fast and witty and Ethel Merman's performance was energetic, loud and brassy. The next morning, I flew to Chicago, to see Mary Martin's performance.

She had taken a different approach. Her Annie had a shy, poignant sweetness about her. My challenge was to write a character that combined the best elements of both.

Working on a hit like *Annie Get Your Gun* had its pitfalls. I could not wander too far from the original material and yet it was necessary to open up the show for the screen. Many of the scenes that worked on the stage would not work on film. New scenes had to be created.

The biggest problem was the gap between Act One and Act Two of the play. On the stage, Act One ended with Annie leaving for Europe. Act Two began with her return. The problem was in deciding what to do in the screenplay to bridge the two acts.

I could show a montage of brief scenes of Annie in different countries, or I could concentrate on one country. Should the interval be long or short? These were not my decisions, because shooting those scenes would involve a great deal of money. It was the producer's decision.

I called Arthur Freed's office and made an appointment to see him, to discuss the problem. One hour later, his secretary called to cancel the appointment. I made another appointment for the following day. His secretary called to cancel that. This happened for three consecutive days. On the afternoon of the third day, Sammy Weisbord dropped by my office.

"I just came from Arthur Freed's office. He's very disappointed in you."

I felt a rising panic. "What have I done?"

"Arthur said you're not turning in any pages."

"But I've been calling to make an appointment to discuss—" and I suddenly understood what was happening. Arthur Freed was not interested in talking about the screenplay. He was interested in the musical aspects of the picture—the songs, the dances, the girls. I had a feeling he was unable to visualize how the scenes would play. I remembered how he had reacted to my screenplay of *Easter Parade*. He had not commented on it until he had heard how the cast felt about it.

Arthur Freed's gift was in selecting the right property and hiring the best people to make it. I took a deep breath. With no guidance, I made my own decisions, and set to work writing the screenplay. It went quickly and, I hoped, smoothly.

I finished the screenplay, turned it in, and held my breath. I wondered who I would hear from first.

The following day, George Sidney, who was directing the picture, came into my office.

"Do you want me to flatter you or do you want the truth?"

My mouth was suddenly dry. "The truth."

George Sidney grinned and said, "I love it! You've done a hell of a job." His eyes were sparkling. "We're going to have a great picture."

After I had gotten comments on my script from everyone in the cast, Arthur Freed said, "You've caught the tone perfectly, Sidney."

Judy recorded the score and production began.

From time to time, when Judy was not shooting, she would come into my office for a chat.

"It's going well, isn't it, Sidney?" She sounded nervous.

"It's going beautifully, Judy."

"It is, isn't it?" she asked.

I took a closer look at her. She seemed clenched and I wondered what she looked like under her makeup.

I began to hear disturbing rumors. Judy was always late and she had not learned her lines. Production was being held up. She would telephone George Sidney at two o'clock in the morning to say she was not sure whether she could make it to the set that day.

Production finally closed down and that same day, the studio announced that Judy Garland was being replaced. I was saddened. I tried to call her when I heard the news, but she had already run off to Europe, devastated.

The part of Annie was offered to Betty Garrett, a talented young actress who had starred in my play *Jackpot* and who was married to Larry Parks, who had played Jolson in *The Jolson Story*.

Benny Thau met with Garrett's agent.

Thau said, "We want an option for Betty's next three movies."

Garrett's agent shook his head. "You can only have her for this picture and no options."

So, because of her agent, Betty Garrett lost the role of a lifetime. Betty Hutton was signed to play Annie and the production went forward without any further incidents.

One morning during the shooting, Irving Berlin came into my office and said, "Sidney, why haven't we done a Broadway show together?"

My heart skipped a beat. Writing a musical with Irving Berlin was a virtual guarantee of a successful show. I tried to sound cool. "I would love to write a show with you, Irving."

"Good. I have an idea."

Irving began to pace and tell me about his idea.

I peeked at my watch.

"I hate to interrupt you," I said, "but I have a luncheon date at twelve-thirty and I have to leave now. Let's pick up this discussion when I get back."

"Where are you having lunch?"

"In Beverly Hills, at the Brown Derby."

"I'll ride over there with you."

And Irving Berlin got into my car and rode with me to the restaurant while his chauffeur followed, so that Irving could keep talking about his idea, instead of waiting until I got back from lunch, in an hour. I had never seen such enthusiasm.

That same afternoon, Irving told me he was going to East Los Angeles because a new young singer was going to sing one of his songs. That was Irving Berlin in his sixties, a dynamic genius at the peak of his creativity.

The years were not kind to him. When Irving Berlin was in his nineties, he became paranoid. One day Tommy Tune, the talented Broadway producer and choreographer, telephoned him.

"Irving, I want to do a Broadway musical based on some of your songs."

"No. You can't."

Tommy Tune was surprised. "Why not?"

Irving Berlin said in a whisper, "Too many people are singing my songs."

To my regret, we never did get around to doing that musical together.

One of the many pleasures of writing *Annie Get Your Gun* was meeting Howard Keel, a tall, rugged leading man with an incredible voice. Howard had to practice shooting skeet for a scene in the movie, so he and I would go to a skeet range and compete with each other.

He always won.

The production went well under George Sidney's direction, and the post-production was finally finished.

When *Annie Get Your Gun* opened in 1950, the reviews were unanimously ecstatic. The New York critics called it the "Top screen musical of the year."

"*Annie Get Your Gun* puts movies back on must list."

"Screen's *Annie* better than stage version."

"Give credit to Berlin and the Fieldses. Runaway hit."

Betty Hutton received the Photoplay Award as the Most Popular Actress and I received the Writers Guild of America Screen Award for my screenplay.

In 1950, Variety published a list of the highest grossing films of all time. On the list were three movies that I had written: *The Bachelor and the Bobby-Soxer, Easter Parade,* and *Annie Get Your Gun.*

My periods of depression had stopped and I decided that the psychiatrist had been wrong about my being manic-depressive. I was fine. I continued to date Dona Holloway and looked forward to her company.

One evening at dinner, Dona said, "How would you like to meet Marilyn Monroe?"

"I'd like it," I told her.

She nodded. "I'll set it up."

Marilyn Monroe was a sex symbol, superstar. Her troubled background included an insane mother, growing up in foster homes, a failed marriage, and a battle with alcohol and pills. But she had something that no one could take away from her: talent.

The next day, Dona called me. "You're having dinner with Marilyn Friday night. Pick her up at her apartment."

She gave me the address.

I was looking forward to Friday night. Marilyn Monroe had already had big hits in *Gentlemen Prefer Blondes*, *How to Marry a Millionaire*, and *Monkey Business*, with Cary Grant.

The evening did not turn out as I expected. I went to Marilyn's apartment at the appointed time and a woman who was her companion let me in.

"Miss Monroe will be with you in a few minutes. She's getting dressed."

The few minutes turned out to be forty-five minutes.

When Marilyn finally emerged from the bedroom, she looked stunning.

She took my hand and said softly, "I'm happy to meet you, Sidney. I admire your work."

We had dinner at a restaurant in Beverly Hills.

"Tell me about yourself," I said.

She began to talk. To my surprise, the thrust of the conversation was Dostoyevsky, Pushkin, and several other Russian writers. What she was saying seemed so incongruous coming from this beautiful young woman, that it was as though I were having dinner with two different people. I felt she had no real grasp of what she was talking about. It was only later that I learned that she was dating Arthur Miller and Elia Kazan, and that they were her mentors. It was a pleasant evening, but I never called her again.

Shortly after our dinner, she married Arthur Miller.

On an evening in August 1962, I was having dinner with Hy Engelberg, my doctor, at his home. In the middle of dinner, he was called to the telephone. He came back to the table and said, "I have an emergency. I'll be back."

It was almost two hours later before he returned.

"I'm sorry," he apologized, "a patient of mine." He hesitated. "Marilyn Monroe. She's dead."

She was thirty-six years old.

I had first met Harry Cohn, the head of production at Columbia Pictures, with Dona Holloway. Cohn had the reputation of being the toughest studio head in Hollywood. He had once bragged, "I don't get ulcers, I give them."

It was reported that there was only one man he feared: Louis B. Mayer. Mayer called Cohn one day and said, "Harry, you're in trouble."

Fearfully, Cohn asked, "What's the problem, L.B.?"

"You have an actor under contract that I need."

Relieved, Cohn said, "Take him, L.B., anyone you want."

During World War II, there was a saying: Any writer at Columbia who quits to join the Army is a coward.

When Harry Cohn was in his early twenties, his best friend was Harry Ruby. The two of them worked together on a streetcar in New York. Harry Cohn was the conductor and Harry Ruby was the ticket-taker. They were inseparable.

Years later, when they were both in Hollywood, they went out on a double date, reminiscing about the old days. Harry Cohn was now running a studio and Harry Ruby was a successful songwriter.

"Streetcars have gone the way of the dinosaurs," Harry Ruby said that evening. "When you and I worked on them, it was fun."

Harry Ruby turned to the girls and nodded toward Cohn. "He was making eighteen dollars a week and I was making twenty."

Harry Cohn's face turned red.

"I was making twenty and *you* were making eighteen," Harry Cohn snarled.

Harry Ruby never saw Harry Cohn again.

I had seen Harry Cohn at several dinner parties. The first time we met he was saying disparaging things about writers and how lazy they were.

"I make my writers come in at nine o'clock every morning, just like the secretaries."

"If you think that's going to get you good scripts, you should be in another business," I said.

"What the hell do you know about it?"

And we began to argue. The next time I saw him at a party, he sought me out. He enjoyed confrontations. He invited me to lunch.

"Before I hire a producer, Sheldon," Harry Cohn told me, "I always ask his golf score."

"Why should that interest you?"

"If he has a low score, I don't want him. I want producers who are only interested in producing for me." Another time he told me, "Do you know when I hire an expensive director? When he's just had a flop. His price comes down."

One day, when I was in Harry Cohn's office, the voice of the studio manager came over the intercom.

"Harry, I have Donna Reed on the line. Tony's regiment is being sent overseas and Donna wants to be with him in San Francisco until he leaves."

Tony Owen, Donna's husband, was a producer. "She can't go," Cohn said, and turned back to me.

A minute later, the studio manager came on again. "Harry, Donna is very upset. It may be years before she sees her husband again, and we don't need her now."

"The answer is no," Cohn said.

The studio manager came on for the third time.

"Harry, Donna is in tears. She says she's going anyway."

Harry Cohn grinned. "Good. Put her on suspension."

I looked at him, stunned, and wondered what kind of monster I was sitting with.

I read a brilliant novel by George Orwell called *1984*, which predicted the future of Russian dictatorships thirty-five years ahead. It was a horrific scenario. I decided it would make a wonderful Broadway play. I sent Orwell a letter asking for the stage rights and he agreed.

I went to Dore Schary and told him that I was going to do *1984*. Dore, the liberal, said, "I've read it. It's a good book, but it's anti-Russian. You shouldn't do a play like that."

"Dore, this can be a very important play."

"Why don't you write Orwell and tell him that you don't think it should be anti-Russian—just anti-dictatorship? In other words, it can apply to any country."

I thought it over for a moment. "All right, I'll do that." I wrote to Orwell and he responded:

Dear Mr. Sheldon,

Many thanks for your letter of August 9th. I think your interpretation of the book's political tendency is very close to what I meant. It was based chiefly on communism because that is the dominant form of totalitarianism, but I was trying chiefly to imagine what communism would be like if it were firmly rooted in the English speaking countries, and was no longer a mere extension of the Russian Foreign Office. What I most particularly did not intend was an attack on the British

Labour Party, or on a collectivist economy as such. I have no doubt you do not need telling, but I emphasise this because I see that part of the American press has used the book as a sermon on what Socialism in England must lead to.

Dore kept me so busy that, in the end, I had to abandon *1984.*

Harry Schechtel, the family consigliere

With Natalie, Otto, and my brother, Richard

Ben Roberts and me, with Virginia Vale and Roger Pryor, on the set of our first movie

With my brother Richard, in Chicago

In the Army Air Corps

Ready to take off
from the air base at
Richfield, Utah

Oscar night, with Val Davies and George Murphy

Frank Sinatra and Jule Styne at a dinner party at our home

Discussing a scene with Fred Astaire and Judy Garland on the set of *Easter Parade*

Betty Hutton getting ready to shoot 'em up in *Annie Get Your Gun*

On the set of *Rich, Young and Pretty*, with Danielle Darrieux

On the set of *Rich, Young and Pretty*, with Fernando Lamas, Danielle Darrieux, Jane Powell, and Vic Damone

With Jane Wyman in
Three Guys Named Mike

Working with
Barry Sullivan in
Three Guys Named Mike

I get the girl! Watching
Jane Wyman with me are
Van Johnson, Barry Sullivan,
and Howard Keel

Looking over the script of
Just This Once, with
Janet Leigh and Peter Lawford

Enjoying Cary Grant's
musical talents on the
set of *Dream Wife*, with
Deborah Kerr

Deborah Kerr and I are
entertained by Betta St. John on
the set of *Dream Wife*

Discussing *Dream Wife*
with Dore Schary
and Cary Grant

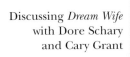

With my darling daughter, Mary

Jerry Lewis and me discussing a scene from *You're Never Too Young,* with director Norman Taurog

Dean Martin and Jerry Lewis, saving the West in *Pardners*

With George Gobel
on a bicycle built
for two

With the cast of *Anything Goes*:
Donald O'Connor, Mitzi Gaynor,
Zizi Jeanmaire, and Bing Crosby

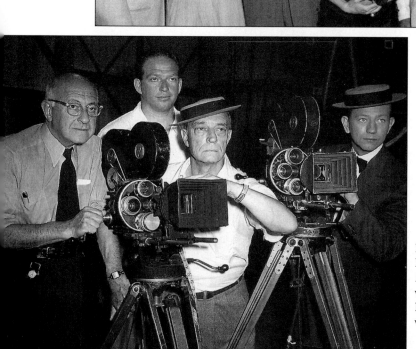

Directing Cecil B.
DeMille in *The
Buster Keaton Story*,
while Buster and
Donald O'Connor
watch

Gwen Verdon
doing her magic
in *Redhead*

Robert Sterling fighting
Inger Stevens's charms in the
Broadway show *Roman Candle*

On the set of *Jumbo* with Doris Day

Chatting with Patty Duke, discussing the series I created for her

Patty Duke with my daughter, Mary

Barbara Eden and Larry Hagman up to no good in *I Dream of Jeannie*

Jorja as Madame Zolta, conducting a séance in an episode of *I Dream of Jeannie*

Groucho Marx
with Jorja and me

With Walter Matthau at
the publication party for
my daughter Mary's
first novel

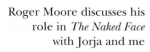

Roger Moore discusses his
role in *The Naked Face*
with Jorja and me

Spending an evening
with Kirk Douglas

Alexandra and me
on a book tour

SIDNEY SHELDON
THE DOOMSDAY CONSPIRACY
THE NEW NOVEL

Fishing with my treasured
friend Bob Schiffer

With my eldest granddaughter, Lizy

With my
granddaughter
Rebecca and her
fuzzy friend

CHAPTER

21

Kenneth McKenna assigned me to write *Rich, Young and Pretty*, a musical that was to star Jane Powell, Danielle Darrieux, Wendell Corey, and a young singer named Vic Damone. A very talented cast.

It was a story about a young woman who falls in love during a trip to Paris. A story that had to keep moving quickly and required a light touch.

One morning, Jules Stein called me. "Doris and I are having dinner with you tonight. Do you mind if I bring someone with us?"

"Of course not," I said.

One more person wouldn't matter because there was never enough room for everybody, anyway.

That evening, Jules and Doris arrived with a handsome young man.

"I want you to meet Fernando Lamas. He's going to be in your movie."

Fernando had a South American accent and turned out not only to be a charming man, but a very intelligent one. Once, when he appeared on *The Tonight Show,* Johnny Carson started to make fun of Fernando's accent and Fernando stopped him.

"When someone has an accent," he informed Carson, "it means he knows one more language than you do."

The studio audience applauded.

I was on the set of *Rich, Young and Pretty* the first day of shooting. I had written the script with Dorothy Cooper, a wonderful contract writer. It was Vic Damone's first movie and he was understandably nervous. The director was Norman Taurog, a tough old pro.

"All right. This is a take," Taurog called out.

Vic Damone said nervously, "Excuse me, Mr. Taurog. Could I have a drink of water first?"

Norman Taurog glared at him and said, "No. Roll 'em!"

Rich, Young and Pretty began shooting.

The movie was a modest success at the box office. That same year I also wrote a musical comedy, *Nancy Goes to Rio,* starring Ann Sothern, Jane Powell, and Barry Sullivan. It was the story of a mother and daughter who fall in love with the same man. When I finished the screenplay, I wrote *No Questions Asked,* starring Barry Sullivan, Arlene Dahl, and George Murphy.

A studio executive had been on a flight to New York when he encountered Pug Wells, a stewardess who fascinated him. She was cheerful and effervescent, and when the executive started to question her about her life, he became even more fascinated. When he returned to the studio, he suggested to Dore that we make a movie based on her character. That was my next assignment.

I was working with Ruth Brooks Flippen, one of the top writers at the studio. The producer was Armand

Deutsch, whom Dore had brought in from the east. Armand, or Ardie, as he was called, had no experience making movies, but Dore was very impressed with his intellect.

When I met Ardie, I liked him immediately. Instead of having the restrained attitude of many producers, Ardie was filled with enthusiasm.

I sat down to begin writing the screenplay. I decided to complicate the life of the Pug Wells character, not with one man, but with three. That gave me my title, *Three Guys Named Mike.*

When I showed Ardie the beginning of my screenplay, he was literally jumping up and down with excitement. The result was that I couldn't wait to show him more. He was wonderful to work with. When I finished the screenplay, he said, "This is a great part for Jane Wyman."

"And the men?"

"Van Johnson, Howard Keel, and Barry Sullivan. That's my dream cast."

Ardie got his dream cast. We started shooting in the spring of 1950, and the picture went well.

For reasons which now escape me, I decided I wanted to act in the movie. I spoke to Ardie about it.

"Fine," he said. "What part do you want to play?"

"I haven't written it yet," I told him.

I knew how to write a part that could not be cut out of a movie. The secret was to play a character who was with the star when he or she was introduced. Since they could not cut out the entrance of the star, they could not cut out the character. I wrote myself a brief part as a gardener in the scene introducing Barry Sullivan.

The next day, at the dailies, when I saw my performance, I would have given any amount of money not to have done it. I was dreadful.

* * *

I was assigned to *Just This Once*, a lovely original idea by Max Trell. It was about a spendthrift who was living a high life running through his inheritance. The executor of his estate was so upset that he hired a conservator to control the man's spending. The conservator happened to be a beautiful young woman.

When I finished this script, I thought it would be perfect for Cary Grant. The studio sent the script to Cary, and he turned it down.

Peter Lawford was cast, along with Janet Leigh and Lewis Stone, who had played Judge Hardy in the famous Andy Hardy series.

One year later, when the picture was released, Cary called me. "Sidney, I just want to tell you that you were right. I should have played that part."

To this day, *Just This Once* remains one of my favorite movies.

In February of 1952, Kenneth McKenna sent for me.

"We just bought a Broadway play, *Remains to Be Seen*."

I had read the reviews. It was a big Broadway hit written by the talented team of Howard Lindsay and Russel Crouse. It was about a female band singer in New York City who moves into an apartment house where the murder of her wealthy uncle took place. When the girl grows suspicious of the murderer, he decides to kill her.

"I'm assigning you to it," McKenna said.

I nodded. "Fine, Kenneth."

He was definitely not a Ken.

"We'll fly you to New York to see the show and meet Leland Hayward, the producer."

Leland Hayward. My mind was spinning. I could still visualize the client list of the Leland Hayward Agency when

I was there. *Ben Hecht, Charles MacArthur, Nunnally John-son.*

Hayward would go on to produce some prestigious movies, *The Old Man and the Sea, The Spirit of St. Louis,* and *Mister Roberts.*

I flew to New York the following day. On the plane, I read the stage play of *Remains to Be Seen* and it was delightful.

The day after I arrived, I had lunch with Leland Hayward at the Plaza Hotel. He had the reputation of being a bon vivant. He had been married to Pamela Churchill, Margaret Sullavan, and Nancy Hawks, all beauties. He was a charismatic man, with gray hair that was carefully styled, and he was always elegantly dressed.

Leland rose from the table to greet me and said, "It's a pleasure to meet you." I saw no point in reminding him that I had been a seventeen-dollar-a-week client with his agency, twelve years earlier. We started lunch and he turned out to be an interesting and witty conversationalist.

We talked about the play.

"I read it. I think it's wonderful."

"Good. I'm glad you're doing the screenplay."

He had arranged for me to see the play that evening. It was an excellent cast, headlined by Jackie Cooper, Harry Shaw Lowe, Madeleine Morka, and Janis Paige. Also in that cast were two relative unknowns, both of whom later went on to have huge careers—Frank Campanella and Ossie Davis. The evening was as delightful as I had expected it to be.

I went back to Hollywood to write the screenplay. Three months later, I had finished it. I turned it in to the producer, Arthur Hornblow. "It's very good," he said. "We'll put it into production right away."

"Do you have a cast in mind?"

"The studio is signing June Allyson and Van Johnson."

"Great."

A few days later, Dore called me into his office. "The part of Benjamin Goodman would be perfect for Louis Calhern."

"I agree," I said. "He's a gifted actor."

"There's one problem."

"What's that?"

"He turned it down. He said it's too small a part."

He's right, I thought.

Dore went on. "You're a good friend of Louis's, aren't you?"

"Yes."

"I'd like you to talk him into doing this. He'd be a big asset to the movie." And that's when I made up my mind. Dore was right.

The next night, I invited Calhern to dinner at a restaurant. He looked around the room and said, "I hope no one sees us together. It would spoil my reputation. I should have worn a mask."

"I understand you turned down the part of Benjamin Goodman."

"You call that a part?" he snorted. "By the way, I liked your script."

I began my pitch. "Louie, it's going to be a big picture and I want you to be part of it. Your character is essential to the plot. Your performance would make the picture. It's going to vault your career to the top. And it would be very good for you—"

I went on for the next half hour being Otto, and when I was through, Calhern said, "You're right. I'll do it."

The reviews and the box office were only fair and it did not vault Calhern's career to the top.

* * *

Once a year, the international distributors and exhibitors of MGM movies were invited to Culver City, to learn about the upcoming projects. It was an exciting time for the studio. The representatives of more than a dozen countries around the world were brought to a huge soundstage to hear about the new films.

Dore addressed the assembly. "This is going to be one of the best years we've ever had," he promised them.

After a short speech, he began to read the list of the upcoming movies, naming the stars, directors, and writers of each one. I was told later that after he had named a few pictures, he came across one of mine.

"*Rich, Young and Pretty*, written by Sidney Sheldon." He named a few more pictures.

Then "*Nancy Goes to Rio*, written by Sidney Sheldon."

"*No Questions Asked*, written by Sidney Sheldon."

"*Three Guys Named Mike*, written by Sidney Sheldon."

The men in the audience began to laugh.

Schary looked up and said, "Sheldon seems to be writing most of our pictures this year."

That afternoon, Dore called me into his office. "How would you like to be a producer?" he asked.

I was surprised. "I've never thought about it."

"Well, think about it, because as of today, you're a producer."

"I don't know what to say, Dore."

"You've earned it," he said. "Good luck."

"Thanks."

I went back to my office and thought, *I'm thirty-four years old, I have an Oscar, and I'm a producer at the biggest motion picture studio in the world.*

It was a moment when I should have felt a sense of jubilation. Instead, I was overcome with a feeling of dread.

I did not know anything about producing. Dore had made a mistake. There was no way I could do this. I would call Dore and tell him that I could not accept it. He would probably fire me and I would soon be looking for a job.

I tried to sleep that night but it was no use. At midnight I got dressed and went for a walk, thinking about all the things that were happening to me. I remembered the night that Otto had asked me to go for a walk with him. *Every day is a different page, Sidney, and they can be full of surprises. You'll never know what's next until you turn the page. I would hate to see you close the book too soon and miss all the excitement that could happen to you on the next page.*

When I woke up in the morning, I decided to at least attempt to produce a picture. If I failed, I could always go back to being a writer.

That morning, when I went to the studio, I found out I had been moved into a larger office. I also learned that being a producer at Metro-Goldwyn-Mayer was very simple. The story department, which had access to all the publishers, sent every producer synopses of the books that were coming out, along with the plays and original stories that were submitted to the studio. All the producer had to do was choose the one he wanted.

Producers were then given a list of writers available to work on their projects. When the scripts were completed, the casting department got into action. They gave the producers a list of stars, and directors. "Who would you like?"

The last step was Benny Thau, who would make the deals with the agents for the writers, stars, and directors. The producers at Metro literally sat in their offices and pushed buttons. Being a producer was going to be easy.

* * *

I still enjoyed giving dinner parties in my home. Friends and actors and directors I had worked with filled my humble abode, and there was never a dull moment.

One night, I decided to make it a musical evening and I invited a group of some of the most talented musicians and composers in Hollywood—all of whom were already successful and went on to have huge careers. Among my guests were:

Alfred Newman, whom we all called "Pappy." He was short in stature but long on talent. He was nominated for more Oscars than any other composer in motion pictures and had won nine times. He scored more than two hundred films, including *Alexander's Ragtime Band, Call Me Madam,* and *The King and I.*

Victor Young, who was nominated for twenty-two Oscars. He wrote the scores for *The Wizard of Oz, The Quiet Man, Around the World in Eighty Days,* and *Shane.*

Dimitri Tiomkin, who scored *Lost Horizon, It's a Wonderful Life, High Noon,* and many other pictures.

Johnny Green, who wrote more than a dozen hit songs, including "I Cover the Waterfront," "Out of Nowhere," "You're Mine You." He scored films for all the major studios.

Bronislau Kaper, who wrote the score for *Three Guys Named Mike.* He went on to score *Green Mansions, Butterfield 8,* and *Auntie Mame.*

André Previn, who found fame as the conductor or musical director of films that included *Silk Stockings, Kiss Me Kate, My Fair Lady, Porgy and Bess,* and *Gigi.*

It was an impressive group. My date that evening was a young actress who was staying at a motel across the street. After dinner, we all gathered in the living room. I decided to entertain them. I sat down at the little spinet piano and I announced to the group, "I'm taking piano lessons by mail. It's a new system—learning to play by the numbers."

I began to play, and behind me I sensed a respectful silence.

In the middle of my playing, my date whispered, "Sidney, I hate to interrupt, but I have an early call tomorrow."

I rose. "I'll take you across to the motel, Janet." Turning to my guests, I said, "I'll be right back."

I took my date back to her motel and was gone no more than five minutes. When I returned, I started to sit down at the piano to finish the song. There was no piano. My guests had moved it into the den.

I looked around at their grinning faces and I felt sorry for them.

Jealousy is a terrible thing.

CHAPTER

22

Now that I was a producer, literary material started coming into my office—plays, screenplays, and original stories. But there was nothing that excited me. I was resolved that the first picture I produced would be something I could be proud of. Three weeks after I had been made a producer, Dore Schary's secretary called me. "Mr. Schary would like to see you in his office."

"Tell him I'll be right there."

Ten minutes later, I was facing Dore.

He hesitated a moment, and then said, "Harry Cohn called."

"Oh?"

"He asked for permission to negotiate a deal with you to become head of production at Columbia."

I was stunned. "I had no idea he was—"

"I talked to Mr. Mayer and we decided that we would say no. There are two reasons. First of all, we're very happy with what you're doing here. Secondly, we feel Harry Cohn would destroy you. He's a very difficult man to work with. I called Cohn back and told him our decision." He looked at me expectantly. "It's up to you."

I had a lot to think about. Running a major studio was the most prestigious job in Hollywood. On the other hand, Schary and Mayer were probably right about my working for Cohn. I remembered the scene in Cohn's office. *Harry, I have Donna Reed on the line. Tony's regiment is being sent overseas and Donna wants to be with him in San Francisco until he leaves.*

She can't go.

Did I want to spend my days working for a man like that? I made a decision. I said, "I'm happy here, Dore."

He smiled. "Good. We don't want to lose you."

When I got back to my office, Harris Katleman, an agent at MCA, the top agency in Hollywood, was waiting for me. "I hear that Harry Cohn wants you to run Columbia."

News travels fast, I thought. "That's right. Dore just told me."

"Our agency would like to represent you, Sidney. We can make a hell of a deal for you and—"

I shook my head. "I appreciate it, Harris, but I've decided not to accept his offer."

He looked surprised. "I've never heard of anyone turning down a chance to run a studio."

"You have now."

He stood there, trying to think of something to say. There was nothing.

I could not help but wonder what my life would have been like if I had accepted Harry Cohn's offer, and I was thinking about how far I had come. I thought about the guard at the entrance to Columbia Studios. *I want to be a writer. Who do I see?*

Do you have an appointment?

No, but—
Then you don't see anybody.
There must be someone I—
Not without an appointment . . .
Harry Cohn wants you to run Columbia.

Shortly after my conversation with Dore, I was having lunch in the studio commissary, when I saw Zsa Zsa Gabor at a nearby table, with a lovely-looking young brunette. I had met Zsa Zsa several months earlier and I found her amusing. She and her sisters, Eva and Magda, were already Hollywood legends, famous for being famous. They had come from Hungary and quickly established themselves in Hollywood as eccentric, talented women. At the moment, it was Zsa Zsa's companion I was interested in. When I finished lunch, I went over to Zsa Zsa's table.

"Darling—" That was her usual greeting to everyone, including strangers.

"Hi, Zsa Zsa." We did the Hollywood air kiss.

She turned to the young woman with her. "I would like you to meet Jorja Curtright. She's a wonderful actress. This is Sidney Sheldon."

Jorja nodded. "Hello."

"Sit down, darling."

I sat. I turned to Jorja. "So, you're an actress. What have you done?"

She said, vaguely, "Different things."

I was taken aback by her response. Actresses usually could not wait to tell producers their credits.

I looked at her more closely. There was something magnetic about her. She was a beauty, with classical features and deep, intelligent brown eyes, filled with promise. Her voice was husky and distinctive.

"Why don't you two come up to my office when you're through with lunch?" I suggested.

"We'd love to, darling."

Jorja said nothing.

On the way to my office, I stopped to see Jerry Davis, my close friend who was a writer on the lot.

"Jerry, I just met the woman I'm going to marry."

"Who is she? I'd like to meet her."

"Oh, no, not yet. I don't need the competition."

Fifteen minutes later, Zsa Zsa and Jorja came to my office.

"Please, sit down," I said.

We chatted idly for a few minutes. Finally, I said to Jorja, "If you're not seeing anyone, why don't we have dinner one night?" I picked up a pen. "What's your phone number?"

"I'm afraid I'm very busy," Jorja said.

Zsa Zsa looked at Jorja in horror. "Don't be a fool, darling. Sidney's a producer."

"I'm sorry," Jorja said, "I'm not interested in—"

Zsa Zsa spoke up and gave me Jorja's telephone number. Jorja glared at her, obviously upset.

"It's just a dinner," I said to Jorja. "I'll call you."

Jorja got up. "It was nice meeting you, Mr. Sheldon."

I could feel the chill in the room. I watched as the two of them left. *This is not going to be easy,* I thought.

I looked up Jorja Curtright's credits. They were formidable. She had appeared in television, motion pictures, and on Broadway. She had just starred as Stella on a road tour of the Broadway hit *A Streetcar Named Desire*. The reviewers were ecstatic.

The *New York Times* said, "As 'Stella,' Jorja Curtright is superb—energetic and decisive in her analysis of the part and glowing with warmth, pity and understanding."

She had also gotten great reviews for the movie *Whis-tle Stop* and a dozen important television shows.

I telephoned Jorja the next morning and invited her to dinner. She said, "I'm sorry, I'm busy."

I telephoned her for the next four days and got the same answer.

On the fifth day, I called and said, "I'm giving a dinner party Friday night. There are going to be a lot of important producers and directors here. I think it might be helpful for your career for you to meet them."

There was a long, long pause. "All right."

I had the feeling that she had accepted because the two of us were not going to be alone.

Now I had to begin putting together a dinner party with important producers and directors.

Somehow I managed to pull it off. A few of the producers and directors who were there had seen Jorja's work and were very flattering.

When the evening was over I said to Jorja, "Did you enjoy yourself tonight?"

"Yes. Thank you."

"I'll drive you home."

She shook her head. "I have my car. Thank you for a lovely evening." She started to head for the door.

"Wait a minute," I said. "Will you have dinner with me one night?"

She thought about it. "All right." There was a definite lack of enthusiasm in her answer.

I called her the following morning. "Are you free for dinner this evening?"

For the first time she said, "Yes."

"I'll pick you up, seven-thirty."

That was the beginning.

* * *

We had dinner at Chasen's. My experience was that when having a conversation with an actress, the talk usually consisted of: "So I said to the director . . ." and "I told the cameraman . . ." and "My leading man . . ." Dinner with an actress was all about show business. With Jorja, show business was not even mentioned. She talked about her family and friends. She had come from a small town—Mena, Arkansas—and still had her small-town roots. She was the antithesis of any actress I had ever met.

As we came to the end of the dinner, I said, "Jorja, why were you so reluctant to go out with me?"

She hesitated. "Do you want a straight answer?"

"Of course."

"You have the reputation of dating too many women. I don't intend to be just another one on your list."

I said, "You're not just another one. Why don't you give me a chance?"

She studied me a moment. "All right. We'll see."

I began seeing Jorja every evening. The more I saw of her, the more I knew that I was in love. She had a wonderful, wicked sense of humor, and we laughed a lot. We became closer and closer.

At the end of three months, I took her in my arms and said, "Let's get married."

We eloped to Vegas the next day.

I arranged for Natalie and Marty to come to Hollywood to meet Jorja, and they all got along beautifully. Natalie asked Jorja a hundred questions, then decided that she was thrilled for me.

I planned a honeymoon for us in Europe. I had bought a small house off Coldwater Canyon in Beverly Hills.

Otto and his wife, Ann, were living in Los Angeles, and when I told Otto the news about Jorja, he clapped me on the shoulder and said, "That's wonderful. I'll tell you what I'm going to do. As a wedding gift, I'm going to put siding on your house."

Otto's latest occupation was the siding business, putting aluminum siding on the outside of houses. It was a generous gift because siding was expensive.

"Great. Thanks."

I told Kenneth McKenna that I was taking three months off, and Jorja and I sailed to Europe. It was a dream honeymoon that included a tour of London, Paris, Rome, and one of my favorite places in the world— Venice. I had never been happier. The dark cloud was behind me.

Finally, it was time to return home. When we arrived back in Los Angeles, Otto was waiting for us. As we drove up to our house, he said, "I think you're going to love this."

He was right. The house looked beautiful, completely covered with shiny aluminum siding.

". . . And I'll tell you what I'm going to do," Otto added magnanimously. "I'm going to give you this at cost."

Jorja was doing a lot of television. She seemed to go from one top show to another.

One night, Jorja had a dream that she was making an impassioned speech to save the life of a man a crowd was about to lynch. She woke up in the middle of the dream and sat straight up in bed. She enjoyed her speech so much that she finished it, wide awake.

Back at MGM, late in the spring of 1952, I found a project that I liked. It was called "Dream Wife," a short story written by Alfred Levitt.

The plot was about the battle of the sexes. A bachelor was engaged to a beautiful State Department official who was too busy with an oil crisis in the Middle East to have time to marry him. Fed up, he decides to marry a beautiful young princess he met in the Middle East. Because of the world oil crisis, complications begin.

I brought an aspiring young writer, Herbert Baker, in to work with me on the screenplay. The writing went well. I had Cary Grant in mind as the leading man, but I knew how busy his schedule was.

When I was involved in a project, I became so absorbed that time had no meaning for me. One evening, I was working late at the studio when I got an idea for a scene that excited me. I picked up the telephone and phoned Herbert Baker.

"Get over here right away," I said. "I have an idea you're going to love." I hung up and I kept working.

An hour later, Herbert Baker still had not arrived. I decided to call him again. As I reached for the phone, I looked at my watch.

It was four o'clock in the morning.

When the *Dream Wife* screenplay was finally finished, I was ready to start casting.

"Who do you want?" the casting department asked.

I did not even hesitate. "My dream cast would be Cary Grant and Deborah Kerr."

"We'll see what we can do."

The screenplay was sent to Cary and I got an answer five days later. "Cary loves the script. He'll do it."

I was thrilled.

"He gave us a list of directors he'll work with, I'll start checking them out."

The bad news came the next day. "All of Cary's

choices are busy directing other movies. Why don't you talk to him?"

I arranged to have lunch with Cary.

"Cary, we have a problem. The directors you want are not available. What do you want us to do?"

He thought it over. "I know who should direct this picture."

I was relieved. "Who?"

"You."

Me? I shook my head. "Cary, I've never directed before."

"I know how your mind works. I want you to direct it."

This was obviously going to be a fantastic year for me. How high could an elevator go?

I went to see Dore Schary.

"Cary wants me to direct *Dream Wife.*"

Dore Schary nodded. "He called me. If that's what he wants, fine. You're the director."

It was like a miracle to me. A few short years ago I had been an usher, watching these glamorous, unreachable stars on the screen. And now I was writing for them, producing, directing them, touching their lives as they had once touched mine.

I was ecstatic. I was joining the roster of all of the talented directors who had worked with Cary—Alfred Hitchcock in *Suspicion* and *Notorious*, George Cukor in *Holiday* and *The Philadelphia Story*, Leo McCarey in *The Awful Truth* and *Once Upon a Honeymoon*, and Howard Hawks in *Bringing Up Baby* and *His Girl Friday*.

I got up to leave.

"Wait a minute, Sidney," Dore said. "This would make you the writer, director, and producer. You really don't need all those credits."

I turned to look at him. "What did you have in mind?"

"Why don't I put my name on as producer," he said.

It made no difference to me. I nodded. "No problem."

It was a decision that would almost destroy my career.

We began casting. Walter Pidgeon was signed to the cast, but we were having trouble finding the Middle East princess. I had heard about an actress named Betta St. John, who was in London, starring in *South Pacific.*

I flew over there to make a test of her. She was perfect for the part and I signed her for the movie. When I returned to the studio, there was a message that Harry Cohn had called. I returned the call.

"Sheldon, I understand that you're going to direct a picture with Cary Grant."

"That's right."

"Be careful."

"What do you mean?"

"Cary Grant is a killer. He likes to run things. Why do you think he picked you to direct the movie?"

"Because he thinks I—"

"He's setting you up. He figures that with an inexperienced director, he can get away with murder. Remember this, Sheldon. There can only be one director on a picture. Tell him that."

I had no intention of telling him that. "Thanks, Harry."

Cary was coming to the house for lunch the following day. I thought about what I was going to say to him.

I want to thank you for being such a good friend . . . I want to thank you for your faith in me . . . I want to thank you for giving me an opportunity like this . . . I'm counting on you to give me all the help you can. I know you won't let me make a fool of myself . . . Working with you is going to be wonderful . . .

Cary walked in, smiling.

"I understand you found our princess in London," he said.

"That's right. She'll be great."

Cary sat down, and I heard myself saying, "I have to talk to you, Cary. There can only be one director on a picture. I want us to be clear on that before we begin. Agreed?"

I had had no intention of saying any of that to one of the biggest stars in the world, who was also my friend. *At times, without any warning, you will lose control of your words and actions.* Cary could have had me fired from the movie in about ten seconds.

He sat there, looking at me, without a word. Then, after a few moments, he surprised me by saying, "Right."

Wrong.

The trouble began before we even started shooting.

Cary walked onto the soundstage one morning and stopped before one of the sets.

He shook his head. "If I had known it was going to look like this, I never would have agreed to do the picture."

When I cut three unnecessary lines from the script, Cary said, "If I had known you were going to cut those lines, I would never have agreed to do this picture."

He saw the wardrobe he was to wear. "If I had known they expected me to wear this, I never would have agreed to do this picture."

The night before we began to shoot, Deborah Kerr called me.

"Sidney, I just want to tell you that Cary said the two of us should gang up on you. I told him I won't do it."

"Thank you, Deborah."

What have I gotten myself into?

When shooting started the next morning, Cary flubbed his first scene.

I said, "Cut—" and Cary turned on me.

"Don't ever say 'cut' when I'm in the middle of a scene."

Everyone on the soundstage could hear him. The harassment went on that way, and in the late afternoon, I said to my assistant director, "This is the last scene. I'm quitting."

"You can't quit. Give it a chance. Cary will calm down."

Cary did, but every day he managed, in little ways, to try to test me.

In a scene between Cary and Deborah, she was explaining to Cary that they could not have dinner together because she had to go to the Middle East on State Department business. Deborah started to say her lines to Cary, and she began to laugh.

"Cut," I said. "Let's try it again."

The camera began to roll.

"I'm sorry I can't have dinner with you," Deborah said. "I have to go to—" She began to burst into laughter again.

"Cut."

I walked up to the two of them. "What's the problem?"

Cary said, innocently, "No problem."

"All right," I told him. "Do the scene with me."

We began the scene. I said, "I'm sorry I can't have dinner with you but—"

Cary was looking at me with such overpowering intensity that I began to laugh.

"Cary," I said, "don't do that. Let's get this scene."

He nodded. "All right."

From then on, that scene went well.

We finished the day's shooting and I was happy with the result. Deborah was enormously talented and she and Cary were wonderful together.

Cary was married to a young actress named Betsy Drake, with whom he had done a movie. Every evening, after each day's shooting, as Cary and I left the sound-stage, Jorja and Betsy would be waiting outside for us. Cary would take Jorja's arm and begin complaining about what I had done that day. I would take Betsy's arm and complain about Cary's behavior.

One day, while shooting a scene with Walter Pidgeon, Cary moved his eyebrows up and down like Groucho Marx.

"Cut! Cary, what are you doing?"

He was all innocence. "I'm doing the scene."

"Do it without your eyebrows."

"Right."

"Action."

The scene started again and so did the eyebrows. It was so ridiculous that it broke me up. I was behind the camera. I did not want to spoil the scene, so I bit my hand to keep from laughing aloud. I had made no sound, but in the middle of the scene, Cary, whose back was to me, turned and said, "Sidney, if you're going to laugh like that, I can't do the scene."

Cary and I reached a kind of détente. The fact was that we liked each other too much to carry on a feud.

One day, Elvis Presley came on the set to watch us shooting. He was at the height of his popularity and I had no idea what to expect. He turned out to be extraordinarily polite and modest. It was "Mr. Sheldon" and "Yes, sir" and "No, sir." Everyone was very taken with him.

What happened to him later on in his life was dreadful. He was on drugs, and ruined his voice, and grew fat and unattractive.

When he died, some cynic said, "Good career move."

When we finished shooting, Cary and I had lunch.

Cary said, "Sidney, anytime you want to direct me in another movie, just tell me. I don't even have to read the script."

This was enormously flattering coming from a star who was eagerly sought after by every studio.

Dore and the rest of the executives saw the finished picture and were ecstatic.

Dore said to me, "I have great news. Radio City Music Hall has accepted the picture."

I was thrilled. It was a director's dream to get into the prestigious Radio City Music Hall, and I had done it with the first picture I directed.

"I'm proud of you," Dore said. "You did a great job."

Eddie Mannix spoke up. "Gentlemen, we have a hit on our hands."

Howard Strickling, head of publicity, agreed. "This calls for a big publicity campaign."

Dore smiled. "Let's get started."

The elevator was at the top floor. Nothing could go wrong.

CHAPTER

23

At a dinner party one evening, I was seated next to Groucho Marx.

I nodded and said, "I'm Sidney Sheldon."

He turned and glared at me. "No." He went back to his shrimp cocktail.

I was puzzled. "No, what?"

"You're a fraud. I know Sidney Sheldon. He's handsomer and taller than you, and he's a great juggler. Can you juggle?"

"No."

"See?"

"Mr. Marx—"

"Don't call me Mr. Marx."

"What do you like to be called?"

"Sally. I've read some of the things you've done."

"Oh?"

"Yes. You ought to be ashamed of yourself." He looked me over again. "You're too thin. Whoever you are, you and your wife should come to my house tomorrow night for dinner. Eight o'clock. And don't be late again."

* * *

I introduced Jorja to Groucho and there was an instant rapport. That was the beginning of our lifelong relationship with Groucho.

At Groucho's dinner parties, there were always some of Groucho's lines for his guests to quote: "I find television very educational. Every time someone turns it on, I go into the other room and read a book."

"Outside of a dog, a book is a man's best friend. Inside of a dog, it's too dark to read."

"I had a wonderful evening, but this wasn't it."

"Marriage is a wonderful institution, but who wants to live in an institution?"

Once, he had to visit a doctor. A beautiful young nurse came up to him and said, "The doctor will see you now. Walk this way." Groucho looked at her swaying hips and said, "If I could walk that way, I wouldn't have to see a doctor."

We saw Groucho often and as we got to know him, I realized that people didn't really understand him. When he insulted them, they thought it was funny. They felt rather proud to be the object of his wit. What they didn't realize was that Groucho meant everything he said. He was a misanthrope and was completely honest about his feelings.

He had had a bitter childhood. He was pulled out of school when he was seven and he and his brothers went to the stage. The Marx Brothers made fourteen pictures together. Groucho made five more on his own.

Groucho and I were walking down Rodeo Drive one day and a man came running up to Groucho and said, "Groucho, do you remember me?"

Typical of his attitude toward people, Groucho turned

on him. "What have you ever done that I should remember you?"

Groucho had a very successful television show that was on the air for an incredible eleven years. It was called *You Bet Your Life*. It was a hit because no one knew what he was going to say next.

One night, a contestant on the show told Groucho that he had ten children.

"Why so many?" Groucho asked.

"I like my wife."

Groucho said, "I like my cigar, but I take it out sometimes."

One day, Groucho's daughter, Melinda, who was then eight, was invited to a country club by a classmate. They put on bathing suits and went into the swimming pool.

The manager of the club came running up and said to Melinda, "You'll have to get out of the pool. We don't allow Jews here."

When Melinda ran home, crying, and told her father what had happened, Groucho got the manager of the club on the phone.

"You're being unfair," Groucho said. "My daughter is only half Jewish. Is it all right if she goes in the pool up to her waist?"

Groucho was married to Eden Hartford, a young actress, and Jorja and I were supposed to have dinner with them one night. Eden had an early call at the studio the next day, and Jorja also had an early call.

Groucho telephoned me. "It's just the two of us for dinner. How do you want me to dress?"

I said, "Groucho, we're going to a nice restaurant, so don't embarrass me."

"Right."

When I picked him up at his house and rang the bell, he opened the door wearing Eden's skirt and blouse and high-heeled shoes and smoking his cigar. I didn't take any notice of it.

He said, "Would you like to come in for a drink?"

I said, "Fine."

We went into the den and Groucho mixed drinks for us. The doorbell rang. What he had forgotten was that he had a date with some television executives to talk about his show. He opened the door and invited them in and we sat chatting for a while and they left.

"I'll change," Groucho said.

And we went out to dinner.

Everyone in show business has the same problem—what to say to a friend whose play or performance we hated. Over the years, a few solutions have worked:

"You'll never be better . . ."

"That was a play . . ."

"I have no words . . ."

"You should have been out front . . ."

"I've never seen anything like it . . ."

"People will remember this evening for a long time . . ."

Dream Wife would not be released to theaters for several months and I decided this was the perfect time to take Jorja on another European vacation.

Jorja was as excited about the trip as I was. We sat down and discussed where we would go. London, Paris, Rome . . . In the middle of our planning, there was a phone call. It was Ladislaus Bush-Fekete, calling from Munich. I had not heard from Laci since the closing of *Alice in Arms*, which was almost ten years earlier. Since that time, Kirk Douglas had become a major star. I was pleased that I had not destroyed his career.

"Sidney," Laci said, in his thick Hungarian accent, "how are you? Marika and I miss you."

"We're fine, Laci. I miss you, too."

"When are you coming to Europe?"

"As a matter of fact, we're leaving next week."

"Good. You must come to Munich and visit us. Can you do it?"

I thought about it for a second. "You bet we can. I want you to meet Jorja."

"Wonderful. Let me know when you're coming."

"I will."

I hung up and told Jorja, "That was Ladislaus Bush-Fekete."

Jorja looked at me. "*Alice in Arms*," she said.

I laughed. "You'll like him, and his wife is lovely. And Munich is beautiful. We'll have a great time there."

Right before we left, Sam Spiegel called.

Sam Spiegel was one of Hollywood's most colorful characters. Born in Austria, he had come to Hollywood to sell Egyptian cotton. He had served time in Brixton Prison for fraud. While in Hollywood, he decided to become a producer, and changed his name to S. P. Eagle. He became the joke of the town. When Darryl Zanuck heard the news, he said, "I'm changing my name to Z. A. Nuck."

The laughter quickly stopped, for Sam Spiegel went on to produce a long list of Academy Award–winning pictures, including *Lawrence of Arabia, On the Waterfront,* and *The African Queen.*

I had met him at one of the lavish parties he gave, and we had become friends.

After his phone call, Jorja and I had dinner with Sam. He said, "I've heard about a foreign film I might be interested in remaking. If you're going to Paris, I'd appreciate it if you'd take a look at it and tell me what you think."

Three days later, Jorja and I flew to New York, to spend a few days before boarding the *Queen Mary*.

There were some interesting plays on Broadway—*The Crucible, Wonderful Town, Picnic, The Seven Year Itch,* and *Dial M for Murder.* Walking into the lobbies of the various theaters gave me a sharp sense of déjà vu. Some of the plays were in theaters that Ben Roberts and I had had plays in. So many incredible events had happened since that time. But the most incredible of all was that a Cary Grant picture that I had directed was going to open at Radio City Music Hall.

One evening, Jorja and I went to see *The Crucible,* Arthur Miller's new play. In the cast were Arthur Kennedy, E. G. Marshall, Beatrice Straight, and Madeleine Sherwood. It was a stunning evening in the theater. Jorja was enthralled.

As the curtain came down, she turned to me. "Who directed this play?"

"Jed Harris. He's directed *Uncle Vanya, A Doll's House, Our Town,* and *The Heiress.*"

"He's incredible," Jorja declared. "I want to work with him one day."

I took her hand. "Only if he's that lucky."

CHAPTER

24

The following morning we sailed for London. It was a perfect, smooth crossing, and it seemed to me that that described my present life. I was married to a woman I adored. I was under contract to a major studio, doing what I loved to do, and I was on my way to Europe, on a second honeymoon.

When the ship docked, we took the boat train to London, spent a few days there, and then went on to Paris, where we checked in at the beautiful Hotel Lancaster on Rue de Berri. The hotel had a spectacular garden where they served drinks and meals.

The first thing I did once we checked in was to call the Paris office of United Artists. I spoke to Mr. Berns, the manager.

"Mr. Spiegel told us to expect your call, Mr. Sheldon. When would you like to see the film?"

"It really doesn't matter. Anytime."

"Would tomorrow morning be satisfactory? Say—ten o'clock?"

"Fine."

Jorja and I spent the day sightseeing and went to the fabled Maxim's for dinner.

The next morning, as I was getting dressed, Jorja was still in bed.

"We're running the film at ten o'clock, honey. You'd better get ready."

She shook her head. "I'm a little tired. Why don't you go? I think I'll stay in and rest today. We're going to dinner and the theater tonight."

"All right. I won't be long."

The United Artists office sent a limousine to pick me up and take me to their headquarters. I met Mr. Berns, a tall, pleasant-faced man with a full head of silver hair.

"Pleased to meet you," he said. "Why don't we go right into the theater?"

We walked into the huge theater that the company used to screen movies. There was only one other person there. He was slight, short, and unprepossessing. The only thing outstanding about his features were his eyes. They were very bright, almost probing. We were introduced, but I didn't get his name.

The movie began. It was a French western, badly done, and I was sure that Sam Spiegel would have no interest in it.

I looked across the aisle, and Mr. Berns and the stranger were deep in conversation.

The stranger was saying ". . . and I said to Zanuck, it will never work, Darryl . . . Harry Warner tried to make a deal with me, but he's such a bastard . . . and at dinner, Darryl said to me . . ."

Who the hell was this man?

I walked over to them. "Excuse me," I said to the stranger, "I didn't get your name."

He looked up at me and nodded. "Harris. Jed Harris."

I must have grinned from ear to ear. "Have I got someone who wants to meet you!"

"Really?"

"What are you doing right now?"

He shrugged. "Nothing special."

"Would you come back to the hotel with me? I want you to meet my wife."

"Sure."

Fifteen minutes later, we were in the garden of the Lancaster. I telephoned Jorja from downstairs.

"Hi."

"Hi. You're back. How was the movie?"

"Underwhelming. Come on down to the garden. We'll have lunch here."

"I'm not dressed, darling. Why don't we have something up in our room?"

"No, no. You must come down. There's someone I want you to meet."

"But—"

"No buts."

Fifteen minutes later, Jorja appeared.

I turned to Jed. "This is Jorja."

I looked at Jorja. "Jorja, this is Jed Harris." I said it slowly and watched her face light up.

We sat down. Jorja was thrilled to meet Jed Harris and they talked theater for half an hour before we ordered lunch. Jed Harris was absolutely charming. He was intelligent and funny and the soul of courtesy. I felt that we had made a new friend.

During the meal he turned to me and said, "I'm impressed with your work. How would you like to write a Broadway play for me?"

Writing a play directed by Jed Harris meant I would be working with a master. "I'd like that very much," I said.

I hesitated. "At the moment, I'm afraid I don't have an idea for a play."

He smiled. "I do." He started telling me various plots that he had in mind. I listened, and after each one I said, "That doesn't excite me," or "I don't think that would interest me," or "That sounds too familiar."

After about six different premises of his, he came up with one that I liked. It was about a female efficiency expert who almost destroys the people in the firm she's sent to examine, and in the end, falls in love and changes.

"That has real possibilities," I told Jed. "Unfortunately, Jorja and I are leaving tomorrow. We're going to be traveling around Europe."

"No problem. I'll go with you and we can work on the play."

I was a little surprised. "Great."

"Where are you going first?"

"We're going to Munich, to meet some friends of ours. He's a Hungarian playwright named—"

"I hate Hungarians. Their plays have no second acts and neither have their lives."

Jorja and I exchanged a look.

"Then Jed, maybe it would be better if you didn't—"

He held up a hand. "No, no. It will be fine. I want us to get going on the play."

Jorja looked at me and nodded.

And it was settled.

When the three of us checked into a hotel in Munich, Laci and Marika were on their way to meet us and I was a little apprehensive. *I hate Hungarians. Their plays have no second acts and neither have their lives.*

It turned out that I had nothing to worry about. Jed Harris was the essence of charm.

When Laci walked in, Jed put his arm around him and said, "You're a wonderful playwright. I think you're better than Molnár."

Laci almost blushed.

"You Hungarians have a very special talent," Jed said. "It's an honor to meet you both."

Jorja and I looked at each other.

Laci was beaming. "I'm going to take you to a famous restaurant here in Munich. They serve wines from almost every country in the world."

"Wonderful."

Jed went to his room to change and Laci, Marika, and I caught up on what we had been doing in the interim since we had last seen one another.

Half an hour later, we were entering an elegant-looking restaurant on the Isar River. We sat down to order. The waiter handed us menus. They were filled with wines from countries all over the world.

"What kind of wine would you like?" the waiter asked.

Before anyone could speak, Jed said, "I'll have a beer."

The waiter shook his head. "I'm sorry, sir. We don't serve beer here. We serve only wine."

Jed glared at him and got to his feet. "Let's get out of here."

I could not believe what I was hearing. "But Jed—"

"Come on. Let's go. I don't want to eat in a place that doesn't serve beer."

Embarrassed, we all got up and left.

"Goddamn Germans," Jed snarled.

Jorja and I were horrified. We all got into a taxi and went back to the hotel, where we had dinner.

Laci apologized to Jed. "I'm sorry about this," he said.

"I know another place where they have great beer. We'll go there tomorrow night."

The following day, Jed and I worked on the new play. We spent part of the time writing in the garden and part of the time writing in our suite. I started developing situations arising from the basic premise and Jed would make a suggestion here and there.

That evening, the Bush-Feketes picked us up.

"You'll like this place," Laci assured Jed.

In the restaurant, they took us to our table and the waiter handed us menus. "What would you like to start with?" he asked.

Jed spoke up. "I'll have some wine."

The waiter said, "I'm sorry, sir. We only serve beer here. We have beers from almost every country in the—"

Jed jumped to his feet. "Let's get the hell out of here."

I was shocked again. "Jed, I thought you—"

"Come on. I won't stay in a crummy restaurant where I can't have what I want."

He went out the door and we all followed him. Mr. Charm was turning into a monster.

The next day Jed came to my suite to work on the play and it was as though nothing had happened.

In the morning, as Jorja and I were on our way down to breakfast, the hotel manager stopped me.

"Mr. Sheldon, could I speak to you for a moment?"

"Of course."

"Your guest is very rude to the maids and housekeepers. He's made them very upset. I wonder if you—"

"I'll talk to him," I said.

When I did, he said, "They're too sensitive. My God, they're only maids and housekeepers."

* * *

The actress in Jorja was enchanted by Harris's talent. She kept asking him about the theater. At dinner one evening she said to him, "You know, there was a moment in *The Crucible* when Madeleine Sherwood walked off the stage, and it was a magnificent exit. What was her motivation? What did you tell her to think?"

He looked at Jorja and snapped, "About her paycheck."

That was the last time he called Jorja by name.

The following day the three of us left for Baden-Baden, the luxurious spa in the middle of Baden-Württemberg, in southwest Germany.

Jed hated it.

From there we went to the beautiful Black Forest, a fantastic mountain range in southwest Germany that extends ninety miles between the Rhine and Neckar Rivers. It is covered by dark pine forests and cut by deep valleys and small lakes.

Jed hated it.

I had had enough. Our play was coming along much too slowly. Instead of working out a story line, Jed would concentrate on one scene we had written, and go over it endlessly, unnecessarily changing a word here and there.

I said to Jorja, "We're going back to Munich without him."

She sighed. "You're right."

I looked over the notes that I had made on the play. They seemed very banal.

When Jed came to my suite to go to work, I said, "Jed, Jorja and I have to get back to Munich. We're going to leave you."

He nodded. "Right. I wasn't going to do the play with you, anyway."

A few hours later Jorja and I were on a train, heading for Munich.

* * *

When we arrived at our hotel, I reached for the phone to telephone Laci and my disc slipped out. I fell to the floor in terrible pain, unable to move.

Jorja was frantic. "I'll call a doctor."

"Wait," I said. "I've had this before. If you can help me get into bed, all I have to do is lie still and after a day or two, it will go away by itself."

She finally managed to help me get into bed. "Let me call Laci."

An hour later, Laci was in our hotel room.

"I'm sorry about this," I said. "I had big plans for us."

He looked at me and said, "I can help you."

"How?"

"I know a man here, Paul Horn."

"Is he a doctor?"

"No, he's a physiotherapist. But he's worked on some of the most famous people in the world. They come here to see him. He can fix you up."

I spent the next two days in bed and on the third day, Laci was walking me into an office at 5 Platenstrasse, the offices of Paul Horn.

Paul Horn was in his forties, a tall, tousled man with a mop of wild hair.

"Mr. Bush-Fekete told me about you," he said. "How often does this happen to you?"

I shrugged. "It's very irregular. Sometimes it happens twice a week. Sometimes it doesn't happen for years."

He nodded. "I can cure you."

An alarm went off in my mind. The doctors at Cedars of Lebanon and UCLA had told me there was no cure for what I had. *Put off the operation as long as you can. Finally, when you can't stand the pain, we'll have to operate.* And this man who was going to cure me was not even a doctor.

"You'll have to stay here for three weeks. I will treat you every day. Seven days a week."

It did not sound promising. "I don't know," I said. "Maybe we should forget this. I'll see my doctors at home and—"

Laci turned to me. "Sidney, this man has worked on rulers of countries. Give him a chance."

I looked at Jorja. "We'll see."

The treatment began the following morning. I would go in and lie on a table with a heat lamp warming my back for two hours. Then I would rest and repeat the procedure. This went on all day.

On the second day, something was added. Paul Horn helped me into a kind of hammock he had devised, which let all the muscles of my back relax. I lay there for five hours. Every day was the same procedure.

The waiting room was always crowded with people from all over the world, some of them speaking languages that I could not even identify.

Three weeks later, on the last day of treatment, Paul Horn asked, "How do you feel?"

"I feel fine." But I knew I would have felt fine without the treatments.

"You're cured," he said, happily.

I was skeptical. But he was right. In all the years that have passed since that time, I have not had one attack. It turned out that Paul Horn, who was not a doctor, had cured me.

It was time to return to Hollywood.

Returning to MGM was like going home again.

"You have a homecoming present," Dore said. "We're previewing *Dream Wife* at the Egyptian Theatre."

Dore saw my grin and said, "This is going to be a big one."

It was customary for the trade papers, *Variety* and the *Hollywood Reporter*, to review movies before the other reviews came out. We were all looking forward to the reviews with great anticipation. They could make or break a movie.

The Egyptian Theatre was filled with people anticipating the pleasure they were about to have. The picture began and we watched the screen, happily listening to the laughs in all the right places.

Jorja squeezed my hand. "It's wonderful."

When the picture ended, there was applause. We had a hit. We went to Musso & Frank's to celebrate. The only reviews would be in the trade papers, *Variety* and the *Hollywood Reporter*. We were making bets about which one would be better. Early in the morning, I went out and got the trades.

Jorja was still in bed when I returned. She saw the trade papers and smiled. "Read the reviews out loud. Slowly. I want to enjoy them."

I handed Jorja the papers. "You read them."

She looked at my face and quickly started reading the reviews.

"First, *Variety* . . ."

Part of the review read: ". . . highly contrived piece of screen nonsense. Able performers helped to carry the script's silliness through the frenetics, but director Sidney Sheldon let the action slop over into very broad slapstick too often. This loose handling reflects occasionally in the performances, most notably in Grant's.

"*Dream Wife* was made under the personal supervision of Dore Schary, and Cary Grant is on hand to get laughs where it isn't always possible to find them in the script. This uneven mixture of sophisticated humor and downright slapstick amounts to little more than a fairly amusing comedy. Sidney Sheldon has gone out of his way for comic situations and not succeeded too well."

The review in the *Hollywood Reporter* was worse. I was devastated.

Howard Strickling, the head of publicity at MGM, called me and said, "Sidney, I have some bad news for you. I have orders to kill the picture."

I was shocked. "What are you talking about?"

"Dore pulled the picture out of the Music Hall. We're not going to give it any publicity. We're just going to let it die."

"Howard, why—why would you do that?"

"Because Dore's name is on it as producer. As head of the studio, he tells the other producers what they can or cannot make. He can't afford to have his name on a flop. He's going to let *Dream Wife* fade away as fast as possible."

I was furious. There would be no previews, no bookings or interviews or merchandising. The ship had sailed and the cast and crew had drowned in a sea of ego. It was Dore who had suggested that he put his name on the movie and because of that, he was going to destroy it.

I called Jorja and told her what had happened.

"I'm so sorry," she said. "That's awful for you."

"Jorja, I can't work for a man like that."

"What are you going to do?"

"I'm going to quit. Is that all right with you?"

"Anything you want to do is all right with me, darling."

Fifteen minutes later, I walked into Dore Schary's office.

"I want to get out of my contract."

The man who, a few months earlier, said he didn't want me to leave to run another studio, now said, "Fine. I'll talk to the legal department."

The following day I got a formal release from MGM.

I was not concerned about getting a job. After all, I had an Oscar and a list of wonderful credits. I was sure that any studio in town would be happy to get me.

As it turned out, I was wrong. The elevator had stopped at the bottom.

C H A P T E R

25

I rented an office on Beverly Drive. When Groucho
heard about it, he said, "What are you going to do, become a dentist?"

I called my agent, told him I was available, and sat
back and waited for the calls to pour in.

The phone never rang.

In the theater, a playwright is judged by his best play,
no matter how many failures there are after that. In Hollywood, a writer is judged by his last movie, no matter
how many hits he might have written before. I was being
judged for *Dream Wife*. I had gotten a release from my
MGM contract at the worst possible time, when the film
business was going downhill. The end of block booking
was hurting the studios.

Block booking was the practice that the studios had
for putting their movies into theaters. If they had a picture coming out with a popular star, the theaters that
were eager to acquire that picture were forced to also
take four minor movies from the studio, so there was al-

ways a block of five. When the exhibitors filed a lawsuit, the government stepped in and stopped the practice.

There were other problems, as well. During the war, people were starved for entertainment and they would flock into theaters. Now that the war was over, they were more particular. Television had become a new form of entertainment and its popularity was costing the theaters money. One more problem was added to the mix: Foreign income had always been a big part of a picture's gross. Now, England and Italy and France were making their own movies, and that cut into the foreign revenue of the Hollywood studios.

I went into a deep depression. Jorja was doing an occasional television show, but not nearly enough to cover our expenses. I had not been concerned about money for a long time, but now I had a wife to support and the situation was different. The longer I was out of work, the more pressure I was under. The weeks were dragging by and there were no job offers.

Natalie would have said, "Hollywood doesn't know talent when they see it."

William Goldman said it differently: "Nobody in Hollywood knows anything . . ."

Clark Gable was turned down by MGM, Fox, and Warner Brothers.

Darryl Zanuck said, "His ears are too big. He looks like an ape."

Cary Grant was rejected by several studios. "His neck is too thick."

Of Fred Astaire, a casting director said, "He can't act, can't sing, he can dance a little."

Deanna Durbin was fired from MGM and went to Universal the same day Judy Garland was fired from Universal and went to MGM. Each of them made fortunes for their new studio.

When a network executive saw *Star Trek*, his only comment was, "Get rid of the idiot with the pointed ears."

A studio chief tried to sell *High Noon* because he thought it was a disaster. No one wanted it. It became the most successful picture United Artists ever made.

Y. Frank Freeman, at Paramount, thought *Shane* with Alan Ladd would be a flop. He tried to sell it to other studios. They all turned it down. The picture became a classic.

When the phone finally did ring, it was Judy Garland.

"Sidney, I'm going to do a remake of *A Star Is Born* and I want you to write the screenplay."

My heart was jumping, but I tried to sound cool.

"That's wonderful, Judy, I'd love to do it." I hesitated a moment and added, "I just directed a picture with Cary Grant, you know. I'd like to direct you in *A Star Is Born*."

"That would be interesting," Judy said.

I was elated. This was going to make up for the debacle of *Dream Wife*. I called my agent.

"Judy Garland wants me to write and direct *A Star Is Born*. Let's make the deal."

"That's good news."

I started planning what I was going to do with the screenplay. *A Star Is Born* was a classic movie that had been made years earlier with Fredric March and Janet Gaynor.

Two days later, when I had not heard from my agent, I called him.

"Did you close the deal?"

There was a silence, and then he said, "There is no deal. Judy's husband, Sid Luft, just signed Moss Hart to write the screenplay and George Cukor to direct the picture."

A writer has an advantage over an actor or director. In order for actors and directors to work, someone has to hire them. But a writer can work anytime anywhere, writing on speculation. There is one important caveat: he or she has to have the confidence to believe that someone is going to buy a story. I had lost that confidence. Hollywood was full of working writers, but I was not one of them. No one wanted me.

Jorja tried to console me. "You've done some great things, you'll do them again. You're a wonderful writer."

But belief in oneself can't be instilled by others. I was paralyzed, unable to write. Hollywood was full of stories of careers that had gone sour. Emotionally, I was at a dead end. I had no idea how much longer I could hold out.

On July 30, 1953, four months after the *Hollywood Reporter*'s and *Variety*'s negative reviews, *Dream Wife* opened wide around the country. There had been no publicity about the movie and no star appearances and no attempt to find bookings for the picture.

We're just going to let it die.

The national reviews started to come out and I was stunned.

Bosley Crowther of the *New York Times*: "As gay a movie mix-up as the summer is likely to bring . . . Nicely escorted to the screen with just the right amount of unmistakable winking under Mr. Sheldon's directorial command."

Time magazine: "A merry little barbeque of *Adam's Rib*."

St. Paul Minneapolis Dispatch: "As delightful a comedy as ever you'd care to see."

Chicago Tribune: "A tight script and good direction."

Los Angeles Daily News: "Writer/director Sidney Sheldon, whose talent for light comedy stirs our memories of the late Ernst Lubitsch . . ."

Showmen's Trade Review: "A beautifully done feature that will draw audiences into any house regardless of size or locale."

Dream Wife was nominated for the Exhibitors Laurel Award, but it was too late to revive the picture. It was over. Dore had killed it. How did I feel about the reviews? It was like winning the lottery and losing my ticket.

The telephone rang early one morning and before I picked it up, I wondered what more bad news there could be. It was my agent.

"Sidney?"

"Yes."

"You have a ten o'clock appointment at Paramount tomorrow morning with Don Hartman, the head of production."

I swallowed. "Good."

"Don is very punctual, so don't be late."

"Late? I'm leaving now."

Don Hartman had started as a writer. He had written more than a dozen movies, including the *Road* pictures, with Crosby and Hope. Y. Frank Freeman, who was the head of Paramount, had put Don Hartman in charge of the studio two years earlier.

Every studio has its own aura. Paramount was one of the top majors. Beside the Hope and Crosby *Road* pictures, the studio produced *Sunset Boulevard, Going My Way,* and *Calcutta.*

Don was in his early fifties, upbeat and cordial.

"I'm glad to have you here, Sidney."

He had no idea how glad I was to be there.

"Have you ever seen a Martin and Lewis movie?"

"No." But I certainly knew about Martin and Lewis.

Dino Crocetti had been a boxer, blackjack dealer, singer, and would-be comic. Joseph Levitch had been a stand-up comic in small nightclubs around the country. They met in 1945 and decided to work together, changing their names to Martin and Lewis. Individually, their careers had been unsuccessful. Together they were magic. I had seen a newsreel clip of them when they were playing at the Paramount Theatre in New York, and the streets had been jammed for blocks with screaming admirers.

"We have a picture for them we'd like you to write. It's called *You're Never Too Young.* Norman Taurog is directing."

I had worked with Norman on *Rich, Young and Pretty.*

It felt wonderful to be working at a studio again. I had a reason to get up in the morning, knowing that the work I loved to do was waiting for me.

When I got home that first evening, Jorja said, "You look like a different person."

And I felt like a different person. The frustration of being out of a job so long had been corrosive.

Paramount was a very friendly studio and it seemed to me there was much less pressure than there had been at MGM.

You're Never Too Young was the story of a young barber's assistant who is forced to disguise himself as a twelve-year-old boy after getting involved in a jewel robbery. It was a remake of *The Major and the Minor,* a 1942 film directed by Billy Wilder, and starring Ginger Rogers and Ray Milland.

When I finished the screenplay, we had a reading with the cast, the producer, and the director.

I said to Dean and Jerry, "If there are any lines that bother you, please let me know and I'll be happy to change them."

Dean got to his feet. "Great script. I've got a golf date. Bye."

And he was out the door.

Jerry said, "I have a couple of questions."

We sat there for the next two hours while Jerry asked about the sets, camera angles, our approach to some of the scenes, and what seemed to be a hundred other questions. Obviously the two partners had different priorities.

No one knew it then, but this was a foretelling of why Jerry and Dean split up years later.

You're Never Too Young opened to good reviews and big box office numbers. As a celebration of my newly restored career, I bought a beautiful house in Bel Air, with a swimming pool and lovely grounds. All was right with the world again. I decided it was time for Jorja and me to take another vacation in Europe.

The elevator was up.

"Mr. Hartman wants to see you."

When I walked into Don's office, he said, "I have a project I think you're going to enjoy. Did you ever see *The Lady Eve?*"

Indeed, I had. It was a Preston Sturges movie starring Barbara Stanwyck and Henry Fonda, about a card shark and his attractive daughter who fleece a naive millionaire during a transatlantic cruise. Complications begin when the daughter falls in love with the victim.

"We're going to remake it with George Gobel," Don said, "and call it *The Birds and the Bees.*"

George Gobel was a young comedian who had had a meteoric rise in television, using a low-key, self-effacing style. Norman Taurog was to direct.

The adaptation of Preston Sturges's screenplay went quickly. David Niven, a charming and amusing man, was signed for the part of the father and Mitzi Gaynor for the daughter, and the picture went into production.

In the middle of shooting, Don called me into his office. "I just bought *Anything Goes*," he said. "I want you to write the screenplay."

It was a smash Broadway musical, with music and lyrics by Cole Porter, and a libretto by P. G. Wodehouse and my former collaborator Guy Bolton.

The score was one of Cole Porter's best. The problem was the libretto. The story involved a group of people who came in contact with public enemy number thirteen, who had slipped onto the ship to avoid the FBI. I felt that the libretto was old-fashioned and unworkable for a movie, and I told that to Don.

He nodded. "That's what you're here for. Make it work."

I came up with a new story line about two partners who were producing a Broadway play. Each partner, unbeknownst to the other, had met an actress and promised her the starring role in their new production. I showed my outline to Don.

He nodded his approval. "Fine. This will work great with our cast."

"Who's our cast?"

"Oh, didn't I tell you? Bing Crosby, Donald O'Connor, Mitzi Gaynor, and a beautiful ballet dancer named Zizi Jeanmaire. She's married to our choreographer, Roland Petit."

Bing Crosby! A whole generation had grown up listening to his songs.

Bing Crosby had started out with a singing group and when he was too drunk to show up for a broadcast one night, he was banned from the airwaves. That should have been enough to finish any singer's career, but Bing Crosby was not just any singer. He had an inimitable style that captured people's approval. He was given a second chance and he shot to the top. Before his career was over he had sold more than four hundred million records, and had made one hundred eighty-three films.

I went to his dressing room to meet him. Bing was charm itself, friendly and easygoing, with a relaxed, laid-back manner.

"I'm glad we're going to be working together," he told me. He had no idea how glad *I* was. It was a dream come true.

The shooting of my script, *Anything Goes*, went smoothly. Roland Petit was a world-famous choreographer and Zizi Jeanmaire did full justice to his work. Donald O'Connor was incredibly talented. It seemed to me that he could do anything, and he and Crosby complemented each other very well.

The production went off without a hitch. When it opened, everyone was happy with the movie, including the critics.

It was not until years later that Bing Crosby's dark side was revealed. His first wife, Dixie, who was dying of ovarian cancer, told friends that Bing neglected her. After she passed away, Bing became a single dad, and a strict disciplinarian. Two of his sons, Lindsay and Dennis, committed suicide.

While I was working on *Anything Goes*, Jorja was at Twentieth-Century-Fox, co-starring with William Holden and Jennifer Jones in *Love Is a Many-Splendored Thing*. Shortly after Jorja started the picture, she said to me, "I have some news for you."

"About the picture?"

"No, it's about us. I'm pregnant."

The two most exciting words in the English language.

I grinned like an idiot, hugged her, and then quickly backed away. I didn't want to hurt our baby.

"What are you going to do about the movie?" I asked. *Love Is a Many-Splendored Thing* was in the middle of production.

"I told them this morning. They said they could shoot it so that they won't have to replace me."

I was ecstatic. I had a wonderful sense of well-being.

As Jorja's due date approached, she fixed up a nursery at the house. As it turned out, Jorja was a brilliant decorator—a talent that would come in handy later on, when we kept moving between Hollywood and New York. She also hired a lovely African-American maid named Laura Thomas, who was destined to become a big part of our lives.

One morning, after seeing the rushes of *Anything Goes*, Don Hartman asked, "How would you like to write another picture for Dean and Jerry?"

"Sounds great, Don." I had enjoyed working with them.

"We just bought a western for them, called *Pardners*. I think you'll like it."

I hesitated a moment. "If you don't mind, I'd like to bring someone in to work with me."

He was surprised. "Who?"

"Jerry Davis." Jerry had not worked in a while and this was a chance to help him.

"I know Jerry. If you want to bring him in, that's fine."

"Thank you."

Jerry was delighted with the news, and I was happy to have him around. He was always upbeat and amusing. He was very attractive to women, and when he broke up with someone, they always remained friends.

One time, an ex-girlfriend named Diane called Jerry to tell him she was getting married. Jerry, who was very protective, said, "Tell me about him."

"Well, he's a writer. He lives in New York."

"Diane, successful writers don't live in New York. All the action is in Hollywood. He has to be a loser. What's his name?"

"Neil Simon."

Jerry and I began work on the screenplay and everything went well. What no one knew was that this was going to be one of Lewis and Martin's final pictures as a team. There were many reasons given for their breakup, but the truth was that their personalities were too disparate.

Both men were besieged with invitations for them to host charity events all over the country, and Lewis, who was very gregarious, always said yes. When he told Dean they were going to do it, Dean was upset. He preferred playing golf. Finally their different temperaments led to a permanent break, but first they agreed to do *Pardners.*

Pardners was a western comedy, and Dean and Jerry

were ideal for it. Paul Jones, one of the nicest men in the business, produced the picture.

The reviews were excellent and the picture was a box office hit.

On October 14, 1955, our daughter, Mary Rowane Sheldon, came into the world. Because of me, Jorja almost did not get to the hospital on time. I inadvertently turned the big event into a situation comedy.

It had started years earlier, when I had called Information and asked for the address of the Beverly Hills Public Library.

"I'm sorry," the operator told me, "we do not give out addresses."

I thought she was joking. "It's not CIA headquarters, it's the public library."

"I'm sorry, we do not give out addresses."

I could not believe it. That was too big a challenge to ignore. I was determined that they were going to give me that address.

I waited a moment, then dialed Information again.

"I'd like the telephone number of the public library in Beverly Hills," I said. "It's on Beverly Drive."

The operator came back on the line. "We don't have a public library on Beverly Drive. There's one on North Crescent Drive."

"That doesn't sound right," I said. "What address on North Crescent Drive?"

"At City Hall, 450 North Crescent Drive."

"Thank you." I had been given the information I needed.

From that time on, whenever I wanted the address of a place, I would always use that technique and outwit the telephone company's stupid rule.

On the night of October 14, my brilliant ploy back-fired. I heard Jorja cry out, and I rushed into the bedroom.

"It's happening," she said. "Hurry!"

Her bag was packed and waiting at the door. I had made arrangements to take her to St. John's Hospital in Santa Monica. The problem was that I was not sure what street it was on. I called Information.

"I would like the telephone number of St. John's Hospital, on Main Street." I had chosen a street at random, so that she would give me the correct street.

The operator returned a moment later, with the telephone number.

"And it's on Main Street?"

"Yes," she said.

I had happened to guess right. I put Jorja in the car and started racing into Santa Monica, where the hospital was. She was groaning in pain.

"We'll be there in a couple of minutes," I assured her. "Hang on."

I reached Main Street and turned on to it. I went up and down the street. There was no St. John's Hospital. I began to panic. It was late at night and the streets were deserted. The gas stations were closed. I had no idea where I was going. I started racing up and down every street until I finally stumbled onto the hospital—at Twenty-second and Santa Monica Boulevard, over twenty blocks away from Main Street.

Two hours later, Mary was born.

We had a healthy, beautiful baby. It was an incredible joy. Shortly after Mary was born, Jorja and I asked Groucho if he would be her godfather. When he agreed, we were delighted. We could not think of anyone more perfect.

When we brought Mary home from the hospital three days later, Laura, our maid, took her from Jorja's arms.

"I'll take care of her," she said.

From that point on, everyone took care of the baby. Mary would cry in the middle of the night and Jorja would rush into the room, only to find me, sitting in a chair, holding Mary. Or I would hear the baby cry and I would hurry into her room to find Jorja sitting there, rocking her. We all raced to pick her up at the first sign of her crying, day or night. The minute we picked Mary up, she would stop crying.

Finally, I said to Jorja, "Honey, I think we're spoiling her. We're giving her too much love. We should cut out half of it."

Jorja looked at me and said, "All right. You cut out your half."

That was the end of that discussion.

CHAPTER

26

One Monday morning, my assistant buzzed me. "There's a Mr. Robert Smith here to see you."

I had never heard of him. "What does he want?"

"He's a writer. He wants to talk to you."

"All right. Send him in."

Robert Smith was in his thirties, small, tense, and nervous.

"What can I do for you, Mr. Smith?"

"I have an idea," he said.

In Hollywood, everyone had ideas and most of them were terrible. I pretended to be interested. "Yes?"

"Why don't we make a movie about Buster Keaton."

I was immediately excited.

Buster Keaton, the silent screen's "Great Stone Face," was one of the top stars of silent pictures. His trademark was a porkpie hat, slap shoes, and a deadpan expression. He was a short, slender, sad-faced actor who had been instrumental in the production and direction of his movies, and who had been compared to Chaplin.

Buster Keaton had been an enormous success and

then, when sound came in, his luck began to change. He made several unsuccessful movies and was finding it difficult to get work. He starred in a few unmemorable shorts and was finally reduced to creating stunts for other actors. I thought that his story would be fascinating to put on the screen.

Robert Smith said, "You and I can produce it, write the screenplay, and you should direct it."

I held up a hand. "Not so fast. Let me talk to Don Hartman."

I went in to see Hartman that afternoon.

"What's up?"

"A writer named Bob Smith came to me with an idea I like. He suggested we do *The Buster Keaton Story*."

There was no hesitation. "That's a great idea. I wonder why someone didn't think of it before."

"Bob and I will produce it and I'll direct it."

He nodded. "I'll start working on getting the rights. Who did you have in mind to play Buster?"

"I haven't had time to give it much thought."

Don Hartman said, "I'll tell you who should play him. Donald O'Connor."

I was excited. "Donald would be wonderful. I worked with him on *Anything Goes*. He's a great talent."

Don Hartman hesitated. "There's a problem. Donald is committed to another movie at the beginning of the year. If we get him, we'd have to start shooting this within the next two months."

That was a major problem. We did not even have a story line. But I wanted O'Connor.

"Do you think you can have the script ready in time?"

"Sure." I sounded more confident than I felt. Rushing a script to get a certain actor is always counterproductive. The audience does not care how long it took to write a script. They only care about what they see on the screen. I had given Bob and myself an impossible deadline.

Getting the rights to Buster Keaton's life turned out to be easy.

Bob and I started on the screenplay immediately. There was a lot of material to work with because Buster's life had been very dramatic. He had come from a dysfunctional family and he had gone through divorces and a struggle with alcoholism. I had watched him in his early classics, *The General, The Navigator,* and *The Boat.* They were filled with dangerous stunts and Buster had insisted on doing them all himself.

I called Don Hartman. "Bob and I would like to meet Buster. Will you set it up?"

"Certainly."

I was looking forward to the meeting.

When Buster Keaton walked into my office, it was as though he had stepped right off the screen. He had not changed at all. He was the same little sad-faced man who had enchanted the world with his deadpan humor.

After the introductions, I said, "We would like you to be the technical advisor on this picture, Buster. What do you say?"

He almost broke tradition by smiling. "I think I can handle it."

"Great. We're going to film a lot of your stunts. I'll get a trailer on the lot for you and I want you to be on the set all the time we're shooting."

He looked, to me, as though he was trying not to cry but perhaps it was my imagination. "I'll be there."

"Thank you."

"Bob and I are working on the screenplay. We want it to be as accurate as possible. Are there any anecdotes that you'd like to tell me about, that we can use in the picture?"

"Nope."

"Perhaps some special things that happened to you in your life that you think might be exciting?"

"Nope."

"Something about your marriages or romances?"

"Nope."

The whole meeting went like that.

When he left, I said to Bob, "I forgot to mention something. If we want Donald O'Connor, we have to start shooting in two months."

He looked at me. "You're joking."

"I've never been more serious."

He sighed. "Let's see how fast we can write a screenplay."

Bob and I ran Buster's old movies. The stunts in them were incredible. I selected the ones I wanted to use, knowing that Buster would be on the set to show me how they were done.

Donald O'Connor came in to see me. "It's a great part," he said. "Buster Keaton is one of my idols."

"Mine, too."

"The Great Stone Face. This is going to be wonderful."

There was one problem. Bob and I needed more time to work on the screenplay, and there was no more time. We had a shooting date coming up that we had to keep, so we started working day and night.

Finally, it was time to begin production.

We had stayed as faithful as we could to Buster Keaton's life, but to increase the drama, we had taken some liberties. I showed Buster the screenplay and when he finished reading it, I said, "Do you have any problems with it?"

"Nope."

That was the full extent of our conversation.

The sets were built and production began.

The shoot was going well. The cast was wonderful. Besides Donald, we had Peter Lorre, Rhonda Fleming, Ann Blyth, Jackie Coogan, and Richard Anderson. The chemistry was good.

Bob and I had written a scene in which an old-time director appears. We had not cast him yet. The assistant director came up to me. "Would you like to have the old man play the part?"

I was puzzled. "What old man?"

"Mr. DeMille."

Cecil B. DeMille was, without question, one of the most important directors in Hollywood. Among many others, his recent pictures had included *Samson and Delilah, The Greatest Show on Earth,* and *The Ten Commandments.*

He was a legend and there were dozens of stories about him floating around town. He was known to be ruthless and demanding. He terrorized actors. There was a story that while he was shooting a scene in one of his epics, standing high on a platform, looking down at the hundreds of extras, he started to explain what he wanted, and saw two young women extras talking. He stopped. "You two," he called, "step up."

The two women looked at each other in horror.

"Us?"

"Yes, you. Step forward."

Nervously, they took a few steps forward.

"Now," DeMille thundered, "since you obviously think

that what you were saying was more important than what I was saying, I think everyone should hear it."

The women were embarrassed and terrified. "Mr. De-Mille—we weren't saying anything."

"Yes, you were. I want everyone to hear what you were saying."

One of the girls spoke up, and said defiantly, "All right. I was saying, 'When is that son of a bitch going to call lunch?'"

There was a shocked silence throughout the set.

DeMille stared at her for a long moment and then said, "Lunch."

"You're mad," I said to my assistant director. "DeMille is not going to play this part. It's four lines."

"Do you want me to talk to him?"

"Sure." I knew there was no chance.

Late that afternoon, the assistant director came to me. "We're shooting the scene tomorrow. He'll be here."

I was stunned. "He's going to do it?"

"Yes."

"*I'm* going to direct Cecil B. DeMille?"

"That's right."

The following day, I was shooting a master shot with Donald and Ann Blyth. When I finished the shot, we were going to go in for a close angle. My assistant director came up to me.

"Mr. DeMille is on his way to the set. Let's move to the other side of the stage where we're going to do his scene."

"I can't do that now," I told him. "I have a close-up to get first."

He looked at me for a moment. "Mr. DeMille is on his

way to the set. I suggest we move over to where he's going to do his scene."

I got the message. "We're moving," I called out.

A few minutes later, Cecil B. DeMille walked in with his entourage. He came up to me and held out his hand.

"I'm Cecil DeMille."

He was taller than I had expected, broader than I had expected, and had more charisma than I had expected.

"I'm Sidney Sheldon."

"If you'll show me what to do—"

I was going to show Cecil B. DeMille what to do? "Yes, sir. It's about—"

"I know," he said. "I've learned my lines."

"Good."

I set the scene up and said, "All right. Camera . . . Action."

The scene was finished but I felt it could be improved. How do you tell Cecil B. DeMille it wasn't good enough?

He turned to me. "Would you like me to do the scene again?"

I nodded gratefully. "That would be great."

"Why don't I take off my jacket?"

"Good idea."

"And I'll be a little more forceful."

"Good idea."

We shot it again and it was perfect. There was one thing I was unsure of, though: Had I directed Cecil B. De-Mille or had Cecil B. DeMille directed me?

The stunts that Buster Keaton had created for his silent movies were incredible. One in particular seemed absolutely impossible. The scene started with Buster running along a wooden fence, being chased by the police. Standing against the fence, with her back to it, was a rather stout woman, wearing a very full skirt. Buster stopped in front of her, saw the policemen closing in on him, and dived through the woman's legs to the back of the fence. The woman instantly moved away, revealing that the fence was solid.

It was a fantastic effect. "How the hell did you ever do that?" I asked.

Buster almost smiled. "I'll show you."

The secret was simple when you knew it. Directly behind the woman, three of the fence panels were on hinges that enabled the panels to swing backward, away from the audience, at a forty-five-degree angle. As Buster reached the woman, two crew members in back of the fence quickly raised the panels, which were hidden from audience view by the woman's skirt, thus making an opening in the fence behind her. Buster simply dove under her skirt and scurried through the opening in the fence. Once he was through, the men hurriedly replaced the panels, thereby closing the fence behind the woman. She quickly walked away, revealing to the audience a fence that was completely intact, and Buster had disappeared. This was all accomplished in a split second and was quite fantastic when done correctly.

Donald did the stunt superbly.

A later scene in the movie was another Buster Keaton classic. It took place at the shipyards and we went to the oceanside to shoot it. It was the launching of a boat, and Donald proudly stood at the prow as the boat came off the ramp.

The front of the boat slowly slid under the water, going deeper and deeper, and Donald stood there without expression as he slowly submerged until only his hat floated.

* * *

During the shooting of the picture, I learned how shy Buster was. Jorja and I had invited Buster and his wife, Eleanor, to dinner. The guests included a studio head, some directors, and several well-known actors and actresses.

I knew Buster had arrived at the house, but I had not yet seen him. I walked into the den. He was alone, reading a newspaper.

"Are you all right, Buster?"

He looked up. "I'm fine." And he went back to reading his newspaper.

When the picture was finished, Buster said, "I want to thank you."

"What for?"

"I was able to buy a house."

Everyone at the studio was very happy. *The Buster Keaton Story* was my last picture under my contract at Paramount, but they were already talking to my agent about a new contract. My life had never been so serendipitous.

I had discussed with Don Hartman an idea I had for a suspense movie called *Zone of Terror* that would be shot in Europe.

In April 1957, an article appeared in *Daily Variety*:

Where to go in April? That's the problem facing Sidney Sheldon.

Buster Keaton, which he directed, co-produced and co-scripted at Paramount, will be opening next month. On April 27, his play, *Alice in Arms*, will open in Vienna. At the same time, rehearsals start in New York on his revised version of *The Merry Widow*, with the Kiepuras, set for a mid-May opening. Sheldon is at work on his next project, *Zone of Terror*, slated to go before the cameras in Germany next year.

I knew how I was going to spend my time in April. I was going to take Jorja and Mary to Europe to celebrate.

The Buster Keaton Story opened to good reviews for Donald O'Connor, Ann Blyth, Peter Lorre, and the rest of the cast. The script did not fare so well. Most of the critics attacked it, saying there should have been more of Buster's routines and less story.

"The screenplay is a rehash of too many old Hollywood movies."

They were right. We had written it too quickly. The picture opened well because people were intrigued by Buster Keaton's name. But word of mouth quickly spread and the picture soon faded at the box office.

My agent called. "I just talked to Don Hartman. The studio is not going to renew your contract."

I knew where the reporter from *Variety* could find me in April. In the unemployment line.

Reluctantly, I canceled our reservations to Europe. I called my agent once a week, and tried to sound cheerful.

"What's happening on the battlefront?"

"Not much," he said. "There aren't any assignments around, Sidney."

That was a kind lie. There were always assignments around, but none for me. Just as I had been prematurely judged for *Dream Wife*, I was now being judged for the failure of *The Buster Keaton Story*. Again I was traumatized by the thought that I might never work again. During the times I was out of work, friends came and went, but Groucho was always there with a cheery word.

I waited for the call that never came, weeks went by, then months, and soon I had a major money problem.

I enjoyed living well, but I had never been interested in money per se. My philosophy about money was a combination of Natalie's thrift and Otto's spendthrift ways. I found it difficult to spend any money on myself, but I had no problem helping others. The result was that I had never been able to save any money.

The Bel Air house had a mortgage on it and I was hard pressed to also pay the salaries of a gardener, a pool man, and Laura. Our financial situation was rapidly deteriorating.

Jorja was getting concerned. "What are we going to do?"

"We have to start economizing," I said. I took a deep breath and added, "We're going to have to let Laura go. We can't afford a maid anymore."

It was a terrible moment for both of us.

"You tell her," Jorja said. "I can't."

Laura had been wonderful. She was always cheerful and helpful. She adored Mary and Mary adored her.

"This is going to be very difficult."

I called Laura into the library. "Laura, I'm afraid I have some bad news."

She looked at me in alarm. "What is it? Is someone sick?"

"We're fine. It's just that . . . I'm going to have to let you go."

"What do you mean?"

"I can't afford you anymore, Laura."

She looked shocked. "You mean you're firing me?"

"I'm afraid so. I'm terribly sorry."

She shook her head. "You can't do that."

"You don't understand. I can't afford to pay you any-more and—"

"I'm staying."

"Laura—"

"I'm staying." And she walked out of the room.

Jorja and I had been forced to cut down on our social life, and we went out very seldom. There were plays that we wanted to see, but they were too expensive. Laura heard Jorja and me talking about it.

As we debated going out one evening, Laura said, "Take this," and she handed me twenty dollars.

"I can't take that," I said.

"You'll pay me back."

I was near tears. She was working hard, getting no salary, and she was giving me money.

The day arrived when I had no money to make the mortgage payment.

"We've lost the house," I told Jorja.

She could see my pain. "Don't worry, darling. We'll be fine. You've written hits before, you'll write them again."

She did not understand. "Not anymore," I said. "It's over."

I remembered the first house my family had ever rented, on Marion Street, in Denver. *I'm going to get married here and my children will grow up here* . . . By now, counting houses, apartments, and hotels, I had moved thirteen times.

The following week we gave up the house with the swimming pool and the beautiful gardens, and I rented an apartment for us. I was living Otto's life, on a roller coaster that took me from prosperity to poverty in a seemingly never-ending cycle. I was suicidal again. I had kept up payments on a life insurance policy that would take care of Jorja and Mary. *They're better off without me,* I decided. And I began to pursue that thought.

I knew I would never have the life I once had. There would be no more Europe, no more wonderful parties, no more successes. I would miss all that, and I wondered whether it was better to have been a success and lost it all or never to have tasted success, so it would not be missed. I was in a deep depression and suicide was the only way I could think of to escape it. *You're suffering from manic depression . . . Approximately one in five people who are manic-depressive eventually commit suicide.*

I was living through a nightmare that I felt would never end. Was I serious about committing suicide?

I tried to think of all the successes I had had, instead of the failures, but it was no use. The mysterious, dark chemistry in my brain would not allow it. I was unable to control my emotions.

But the more I thought about it, the more I realized I could not bear to leave Jorja and Mary. *I have to create something,* I thought. The motion picture studios obviously did not want me. What about television?

My favorite show was *I Love Lucy,* which was a brilliantly done comedy that Lucille Ball and her producer husband, Desi Arnaz, put on every week. It was the most popular comedy on television. Maybe I could write something that Desi would be interested in. I thought of a title and an idea, *Adventures of a Model.* It would be a romantic comedy with all the situations that a beautiful model would get involved in.

It took me one week to write the pilot script. I made an appointment to see Desi Arnaz.

"It's nice to meet you," he said. "I've heard about you."

"I have an idea for a pilot, Mr. Arnaz." I took out the script and handed it to him.

He looked at the title and his face lit up. "*Adventures of a Model.* That sounds great."

I stood up. "When you have a chance to read it, I would appreciate it if you would call me."

"No, no. Sit down," he said. "I'm going to read it now."

I watched his face as he read it. He kept smiling. *That's a good sign*, I thought. I was holding my breath.

He read the last page and looked up at me. "I love it," he said. "We're going to do it."

I could breathe again. It felt as though a giant weight had been lifted from my heart. "You mean it?"

"It's going to be a smash. There's been nothing like it on the air. We can still make this season," he told me. "CBS has one time slot left. Let's see if we can get it."

CHAPTER

27

I did not need a car to take me home. I was walking on air. Jorja was waiting for me at the door when I got home. She looked at my face and said, "Good news?"

"Great news. Desi Arnaz is going to produce *Adventures of a Model.*"

She hugged me. "That's wonderful."

"Do you know what it means to get a successful show on television? It could go on for years."

"When will you know?"

"In the next day or two."

Two days later I got a call from Desi. "We're in," he said. "CBS has given us their last time slot."

"We're going out to celebrate tonight," I told Jorja.

Laura was listening, her face beaming. "You two have a good time," she said, and she handed me twenty dollars. "It's on me."

"I can't. You've already been—"

"Yes, you can."

I hugged her. "Thank you."

"I knew you could do it all the time."

Jorja and I went to an Italian restaurant and had a wonderful dinner.

"I can't believe it," I said. "We're on CBS. I'm going to produce the show and write the scripts."

On the way home, Jorja said, "I'm so proud of you, honey. I know what you've been through and how hard it's been, but that's all over now."

Desi called me the next morning. "Can you come to the office?"

I grinned. "Certainly." I was there thirty minutes later.

"Sit down," Desi said.

"Right. When do we start?"

He studied me a moment. "Sidney, CBS had one opening left and we got it. They canceled *The Dick Van Dyke Show* and put us in that time period. Danny Thomas, who owns *The Dick Van Dyke Show* and a few other shows on CBS, put pressure on them and insisted they give *The Dick Van Dyke Show* another year. The network finally agreed. They put them back in the time slot. We're out."

I sat there, not moving, unable to speak.

"I'm sorry," Desi said. "Maybe next season."

I was faced with the same choice: Give up or try again. I was damned if I was going to give up.

I needed another project, and I sat down to create one. I sat in my study for a week, discarding idea after idea. Finally, I thought of one that might work. There had been no shows on Broadway about Gypsies. I had a title, *King of New York.* It would be about a Gypsy family with a beautiful daughter falling in love with a non-Gypsy and the situations that that could lead to.

I knew nothing about Gypsies and I had to do research. Where could I find out about them? I called the police station and asked to speak to a detective.

"What can I do for you?"

"I would like to interview some Gypsies. Do you know where I can find some?"

He laughed. "Yeah, usually we have them locked up in the station. At the moment they're all out. I can give you the name of the man who calls himself 'the King.'"

"Perfect."

His name was Adams and the detective told me where to get in touch with him. I called Adams and told him who I was, and invited him over to the apartment. He was a tall, burly man, with black hair and a deep, gravelly voice.

"I'd like to talk to you about Gypsy customs," I said. "I want to know all about the way you live."

He sat there, silently.

"I'll pay you for it," I said. "If you talk to me and tell me everything I need to know, I'll pay you—" I hesitated "—a hundred dollars."

His face lit up. "Fine. You can give me the money now, and—"

And I knew I would never see him again. "No. I want you to come here once a week and we'll talk and I'll give you some money each time you come for an hour."

He shrugged. "Okay."

"Now, start talking."

He talked and I made notes. I wanted to know the Gypsy customs, how they lived, dressed, talked, and thought. At the end of three weeks, I knew enough about Gypsies to start writing the play. When I finished it, I showed it to Jorja.

"It's lovely," she said. "Who are you going to take it to?"

I had already decided that. "Gower Champion." He had just directed a Broadway hit called *Bye Bye Birdie*.

I went to see Gower. He had been a musical star at MGM, had gone on to Broadway as a director, and had become a big success.

"I have a play I'd like you to read," I told him.

"Fine. I'm leaving for New York tonight. I'll take it with me, and read it on the plane."

I had foolishly hoped that he would do what Desi Arnaz did and read it immediately. "Thank you."

When I got home, Jorja said, "What did he say?"

"He's going to read it. The problem is that I heard he has a lot of other projects in the works. Even if he's interested, it may be a long time before he does this."

Gower Champion called the next morning. "Sidney, I think it's great," he said. "It's going to make a wonderful musical. There's been nothing like it on Broadway. I'm going to call Charles Strouse and Lee Adams, who wrote the score for *Bye Bye Birdie,* and bring them on board."

For some reason, I felt no excitement. I had had too many disappointments. I managed to sound enthusiastic. "That's great, Gower."

I hung up the phone and thought of all the dreams that had never come true.

I waited to hear from Gower, and five days later he called. He sounded angry.

"Is everything all right?" I asked.

"No. I told Strouse and Adams that I wanted them to do the music for this show and they're asking for a bigger percentage. They're ungrateful bastards. I told them I wouldn't give it to them."

"So who do we—?"

"I'm not going to do the show."

A year later, someone else opened a show on Broadway called *Bajour.* It was about Gypsies living in New York.

* * *

At a time when I should have been depressed, I felt elated. I remembered what Dr. Marmer had said about manic depression. *It's a brain deviation that involves episodes of serious mania and depression, where moods swing from euphoria to despair . . . a major contributing factor in thirty thousand suicides a year.* I was euphoric. I felt that something wonderful was going to happen.

It came in the form of a phone call.

"Sidney Sheldon, please."

"Speaking."

"This is Robert Fryer." A very successful Broadway producer.

"Yes, Mr. Fryer?"

"Dorothy and Herbert Fields asked me to phone you. They're writing a musical for me called *Redhead,* and they would like to know whether you would be interested in working on it with them. Are you interested?"

Was I interested in working with Dorothy and Herbert Fields again? Was I! I tried to sound cool. "Yes, I would be very interested."

"That's wonderful. How soon can you come to New York? We want to get started as quickly as possible."

Two weeks later, Jorja, Mary, and I were moving into a rental apartment in Manhattan. Our one disappointment was that Laura was unable to travel with us. I had paid her all the salary I owed her, plus a large bonus. It was an emotional farewell.

"I can't leave my family, Mr. Sheldon. I'll miss you and pray for you."

That was Laura.

Robert Fryer was in his middle forties, a handsome, elegantly dressed man with a passion for the theater. We met in his office on Forty-fifth Street.

"*Redhead* is going to be a really great show," he said enthusiastically. "I'm glad you're going to work with us."

"So am I. Tell me about the show."

"Dorothy is writing the lyrics. The music is being written by Albert Hague. You and Herbert will write the book. The play takes place in turn-of-the-century London. Our lead is a young woman who makes figures that are exhibited in the chamber of horrors in a wax museum. A serial killer is loose, and he leaves no clues. When he murders his latest victim, our heroine sees him and makes a wax model of him. He sets out to murder her. It's a mixture of mystery, suspense, and songs and dances."

"That sounds exciting."

We met Dorothy at her home.

After the greetings were over, Dorothy said, "Let's go to work."

Dorothy and Herbert had conceived a dream of a plot. I had not seen them since *Annie Get Your Gun* and it was a joy to be working with them again.

The Fieldses introduced me to Albert Hague, the composer, who had done half a dozen Broadway shows. He was a brilliant musician.

Hague later gained fame as Mr. Benjamin Shorofsky in the television series *Fame*.

Because the basic idea the Fieldses had was so exciting, the writing of the book went smoothly. Herbert and Dorothy were professionals who worked business hours. We worked from nine in the morning until six P.M. and then everybody went home. I thought of the frantic days when Ben Roberts and I were working on several shows at once, until the wee hours of the morning.

Jorja and I got a nurse for Mary, and when I was not

working, we explored New York. We went to the theater and the museums and enjoyed some of the restaurants. The first one I took Jorja to was Sardi's, and Vincent Sardi was still there, as warm as ever. We had a wonderful meal, with a complimentary bottle of champagne.

Herbert and I finished the first draft of the libretto as Dorothy and Albert were finishing the score.

When we were ready, we gathered in Robert Fryer's office and ran through the book and score.

"Great," Fryer said. "It's everything I hoped it would be. Now, who are we going to cast in it? Who is going to play the lead?"

We needed a leading lady who was attractive, sympathetic, and could sing and play comedy. Not an easy combination to find. We went through a list of actresses and finally came across a name that we all liked: Bea Lillie. She was an English stage star who played comedy, and sang and danced.

"She would be perfect. I'm going to send her the book and the score," Fryer said, "and pray."

Five days later, we were meeting again in Fryer's office. He was grinning. "Bea Lillie loves it. She's going to play it."

"That's great."

"Now we need a choreographer and we're in business."

It was not to be. Bea Lillie wanted her boyfriend to direct the show.

We went through the list of available actresses again.

"Wait a minute," Dorothy said. "What about Gwen Verdon?"

The room lit up.

"Why didn't we think of her before? She's perfect.

She's a beautiful, talented musical star—and she's a red-head. I'll get the play to her this afternoon."

This time there was only a two-day wait.

"She'll do it," Robert Fryer said. He sighed. "But there's a catch."

We all looked at him. "Oh?"

"She wants her boyfriend to direct it."

"Who's her boyfriend?"

"Bob Fosse."

Bob Fosse was a brilliant choreographer. He had just choreographed two hit shows, *The Pajama Game* and *Damn Yankees*.

"Has he ever directed anything?" I asked.

"No, but he's damn talented. If you all agree, I'm willing to take a chance on him."

I said, "I'd hate to lose Gwen Verdon."

Dorothy said, "Let's not lose her." She looked at Robert Fryer. "Let's talk to Bob Fosse."

Bob Fosse was in his early thirties, a small, intense man who had been a dancer and actor in several Hollywood films. He had gone on to be a choreographer and had his own exciting style. His trademark, when he danced, was wearing a hat and gloves. He wore hats to cover the fact that he had started going bald. It was said that he wore gloves because he did not like his hands.

We met in a rehearsal room off Broadway. Bob Fosse knew exactly what he wanted to do with the show. He was filled with exciting ideas and by the time the meeting was over, we were delighted to have him. It was a two-in-one deal. He would choreograph and direct.

We rounded out the cast with Richard Kiley and Leonard Stone, and rehearsals began.

Along with the problems.

Bob Fosse, like all good choreographers, was dictatorial. He had his own vision of the show. The libretto was written, the sets were being built, costumes were ordered, and Fosse was dissatisfied with everything. He was opinionated and stubborn and he was turning all of us into nervous wrecks. Why we stood for it was simple: He was a genius. His choreography was brilliant enough to light up the show. But when Fosse tried to rewrite the book, I put my foot down. Herbert agreed with me. We decided to let him bring in another writer, David Shaw.

The rehearsals looked wonderful. Gwen was brilliant. The dances were spectacular and the book worked like a dream. I held my breath, waiting to see what was going to go wrong.

Natalie and Marty came to New York for the opening, and Richard flew in with his wife, Joan. They sat in the audience with Jorja and me. This time none of them was disappointed.

We opened at the 46th Street Theatre, in New York, on February 5, 1959, and the critics were unanimous in their praise. They raved about Gwen, loved the songs and dances, and enjoyed the book.

"Best musical comedy of the season . . ." Watts, *New York Post*

"The musical triumph of the year, perhaps several years . . ." Aston, *New York Telegram and Sun*

"The best musical of the season to date! . . ." McClain, *New York Journal-American*

"A tip-top musical! . . ." Chapman, *New York News*

"Red-hot hit! . . ." Winchell

"Firecracker of a musical . . ." Kerr, *New York Herald Tribune*

Redhead garnered seven Tony nominations that year and five wins. Needless to say, we were thrilled.

Three months later, Gwen Verdon and Bob Fosse were married.

The elevator was at the top again, and I decided it was time to move back to Hollywood. I was not going to wait around for a studio to hire me. I was going to write a play that the studios would want to buy.

It is very easy to have a hit play on Broadway. I had always been interested in extrasensory perception. The movies and plays that had been done about it were always very serious. I decided it would be fun to write a romantic comedy about a beautiful young psychic. I wrote the play and called it *Roman Candle*. My agent sent it to various studios and Broadway producers and the excitement it generated stunned me. Four Broadway producers made offers for it.

Moss Hart, who was one of the top directors on Broadway, wanted to direct it. Moss Hart had just directed the Broadway smash musical *My Fair Lady*. He wanted the producer he worked with, Herman Levin, to produce *Roman Candle*. Sam Spiegel also wanted to produce it.

My agent was Audrey Wood. Audrey was a small, dynamic woman and one of the preeminent theatrical agents on Broadway. She worked with her husband, Bill Liebling, and they represented some of the top playwrights, including Tennessee Williams and William Inge.

Audrey said, "This is going to be a big play. Sam Spiegel called again. He's ready to make a deal. He's a friend of Moss Hart and Moss will direct it for him."

I was thrilled. There was no one better.

Audrey called me again. "I have some more news for you," she said. "William Wyler read your play and wants to direct the movie."

William Wyler was a top director in Hollywood.

Among other classics, he had directed *Mrs. Miniver, Ben-Hur, The Best Years of Our Lives*, and *Roman Holiday*. He was with the Mirisch Company, and they were going to produce the picture. They also wanted to invest in the Broadway play. I had a choice to make: Sam Spiegel and Moss Hart, or William Wyler and the Mirisch Company?

"Since Moss wants to do the play," I told Audrey, "why don't we have Sam Spiegel produce the play and Moss will direct it and the movie will be done by William Wyler and the Mirisch Company."

She shook her head. "I doubt if Sam will produce the play if he can't have the picture rights."

"Try him," I urged.

The following day she said, "I was right. Spiegel wants the picture rights, too. But I have a producer for you who will be great for this play. She just produced a big hit, *Candide*. Her name is Ethel Linder Reiner."

I met Ethel Linder Reiner. She was in her fifties, gray-haired, and very aggressive. "I love your play," she said. "We're going to have a big hit."

I had heard that Alan Lerner and Frederick Loewe had written a Broadway show about a psychic that was ready to be produced. They had put it on hold because of *Roman Candle*. In movies or television, a success quickly breeds imitators, but on Broadway originality is the key. Lerner and Loewe did not want to put on a show about a psychic when it had just been done by someone else. They were waiting to see how *Roman Candle* turned out.

I had met Alan when we were at MGM together and I liked him. He and Frederick Loewe were enormously gifted and I felt sorry that they had wasted their time and talent on a show that would never be put on.

Everyone was saying that we were going to have a big

hit. With Moss Hart directing *Roman Candle*, it was going to be a smash.

I said to Audrey, "Will you call Moss and tell him we're moving ahead?"

"Sure," she said. "The sooner we get this play on, the better."

The following day I had a meeting with Audrey Wood and Ethel Linder Reiner.

"I got a telegram from Moss," Audrey said. She read it aloud.

"Dear Audrey, I received your ultimatum, but I am in the middle of writing an autobiography called *Act One*, and it will be another six months before I am finished and able to direct Sidney's play."

She looked up at me. "We'll get another director."

That was the time for me to speak up. *There is no Broadway director better than Moss Hart. There is no hurry to get the play on. Let's wait for him.* But I hated confrontations. Ever since I was a small boy, listening to the bitter fights between Natalie and Otto, I had dreaded arguments. So, I nodded. "Whatever you say."

That was one of the biggest mistakes of my life. It turned out that Ethel Linder Reiner was a dilettante. She did not understand Broadway or Hollywood. When I introduced her to William Wyler, who was going to direct the movie, she said, "I loved *Sunset Boulevard*," a classic picture that of course was directed by Billy Wilder.

We started casting the play. She chose Inger Stevens, a beautiful young actress who had done some television series, and Robert Sterling and Julia Meade. The director was David Pressman, who had had very little directing experience. As the playwright, I had the right to approve the director and the casting, but I did not want to make waves. Inger Stevens and Robert Sterling flew to New York, and the rehearsals began.

William Wyler called. "Sidney, we have a problem."

I took a deep breath. "What happened?"

"Audrey Hepburn and Shirley MacLaine read your play. They both want to do the picture."

"Willie—may problems like that continue!"

The play opens with a beautiful young psychic coming to New York because she had seen the picture of the man she knew she would marry, on the cover of *Time* magazine. He was a scientist about to get married to a senator's daughter. The complications started from then on. The Army was not thrilled with one of their scientists being involved with a woman who claimed to be a psychic.

The rehearsals went well. The play opened out of town and the reviews could have been written by Natalie.

In Philadelphia: "Sidney Sheldon's happy spoof is a source of sheer delight. Hilarious . . ."

New Haven: "Sidney Sheldon's *Roman Candle* was responsible for a lot of laughter at the Shubert Theatre last night . . ."

The Journal Evening, Wilmington, Delaware: "*Roman Candle*, the most delightful comedy involving the armed forces we've seen since *No Time for Sergeants* . . ."

John Chapman: "*Roman Candle* is a jolly, joke-filled farce about our armed services and a beautiful psychic."

In every theater we played, the walls resounded with the laughter of audiences.

Audrey said, "This play is going to run forever."

I tried to control my enthusiasm. In every town we played, there were rave reviews. I kept working on the play, refining it, sharpening it. The scenes all worked beautifully. We were getting ready to go to New York.

Everyone was brimming with optimism, and with good reason. We had a play that the audience loved.

It was time to open in Manhattan. We had gotten the Cort Theatre, a perfect venue for the play. The glowing out-of-town reviews had preceded us. The entertainment pages of the New York newspapers were filled with photographs of our cast and articles already proclaiming us a huge hit. Telegrams of congratulations were pouring in from family, my friends on Broadway, and in Hollywood. We were all filled with enormous excitement. We started making bets.

"I'll bet it runs for two years," the producer said.

Audrey Wood spoke up. "With road shows, it could run for three years, maybe even four."

They turned to me. I had had too many bitter lessons. "I quit betting on the theater a long time ago," I said.

Opening night went well and the audience was appreciative. Late that night we read the early reviews.

New York Times: "Less spirited than a six-day bicycle race."

Variety: "The characters are astonishingly colorless."

New York Herald Tribune: "Don't let me give you the impression that the show is a dud. It isn't. *Roman Candle* is a mild, modest, stubborn, little show."

Q Magazine: "The actors make the Cort stage more alive and exciting than the script allows."

New York Daily News: "The plot of *Roman Candle* keeps moving, most but not quite all the time."

Some pundit said that a critic is someone who waits until a show in trouble opens, then goes in and shoots the wounded.

Roman Candle closed after five performances.

Soon after our closing, Lerner and Loewe went into

production with their show about a psychic. It was called *On a Clear Day You Can See Forever.*

It was a big hit.

My agent telephoned me from Hollywood. "I'm sorry about the play."

"So am I."

"I'm afraid I have some bad news for you."

"I thought that was the bad news."

"There's more. William Wyler has decided not to direct the movie."

That was the final blow.

It is very easy to *almost* have a hit play on Broadway.

CHAPTER

28

One day a fire broke out in a canyon near our home. If the fire spread out of the canyon, dozens of houses would have been destroyed.

A fire marshal appeared at our door. "The fire is moving pretty fast. Start to evacuate."

Jorja hurriedly gathered the things she needed. I took Mary, who was five years old at the time, by the hand and whisked her out to the car. I had to quickly decide what I was going to take with me. In the den I had a collection of awards, a shelf full of first-edition books, research papers, sport clothes, and my favorite golf clubs. But there was something more important to take.

Rushing back inside, I grabbed a handful of pens and half a dozen yellow pads I could have replaced at any dime store, because somewhere deep inside me I thought we might have to spend a few weeks in a hotel, and I instinctively knew I could not let my writing be interrupted. That was all I took from the house.

"I'm ready."

Fortunately, the fire department was able to control the fire and our house was untouched.

It was a familiar voice on the phone. "The critics are crazy. I read the script of *Roman Candle* and I loved it." It was Don Hartman.

"Thanks, Don. I appreciate it." *Send no flowers.*

"I have a project I'd like you to write. It's called *All in a Night's Work.* Dean Martin and Shirley MacLaine are going to star in it. Hal Wallis is producing it. We have a screenplay that's pretty good, but it has to be rewritten for our stars."

"I enjoy working with Dean."

"Fine. How soon can you start?"

"I'm afraid I can't start right now, Don. I'll need about fifteen minutes."

He laughed. "We'll call your agent."

It was good to be back at Paramount. It had given me so many wonderful memories. There were still a lot of familiar faces around—producers, directors, writers, secretaries. I felt that I had come home again.

I had an appointment with Hal Wallis. I had met him a few times socially, but I had never worked with him. He had produced a string of prestigious movies, among them *Little Caesar, The Rainmaker, I Am a Fugitive from a Chain Gang,* and *The Rose Tattoo.* Hal was a short, compactly built man with a grave manner. Now in his seventies, he was more active than he had ever been.

As I walked into his office, he rose. "I asked for you," he said, "because I think this picture is right up your alley."

"I'm looking forward to working on it."

We discussed the movie and he told me his vision of

it. As I was leaving, he said, "By the way, I read *Roman Candle*. It's a great play."

Too late, Hal. "Thanks."

It was time to go to work.

Edmund Beloin and Maurice Richlin had written the screenplay and it was excellent, but Don was right. It had to be tailored for Dean and Shirley. They were both such distinctive personalities that the adaptation was easy, and I began writing.

One evening, when I got home from the studio, Jorja was waiting for me with a large bouquet of flowers. She was beaming.

"Happy Father's Day."

I looked at her in surprise. "Today isn't—" And then I realized what she was saying. I grabbed her in my arms and hugged her.

"Do you want a girl or a boy?" she asked.

"Two of each."

"That's easy for *you* to say."

I held her closer. "It doesn't matter, darling. Let's just hope the baby turns out to be as wonderful as Mary."

Mary was then five years old. How was she going to feel about having a brother or sister? "Are you going to tell Mary or should I?"

"I've already told her."

"How did she react?"

"Well, she said she was very happy, but a few minutes later I saw her counting the steps from our room to her room, and the steps from our room to where the nursery is going to be."

I laughed. "She'll love being a big sister."

"What are we going to call the baby?" I asked.

"If it's a girl, I'd like to name her Alexandra."

"That's a pretty name. If it's a boy, let's name him Alexander. That means defender of mankind."

Jorja smiled. "Sounds good."

We talked all night about our plans for Mary and the baby. In the morning I was exhausted, but happy. Incredibly happy.

The screenplay for *All in a Night's Work* was coming along well. I conferred with Hal Wallis from time to time and his comments were always helpful. Sets were being built and a director named Joseph Anthony was brought on board.

Cliff Robertson and Charles Ruggles were added to the cast. Although I had worked with Dean before, I had never met Shirley MacLaine. All I knew about her was that she was a very talented actress and that she believed she had lived many previous lives. Maybe she had. But when I met her in her present life, she turned out to be a dynamic redhead with a wellspring of energy.

"Sidney Sheldon."

She looked at me closely. "Shirley MacLaine. It's nice to meet you, Sidney."

I wondered whether we had met in another life.

Dean grinned when he saw me. "You haven't had enough of me yet?"

"Never."

Dean had not changed at all. He was the same relaxed, easygoing man I had known, completely unaffected by his status as a star.

After they split up, Jerry made forty more films and devoted himself to raising money for children with muscular dystrophy. Dean went on making movies and starred in a television show, which was a big success.

Television fit Dean's lifestyle perfectly. His contract

with the network said he did not have to rehearse. He walked in, did the show, and said good night. And the show was terrific.

Jorja and I gave dinner parties and were invited out. In order not to emulate Otto's penchant for using his friends, I went too far the other way and unintentionally hurt some wonderful people. Eddie Lasker was the heir to the fabulous Lord & Thomas advertising agency. His wife, Jane Greer, was a beautiful and successful actress. They would invite us to their home frequently and their parties were lavish. Jorja and I enjoyed being with them.

One night, Eddie said, "We have such a good time to-gether, why don't we have a standing date once a week?"

And I thought: *I can't afford to entertain as lavishly as they do. I would be taking advantage of them.* And I said, "Eddie, let's just see each other when we can."

I could see the hurt on his face.

Another couple we enjoyed was Arthur Hornblow and his wife, Lenore. Arthur Hornblow was a successful pro-ducer.

"I have a project I think you would enjoy," Arthur said one day.

He's very successful and I need a job, but I don't want to take advantage of him. And I said, "Let's just see each other socially, Arthur."

And I lost a friend.

All in a Night's Work was finished and a short time later Jorja was ready to deliver our second baby. This time I was ready. I knew where the hospital was and we left early enough so that there would be no last-minute dash. We were given a room at the hospital and there was nothing to do now but wait for the arrival of our—*Boy? Girl?* It really did not matter.

Our obstetrician, Dr. Blake Watson, had already arrived at the hospital.

At one o'clock in the morning, Alexandra arrived. I was waiting outside the delivery room when Dr. Watson and two nurses came hurrying out. Dr. Watson was carrying the baby, wrapped in a blanket.

"Doctor, how is—?"

He rushed past me. I began to panic. A moment later, Jorja was wheeled out of the delivery room to be taken to her room. She looked very pale.

"Is everything all right?" she asked.

I took her hand. "Everything is fine. I'll be in to see you in a few minutes."

I watched them wheel her down the corridor. Then I hurried to find Dr. Watson.

As I was passing the newborn intensive care unit, I saw him through the window. He and two other doctors were standing over a crib in a heated discussion. My heart began to pound. I wanted to burst into the room, but I forced myself to wait. When Dr. Watson looked up and saw me, he said something to the others. They all turned to look at me. I was finding it hard to breathe. Dr. Watson came out into the corridor.

"What's happening?" I asked. "What's—what's wrong?" I could hardly speak.

"I'm afraid I have bad news for you, Mr. Sheldon."

"The baby is dead!"

"No. But—" He was finding it difficult to go on. "Your baby was born with spina bifida."

I wanted to shake him. "What does that—? Tell me in plain English."

"Spina bifida is a birth defect. During the first months

of pregnancy, the spine doesn't close properly. When the baby is born, it has only a thin layer of skin over its spine. The spinal cord is really protruding through the back. It's one of the most—"

"Well, for God's sake, fix it!" I was screaming.

"It's not that simple. It takes an expert—"

"Then get some experts here. Do you hear me? Now! I want them now!" I was crying, totally out of control.

He looked at me a moment, nodded, and hurried away.

I had to break the news to Jorja. It was probably the most difficult moment of my life.

When I walked into the room, she looked at my face and said, "What's wrong?"

"Everything is going to be all right," I assured her. "Alexandra was born with a—a—problem, but some medical experts are on their way here to take care of it. Everything will be fine."

At four o'clock in the morning, two doctors arrived and Dr. Watson took them into the newborn intensive care unit. I stood outside for a few moments, watching their faces, willing them to nod, to smile reassuringly. Finally, I could stand it no longer. I returned to Jorja. I stayed with her and we sat there, silently, waiting.

Half an hour later, Dr. Watson came in. He looked at Jorja and me a moment and said quietly, "Two of the top experts who deal with spina bifida have examined your baby. They agree that there is very little chance that she can survive. If she should survive, she will probably have hydrocephalus, an accumulation of fluid in the brain." Every word was a hammer. "She will also have bowel and bladder complications. Spina bifida is a permanently disabling birth defect."

I said, "But it's possible that she can live?"

"Yes, but—"

"Then we'll take her home. We'll have twenty-four-hour nurses for her and all the equipment—"

"Mr. Sheldon, no. She needs to be placed in a care center where they're used to dealing with this problem. There's a home we recommend near Pomona, where they can handle this."

Jorja and I looked at each other. Jorja said, "Then we can visit her."

"It would be better if you didn't."

It took a moment for it to sink in. "You mean—"

"She's going to die. I'm sorry. All you can do is pray for her."

How do you pray for your baby to die?

I read everything I could find about spina bifida in medical journals. The prognosis was not good. When Mary asked where Alexandra was, we told her that the baby was sick and would not be coming home for a while.

I had trouble sleeping. I had visions of Alexandra lying in a crib, in pain, in a strange place with no one to hold her, no one to love her. Several times I awakened in the middle of the night and found Jorja in the deserted nursery, crying. But there was hope. The records showed that some children with spina bifida lived into their adulthood. Alexandra would need special care, but we could give it to her. We would stop at nothing. Dr. Watson was wrong. Medical miracles happened every day.

When I came across an article about some new life-saving drug, I would show it to Jorja. "Look. This wasn't even on the market yesterday. Now it's going to save thousands of lives."

And Jorja would look for articles about medical break-throughs. "It says here that new scientific discoveries are about to change the face of medicine. There's no reason they can't find something that will save our baby."

"You bet there isn't. She has our genes in her. She's a survivor. All she has to do is hang in there for a while." I hesitated, then added, "I think we should bring her home."

Jorja's eyes were brimming with tears. "So do I."

"I'll call Dr. Watson in the morning."

I reached him at his office. "Dr. Watson, I want to talk to you about Alexandra. Jorja and I think she—"

"I was about to call you, Mr. Sheldon. Alexandra passed away in the middle of the night."

If there is a hell on earth, it exists for parents who have lost a child. There is an unspeakable grief that never entirely goes away. We could not stop thinking about Alexandra and Mary growing up together, having a wonderful, happy life, sheltered by our love.

But Alexandra would never watch a sunset or walk through a beautiful garden. She would never see a flight of birds or feel a warm summer breeze. She would never taste an ice cream cone or enjoy a movie or a play. She would never wear pretty dresses or ride in a car. She would never know the joy of falling in love, and having a family. Never, never, never.

There is a belief that as time goes on, the pain diminishes. Our pain grew stronger. Our lives had come to a standstill. The only comfort we had was Mary, and Jorja and I found ourselves becoming ridiculously overprotective.

One day, I said to Jorja, "What would you think of adopting a baby?"

"No, not yet."

And a few days later, she came to me and said, "Maybe we should. Mary should have a sibling."

We talked to Dr. Watson about adopting a child. He had just been approached by a pregnant college senior who was about to give birth, and who had broken up with her boyfriend. She wanted to put the baby up for adoption.

"The baby's mother is intelligent and attractive, and comes from a nice family background," Dr. Watson said. "I don't think you can do better."

Jorja, our six-year-old daughter, and I held a family conference. "You have the deciding vote," we told Mary. "Would you like to have a little brother or sister?"

She was thoughtful for a moment. "It won't die, will it?"

Jorja and I looked at each other. "No," I said, "it won't die."

She nodded. "Okay."

And that settled it.

I made the financial arrangements.

Three weeks later, at midnight, Dr. Watson called. "You have a healthy baby daughter."

We named her Elizabeth Aprille, and it fit her perfectly. She was a beautiful, healthy, brown-eyed baby. I thought she had a killer smile, but Jorja told me it was probably gas.

We took Elizabeth Aprille home as soon as we were permitted to, and life started up again. Jorja and I began planning the dreams that we had planned for Alexandra. As far as we were concerned, Elizabeth Aprille was our own flesh and blood, a part of our lives. We would send her to the best schools and let her choose her own career. We were delighted to see that Mary cherished her. We gave Elizabeth Aprille the beautiful little outfits that we had bought for Alexandra. We bought her paints and an easel, in case she showed any inclination to be an artist. Piano lessons would come later.

As the months passed, it was obvious that Elizabeth Aprille adored her big sister. Whenever Mary came to her crib, Elizabeth Aprille giggled. It was wonderful to watch. Jorja and I had done the right thing. They would grow up together and love each other.

When Elizabeth Aprille was one week shy of six months, Dr. Watson telephoned.

"You made a great choice, Doctor," I said. "I've never seen a happier baby. I can't tell you how grateful we are."

There was a long silence.

"Mr. Sheldon, I just received a call from the baby's mother. She wants her child back."

My blood froze. "What the hell are you talking about? We adopted Elizabeth Aprille and—"

"Unfortunately, there is a state law that a mother who puts her baby up for adoption can change her mind within the first six months. The baby's mother and father have decided to get married and keep the baby."

When I told Jorja the news, she went pale and I thought she was going to faint. "They—they—they can't take our baby away from us."

But they could.

Elizabeth Aprille was taken away the next day. Jorja and I couldn't believe what was happening.

Mary, sobbing through her tears, said, "She was great while she lasted."

I am not sure how we got through the excruciating pain of the next few months, but somehow we managed. We found solace in the Church of Religious Science, a nondenominational, rational combination of religion and science. Its philosophy of peace and goodness was exactly what Jorja and I needed. We took courses for a year in practitioner's training, and then a second year. It was a wonderful healing experience. We still felt the vacuum in our lives, but ready or not, life goes on.

CHAPTER

29

Sammy Cahn, a famous lyricist, was once asked, "Which comes first, the music or the lyrics?"

His response was, "Neither. First comes the telephone call."

The telephone call came from Joe Pasternak.

"Sidney, MGM just bought *Jumbo* for me. We want you to write the screenplay. Are you available?"

I was available.

Billy Rose's *Jumbo* had opened on Broadway in 1935. Billy Rose, one of the top producers on Broadway, was not a man to do things in a small way. He had taken over the huge Hippodrome Theatre at Forty-third Street and had rebuilt it like a circus tent, with the audience looking down at the "ring." Jimmy Durante and Paul Whiteman were in the show, Ben Hecht and Charley MacArthur had written the book, Rodgers and Hart had done the score, and George Abbott had directed. The *crème de la crème* all the way.

When the show opened, the reviews were excellent, but there was a catch. The production was so expensive that it was impossible for it to break even, let alone make a profit. It closed after five months.

It had been almost ten years since I was last on the MGM lot. Outwardly, it seemed to me that everything was pretty much the same. I was soon to learn how wrong I was.

Joe Pasternak had not changed at all. He still had the same wonderful exuberance.

"I have already signed Doris Day, Martha Raye, and Jimmy Durante. In order to get Doris, I had to make her husband, Marty Melcher, co-producer. Your old friend Chuck Walters is directing."

That was good news. I had not seen Chuck since we had worked together on *Easter Parade*.

"Who is going to play the male lead?"

Pasternak hesitated. "We don't have anyone yet, but there is an actor playing in *Camelot* on Broadway who might be right for it."

"What's his name?"

"Richard Burton. I want you to fly back to New York with Walters and take a look at him."

"Gladly."

It was when I went into the commissary to lunch that day that I received my shock. The same hostess, Pauline, was still working there. We greeted each other, and as she started to seat me at a table, I asked, "Where's the writers' table?"

"There is no writers' table."

"Well," I said, "then we'll have to start one."

She looked at me a moment. "Mr. Sheldon, I'm afraid you'd be very lonely. You're the only writer on the lot."

From a hundred fifty writers to, "You're the only

writer on the lot." That's how much Hollywood had changed in the last ten years.

I spent the next few days working on an outline to adapt the story of *Jumbo* for the screen. On Friday, Charles Walters and I flew back to New York, to see Richard Burton in *Camelot*.

Camelot was a huge production also starring Julie Andrews and Robert Goulet. Moss Hart had directed it. Burton was brilliant in it.

The studio had arranged for Charles Walters and me to have supper with Burton after the show. We were waiting for him when he arrived at Sardi's. Richard Burton was larger than life—open and gregarious, filled with a hearty Welsh charm. He was well-read, intelligent, and had an eclectic mind. Burton was not a major star, but he was about to become one.

Since I had not had time to write down my story outline, I said, "I have nothing on paper yet, but I would like to tell you the story."

He smiled. "I love stories. Go ahead."

Jumbo was a romantic love story set against the background of a rivalry between two circuses. When I had finished telling Richard Burton the story, he was enthusiastic.

"I love it," he said, "and I'm looking forward to working with Doris Day. Call my agent and tell him to make the deal."

Chuck and I looked at each other. We had gotten our man. Everything was set.

The following morning, we returned to Hollywood. Joe Pasternak told Benny Thau to close the deal for Burton. Thau called Hugh French, Burton's Hollywood agent, and set up a meeting.

When they had exchanged greetings, Hugh French

said, "Richard called me. He likes the project a lot. He's eager to do it."

"Good. We'll draw up the contracts."

"For how much?" Hugh French asked.

"Two hundred thousand dollars. That was the deal on his last picture."

The agent said, "We want two-fifty, Benny."

Thau, who was a tough negotiator, was indignant. "Why should we give him a raise? He's not that important. This part is a break for him."

"Benny, I have to tell you—he has an offer to do another movie. They're willing to pay him the two-fifty."

Thau said, stubbornly, "Fine. Let them pay him. We'll get someone else."

And so it was that instead of starring in *Jumbo*, Richard Burton signed to do *Cleopatra*, met and fell in love with Elizabeth Taylor, and together they created an exciting new chapter in Hollywood romantic gossip. My theory is that if Thau had paid the extra fifty thousand dollars, Richard Burton would have done *Jumbo* and married Martha Raye.

We signed Stephen Boyd for the male lead and the picture was ready to roll. The cast was brilliant. Doris Day was perfect for the part of Kitty Wonder. Stephen Boyd was excellent and Martha Raye was a delight. But my favorite was Jimmy Durante.

Durante had started as a piano player. He had opened a nightclub and formed an act with two other performers, Jackson and Clayton. An insight into Durante was that when he decided to go solo, he kept his former partners on his payroll. He loved to tell stories about the past and I never heard him say an unkind word about anyone.

My screenplay was approved, and production began.

Everything went smoothly during the shooting. When the picture was released, *Jumbo* was nominated for the Writers Guild Award as the best-written American Musical of the Year.

My agent, Sam Weisbord, called me.

"Sidney, we just sold *Patty Duke* to ABC."

I certainly knew that name. At the age of twelve, Patty Duke had gotten the role of Helen Keller in *The Miracle Worker*, had taken Broadway by storm, and when the movie was made, had received an Oscar.

Sam continued. "We already have a time slot. Wednesday nights at eight. We're calling the program *The Patty Duke Show*. Everything is all set. But we have a problem."

"I don't understand. If everything is all set, what's your problem?"

"We don't have a show."

They had sold it on Patty Duke's name alone.

"We want you to create a show."

"I'm sorry, Sammy," I said, "the answer is no."

In the early sixties, people who worked in motion pictures looked down on those who labored in television. When television was in its infancy, the networks had gone to the studios. "We have a great new form of distribution," they said, "but we don't know how to create entertainment. Why don't we become partners?"

The answer was simple. The studios had their own means of distribution. They were called theaters, and most of the studios owned their own chains. They were not about to get involved with an upstart technology that they considered a passing fad. The studios were so anti-television that they would not even permit their stars to be televised going to a movie premiere.

I had been conditioned by that attitude, and I remembered my experience with Desi, so it was natural for me to say, "Sorry, Sammy. I don't do television."

There was a pause. "All right. I understand. But as a courtesy, would you have lunch with Patty?"

I saw no harm in that. As a matter of fact, I was curious to meet her.

We arranged to have lunch at the Brown Derby. Patty was accompanied by four agents from the William Morris office. She was then sixteen years old, smaller than I had expected, and very vulnerable. She sat next to me in our booth.

"I'm very happy to meet you, Mr. Sheldon."

"I'm happy to meet you, Miss Duke."

We talked during lunch and her shyness seemed to disappear, but her vulnerability remained. She held my hand during lunch, and it became obvious to me that she was hungry for love.

Patty had had a terrible background. It was like something out of a Charles Dickens novel. Her mother was psychotic. Her father was a drunk who abandoned the family. At age seven, Patty had moved in with her manager, John Ross, and his wife, Ethel, who were living in an upstairs cold-water flat. Patty had never had a family.

Before *The Patty Duke Show*, John Ross was a struggling, small-time manager. His clientele had consisted of minor character actors. Among them was a young actor named Ray Duke.

One day, Duke came to Ross and asked him if he would represent his young sister, Anna, who had done no acting up to that time. Ross met the seven-year-old girl and agreed to handle her.

A few months later, when Anna's home life became unbearable, the Rosses agreed to let her move in with them, and promptly changed her name to Patty. The order had come from Ethel Ross, who declared, "Anna Marie is dead. You are Patty now."

John Ross read that a play called *The Miracle Worker* was going to be produced on Broadway, and he decided that Patty Duke would be right for the part of Helen Keller, a blind, deaf, and mute girl. He coached Patty for months. When she finally competed against a hundred other girls and won the part, their lives changed completely. The day after the play opened, John Ross's unknown young client had become an overnight star.

Ross began receiving offers for Patty for thousands of dollars a week. Instead of knocking on producers' doors and begging them to hire his clients, Ross was being wooed by producers, directors, and studio executives. He could not believe his good luck.

When lunch was over, I realized how taken I was by Patty. I found her irresistible.

"How would you like to come to my house tonight and have dinner with Jorja and me," I asked her.

She beamed. "I'd love to."

Jorja was just as enchanted with Patty as I was. She was bright and vivacious and kept us laughing throughout the evening.

As Jorja and I were talking, we suddenly realized that Patty had left the table. I got up to see where she was. She was in the kitchen, doing the dishes. That clinched it for me.

"I'm going to write a show for you, Patty."

I got a big hug and a whispered "Thank you."

* * *

I decided that if I was going to have my name on a television show, I wanted to be able to control the quality of it. I held my first meeting with the producers.

"We're delighted that you're going to do the show, Sidney."

"Thank you."

"In addition to being the creator, you'll be the story editor, and supervise the other writers."

"I don't want any other writers."

They stared at me. "What?"

"If I am going to do this show, I want to write it."

"Sidney, that's impossible. We have an order for thirty-nine shows, one show every week."

"I intend to write them all."

They looked at each other, horrified. It was only later that I learned why. No one in the history of television had ever written every script for a weekly half-hour comedy show.

"Is this negotiable?"

"No," I said.

"You have a deal."

Not until months later did I learn that the day I signed the contract, they had hired four other writers to write scripts, so that when I came to them and said, "I don't have a show for next week," they could hand me the scripts and say, "Here you are."

Because Patty was underage and California child labor laws were so strict, we decided to shoot the show in New York, where juveniles could work as many hours as their producer wanted them to.

Jorja, Mary, and I moved back to New York.

Creating a television show for Patty Duke was a challenge, because she was so extraordinarily talented that I did not want to waste her abilities. I hit on the solution of having her play two parts—twin sisters: one a bouncy, outgoing, New York girl; and the other her demure sister from Scotland, who had been separated from her at birth.

Bill Asher was signed on to produce and direct, and he suggested that we make them cousins instead of sisters, to explain them having grown up at a distance from each other. That worked just as well for me.

The Patty Duke Show was produced at an old television studio on Twenty-sixth Street, twelve blocks from the theater where I had worked as an usher and a barker. It was not the best of neighborhoods. One day, a secretary was hired to begin work at nine o'clock. At ten o'clock, a large rat ran over her shoe. At twelve o'clock, she was accosted as she went to lunch, and at one o'clock, she quit.

I had already written half a dozen teleplays in advance. Now it was time to start casting. We got lucky.

The studio signed William Schallert to play Patty's father, Jean Byron to play her mother, Paul O'Keefe for the part of Patty's brother, and Eddie Applegate to play Patty's suitor.

The first day of production, Patty started a ritual that went on until the end of the show. Every morning, before shooting began, the entire cast and crew lined up and sang "Good morning to you. Good morning to you. We're all in our places with bright shiny faces."

It was an interesting sight to see the hard-bitten crew, some unshaven, most in T-shirts, line up to earnestly sing this children's song. Outwardly, Patty was one of the happiest stars in television. It was not until three years later that I learned the truth.

There was an inherent danger in having an actor play two roles. If the audience could not distinguish which character was performing, the confusion could be fatal. In order to avoid this, we dressed Patty in casual attire and made Cathy's clothes much more formal. To further insure that there would be no confusion, I gave Patty dialogue and actions suitable for a young, energetic extrovert, while I made Cathy reserved and proper.

When I saw the first day's rushes, I knew that all our precautions had been unnecessary. Patty did not depend on the clothes or the dialogue. She *became* each character.

I was having a problem with the network. They had assigned an officious young man whom I'll call Todd as the liaison for ABC. Every Monday morning he came into my office and his greeting was always the same. "I read your latest script. It stinks. You're giving the network a disaster."

The last straw came when we were on the scoring stage, recording the music for the first show.

The studio had hired the talented Academy Award-winning arranger and composer Sid Ramin. When the first music take was over, Sid and I were talking at one end of the stage. I looked over and saw Todd hurrying toward us. He stopped in front of Sid and said loudly, "Your music is the only good thing in this show."

That afternoon I put in a call to an executive at the network.

By the following morning, Todd had disappeared from my life.

CHAPTER

30

When John Ross made the deal for Patty to star in the television series, he arranged to have himself put on the payroll as associate producer. Asked what his duties were, he was vague.

The producers said, "His job is to keep Patty happy and to stay out of everybody's way."

One day, Ross came into my office near tears. "What's the matter?" I asked. "What's happened?"

"*Life* magazine is coming to the studio today to cover the rehearsal."

"Well, that's good, isn't it?"

"No." He was trying not to cry. "Now *Life* magazine is going to know that I don't have a secretary."

As the date approached for the first airing of *The Patty Duke Show*, we had a problem. Our producer-director, Bill Asher, was a man who liked to be simultaneously involved in several different projects. As a result, he was behind schedule on our show. None of the shows was completed.

Bill came to me and said, "Ed Scherick, the head of

ABC, wants to take a look at our pilot show. I'm not sure which one he'll like, 'The French Teacher' or 'House Guest.'"

"The French Teacher" starred Jean-Pierre Aumont and the story involved Patty falling in love with him and making plans for her future as his wife. "House Guest" was about an eccentric rich aunt who moved into the Lane household and drove everyone crazy.

"I want you to run the two pictures for Scherick and let him pick out the one that he likes best."

"Fine," I agreed.

The following morning, we set up a running for Ed Scherick and several other executives from ABC. He had brought his wife and his sister and there were cordial introductions all around.

The lights dimmed and the screenings began. "The French Teacher" had not yet been edited or scored because Bill Asher was so busy, and several special effects were missing. "House Guest" had not yet been edited or scored and several special effects were missing. The overall effect was dreadful.

When the lights came up, Scherick got to his feet, glared at me, and said, "I don't give a damn which one you put on first." He and his entourage stormed out of the room.

I sat there, deflated. Maybe Todd had been right.

Our opening night premiere was upon us and we had to make a decision. Asher now worked day and night to complete the two shows. Since the network no longer cared about our show, *we* had to decide which episode to air first.

Things were so chaotic that on the opening night of *The Patty Duke Show,* "The French Teacher" played in the western half of the United States and "House Guest" played in the eastern half.

The Wednesday morning that the show was to air, I was walking through the studio lobby when Eddie Applegate came running in. He hurried over to the pay phone, felt in his pockets, and turned to me, in a panic.

"Do you have a dime?"

"Sure." I took one out of my pocket. "What's wrong?"

"I have to call the president of ABC."

"The president of— Why, Eddie?"

"I just found out that the show I'm in is playing in the east and my folks are in the west."

It took a moment for me to digest this. "You're going to ask the president of ABC to switch the shows around, so that your folks can see you?"

"Yes."

I put the dime back in my pocket. "Eddie, he may be busy with other things today. I would forget it."

The reviews the following morning were generally favorable. Typical of those reviews was the *Hollywood Reporter*'s.

It read: "This could be it—the TV fun the teens and their parents have been waiting for . . . a captivating click."

More importantly, the ratings were even stronger than we had hoped for. We were all thrilled.

The following day, *Daily Variety* carried a two-page ad from ABC. It read: "Nice girls finish first. We always knew that *Patty Duke* was going to be a hit."

Right.

* * *

The shooting of *The Patty Duke Show* the first year was uneventful. I decided it would be fun to use some guest stars. The idea worked well. I wrote scripts around Frankie Avalon, Troy Donahue, Sal Mineo, and others.

During our hiatus, Jorja and I decided to take Mary on a cruise. As a rule, when I am working on a project and I travel, I take all the scripts with me, in case there's a problem. But in this instance I did not feel it was necessary. All the shows for the first year had already been shot.

My mistake.

One morning, onboard ship, I received a cable to call the studio immediately. I could not imagine what the problem was.

When someone in production at the studio answered, I asked, "What's going on?"

"We're a minute short on 'The Green-Eyed Monster,' three minutes short on 'Practice Makes Perfect,' two minutes short on 'Simon Says,' and a minute and a half short on 'Patty, the Organizer.' We need you to expand those scenes and we need it done fast."

I knew the problem now, but I had no solution. When I write a script, I concentrate on it. But when I finish it and move on to the next project, I have pretty well forgotten the first one. As a result, I had no idea what any of those scripts were even about.

I went back to our cabin and told Jorja what had happened. "I don't know what I'm going to do," I said. "I'll probably have to go back to New York and take a look at those scripts, to refresh my memory."

Mary, our eight-year-old genius, spoke up. "No, you won't, Papa. I remember those plots." And she proceeded to recite them, scene by scene.

That evening, I was able to cable the new pages back to the studio.

Near the end of the first year of *The Patty Duke Show,* I received a call from Hollywood. "Screen Gems wants you to create a television series for them."

Screen Gems was a subsidiary of Columbia Pictures.

"Are you interested?"

"Certainly." My attitude about television had completely changed.

"They would like you to come up with an idea for a show and meet with them in Hollywood. How soon can you do that?"

"How about Monday?"

I'd had an idea about doing a show with a genie. I knew that genie projects had been done, but they had always consisted of a giant man, like Burl Ives, coming out of a bottle, saying, "What can I do for you, Master?"

I thought it would be intriguing to make the genie a beautiful young nubile girl, saying, "What can I do for you, Master?" That was the project I decided to create for Screen Gems.

My agent had taken me literally and had made an appointment for a meeting on Monday at Screen Gems. It was now Friday. On Saturday morning, I called in a secretary and started dictating a brief outline of the genie script. As I progressed, however, I began to put in more dialogue and camera angles and soon I thought I might as well write a full teleplay. I went back to the beginning and dictated the entire script. It was finished by Sunday night, just in time for me to race to the airport to catch my plane to Los Angeles.

The meeting at Screen Gems went well. I met Jerry Hyams, one of the top executives, Chuck Fries, and

Jackie Cooper, a former child actor who was now head of Screen Gems Productions. They were enthusiastic about the teleplay.

"How would you like to have your own company and produce it here?" Jerry Hyams asked.

I thought about *The Patty Duke Show*. No one had ever told me that I could not do two shows at once. "No problem," I said.

The deal was made.

When I returned to New York, there was a message waiting for me that Screen Gems had already made a deal with NBC for *I Dream of Jeannie*. I would now have two weekly situation comedies on the air. I was bicoastal.

Jerry Hyams arranged for me to see the pilot of a new show about to go on the air. I loved it. I thought it was charming and was going to be a big hit.

"How would you like to produce it?" Jerry Hyams asked.

I shook my head. Instead of saying yes, which I wanted to do, I said no. *There will be times, with no warning, you will lose control of your words and your actions.*

Bewitched turned out to be an enormous hit.

We were shooting *The Patty Duke Show* in New York and we were going to shoot *I Dream of Jeannie* in Hollywood. Since I was producing *Jeannie* and I was deeply involved, I began hiring some writers for *The Patty Duke Show*. I found myself flying to Hollywood almost every weekend. I spent my time on the plane working on *Patty Duke* scripts, and three days a week preparing *Jeannie*. The Beverly Hills Hotel became my home away from home.

On my next trip to California, all hell broke loose. Mort Werner, the head of NBC, sent for me. He was grim.

"I have a memo here from our standards and practices department, Sheldon." He shoved it at me.

As I started to read it, I realized what had happened. The network had awakened to the fact that in those closely censored days, they had bought a show that was about a nubile, half-naked young woman, living alone with a bachelor, constantly asking, "What can I do for you, Master?" They had panicked. The memo was eighteen pages long. It contained orders like:

They must never touch each other.

We will see Jeannie go into her bottle to sleep alone.

We will see Tony go into his bed to sleep alone.

Jeannie must never go into Tony's bedroom.

Never let Tony go into Jeannie's bottle.

And on and on for eighteen pages.

When I finished reading, Mort Werner said to me, "What are you going to do about it? This network cannot afford to air a show like this." The word "cancellation" hung in the air.

I took a deep breath. "I'm doing a comedy. I don't intend to make it titillating. There will be no sexual innuendoes or double entendres."

He looked at me for a long time. "We'll see."

Hurdle number one.

Hurdle number two: A memo from a vice president of NBC:

I have discussed your pilot script with several of my creative staff. We all agree that this is not going to work. It is a one-joke show, which means that it will be short-lived.

I was beginning to wonder why the network had bought the show in the first place. I sent my reply:

> You are quite right. *Jeannie* is a one-joke show, and that's exactly why it's going to work. *I Love Lucy* is a one-joke show. *The Beverly Hillbillies* is a one-joke show. *The Honeymooners* is a one-joke show. The trick with all these shows is to entertainingly vary the joke each week. We all hope that *Jeannie* will last as long as *I Love Lucy, The Honeymooners,* and *The Beverly Hillbillies.*

I heard no more about it.

It was time to start casting. I found this to be the hardest part of being a producer. It was difficult for me to say no to an actor who came in to read for a part. They all felt that every audition was going to be the breakthrough they deserved. They had had a sleepless night, arisen early in the morning, bathed, dressed carefully, and tried to be optimistic.

I'm going to get the part.
I'm going to get the part.
I'm going to get the part.

And they walked into the audition with clammy hands and bright, fake smiles.

Casting the part of Jeannie was going to be of primary importance because our genie had to be seductive without being blatantly sexy, and likable with a sense of whimsy. We were fortunate because the first and last person we auditioned for the part was Barbara Eden. She was perfect.

She had a warm and naive quality that would appeal

to an audience, along with a wonderful comedic sense. Barbara was married to Michael Ansara, an actor.

The next bit of casting was for the part of Anthony Nelson, her astronaut master. We tested half a dozen actors before Larry Hagman came up for the role. Hagman, the son of Broadway star Mary Martin, had been doing a soap opera, *The Edge of Night*, in New York and had not yet established himself. His screen test was brilliant and we immediately signed him.

We needed a confidant for him and we auditioned dozens of actors. I chose a hyper nightclub comic named Bill Daily who had never acted in television or films.

We had long discussions about directors. Norman Jewison, who later directed the hit movie *The Russians Are Coming, the Russians Are Coming*, read my script. He sent his agent into Screen Gems to make a deal, but when the agent insisted that Jewison get a percentage of the show, we had to start looking for another director.

Gene Nelson, who had starred in musical pictures at Warner Brothers and had directed *The Andy Griffith Show* and other television programs, came in to see me. We spent an hour talking about the show and I felt that he was right for it. He was hired.

Nineteen sixty-five was the year that every show on television changed from black and white to color. Every show, that is, except *I Dream of Jeannie*. I asked Jerry Hyams why *Jeannie* was not going to be shot in color.

"Because each show would cost an additional four hundred dollars."

"Jerry, this show has to be in color. I'll pay the difference out of my own pocket."

He looked at me and said, "Sidney, don't throw your money away."

What he was really saying was that no one expected *Jeannie* to go into a second year.

In 1965, while the studio was getting the *Jeannie* pilot ready to go, I returned to New York for a few days to see how things were going on *Patty Duke*, which was ending its second season.

John and Ethel were determined not to let anything separate them from their windfall. Whenever *The Patty Duke Show* was on hiatus, they took Patty along on their vacations. They arranged it so that Patty would never have an opportunity to meet a young man. When Patty was invited to a social or charity event, they went along to keep an eye on her. She was virtually a prisoner.

There was an assistant director on the show, twenty-five-year-old Harry Falk, who was a nice-looking, pleasant young man. When the Rosses noticed that Patty was spending time with him on the set, they immediately had him fired. Patty was devastated, but she said nothing.

Just before Patty's birthday, the company planned a party for her on the set.

Patty came to see me in my office. "I want to ask a favor of you, Sidney."

"Anything, Patty. What can I do for you?"

"I would like you to invite Harry Falk to my birthday party. Will you do that for me?"

"Of course I will."

The afternoon of the party, Harry Falk came onto the set. John and Ethel were visibly upset, but Patty ignored them. She walked over to greet Falk and they spent most of the time together. The repercussions were soon to come.

31

We rounded out the casting of *Jeannie* with Hayden Rorke playing the psychiatrist, and Barton MacLane as General Peterson.

I felt that the show should open with animation, to tell the story of Jeannie's discovery by an astronaut. One of the best animators in Hollywood was Friz Freleng, but he had worked mostly in motion pictures, and had done very little television. I sent him the pilot script and asked him if he would be interested in animating the opening sequence. He was, and he created a brilliant opening.

I hired Dick Wess, a talented composer, to write the music for the first season, but after hearing it, I felt it was wrong for the show. Instead, I used a bright, upbeat melody written by Hugo Montenegro for the *Jeannie* theme.

The bottle that I selected for Jeannie's home was a Jim Beam liquor decanter, which we painted in bright colors.

The first day of rehearsal went smoothly. We had a reading of the pilot script with the cast and our director,

Gene Nelson, and I asked the actors if they needed any changes, or if they were comfortable with their lines. I wanted to make sure the actors were satisfied because I wanted no ad-libbing when they started to shoot. Everyone was happy.

I Dream of Jeannie was ready to start creating its magic.

In the morning, less than an hour after production on the pilot began, my secretary said, "Mr. Nelson is calling from the set."

I could not wait to hear the good news. "Gene—"

"I'm quitting. Get someone else. Sorry." He started to hang up.

"Wait! Wait a minute!" I was panicky. "Stay right where you are. I'm on my way down there."

Three minutes later, I was on the set. I took Gene aside. "What happened?"

"Nothing. That's the problem. I can't work with actors who don't know their lines. Larry Hagman doesn't know his lines and Bill Daily doesn't know his lines, and—"

"Stay right here." I was furious.

I called Larry over to the side. "How dare you come on this set the first day of shooting and not know your lines."

He looked at me in surprise. "What are you talking about? I know my lines."

"The director says you don't."

"Well, all I did was to expand on them a little. I had some ideas, and I just added a few things here and—"

"Larry! Listen to me and listen carefully. We have a tight schedule. We have a lot of pages to shoot every day. You'll say the lines exactly as they're written. Is that clear?"

He shrugged. "Yeah, sure."

I called Bill Daily aside. "What excuse do you have for not knowing your lines?"

He said, "I'm sorry, Sidney. I—I've never had to learn lines before. I always worked in clubs like The Improv. I did a comedy act."

"This is not The Improv," I snapped. "If you want to stay in this show, you've got to memorize your lines."

He swallowed. "Okay."

I went back to Gene Nelson. "There's been a little misunderstanding, Gene. I think after today, everything is going to be fine. I want you to stay with the show. Larry will be great. I'm going to tape Bill's dialogue and let him play it in the car on his way to and from the studio, so he can learn it. Will you give it another chance?"

There was a long pause. "I'll try, but—"

"Thank you."

The opening scene of the pilot was filmed at Zuma Beach, thirty miles northwest of Los Angeles. The scene consisted of Larry, as an astronaut, stranded on a deserted island when his spacecraft malfunctions. He sees a bottle, uncorks it, and finds a genie inside. Since he has freed her, by the rules of the genie game, he is now her master. She blinks in a rescue ship and he thinks he has gotten rid of her, but she has no intention of leaving him.

The scene went well. The day went well and we were all pleased.

On the way back to the studio, in a company limousine, I got my first glimpse of Larry Hagman's ambition. We had stopped at a red light next to a car full of tourists. Larry rolled down the window of the limousine and, in a loud voice, yelled out at them, "Someday you'll all know who I am."

Larry had some emotional problems to deal with. His

mother was Mary Martin, a top Broadway star, with whom he had a difficult relationship. She had been busy with her career, so Larry was raised by his father, Ben, in Texas.

Some of the time he lived with his grandmother and traveled back and forth to New York, to visit his mother. He wanted to show his mother that he could also be a star. *Someday you'll all know who I am.*

When the pilot was finished but had not yet aired, I received a call from Mary Martin. "Sidney, I would love to see the pilot. Is there any way you could arrange it?"

"Of course."

I was on my way east to work on *The Patty Duke Show*, so I arranged for the pilot of *Jeannie* to be screened for her in New York.

In the projection room were Mary Martin, a few executives from Screen Gems, and John Mitchell, who was head of sales for Screen Gems.

Before the screening started, Mary Martin went up to John Mitchell, took his hand, and said, "I hear you're the best salesman in the world."

I could see John stand visibly taller.

"I've heard so much about you," Mary Martin went on. "They say that you're a genius."

John Mitchell tried not to blush.

"Screen Gems is very lucky to have you."

He barely managed to stammer out the words "Thank you, Miss Martin."

The screening began. When the show had ended, the lights came on. Mary Martin turned to John Mitchell and said, "*Anybody* could have sold that show."

I watched John shrink.

* * *

Jeannie opened to mixed reviews. The critics were mostly dismissive, but the audience was not. The show had a loyal following from the beginning and it grew.

I decided to use guest stars on this show also. Farrah Fawcett did a segment, as well as Dick Van Patten, Richard Mulligan, Don Rickles, and Milton Berle.

I wrote a script about a fake fortune-teller, called "Bigger than a Bread Box and Better than a Genie." I asked Jorja to play the part of a fortune-teller. It was in the spring and Natalie was coming to visit us.

Jorja said, "Why don't you give Natalie a part in the show? She could play one of the characters in the séance scene."

I laughed. "I think she'd enjoy that."

When Natalie arrived, I asked, "How would you like to be on television?"

"I wouldn't mind," my mother said coolly.

"Jorja is going to star as a fortune-teller and you can be one of the characters in the séance scene."

She nodded. "Fine." She was very composed about her debut on national television.

I wrote a few lines for Natalie to read and left them with her. While I was working at the studio, Jorja rehearsed her in her part.

The next morning I auditioned Queenie Smith, a wonderful actress. I decided that she should have Natalie's lines, so I wrote some new lines for Natalie and when I got home that evening, I gave them to her.

She read them and said, "No."

I was puzzled. "No—what?"

"I can't read these lines."

"Why not?"

"Because my character would never say this."

This from a seventy-year-old woman who sold dresses in Chicago.

I argued with her, but I could not take the lines away from her and I had to write something else for Queenie Smith.

The scene went well. Colonel Chuck Yeager played himself in the episode. Natalie was so good that no one knew she was not a professional actress.

Larry had met her at dinner, so when he found out that she was going to be in the show, he jokingly said, "Ahh, I see a little bit of nepotism here."

"You're right, Larry," I told him. "Fair is fair. When *your* mother comes to town, I'll be happy to use her in the show."

The network had moved *Jeannie* from Saturday night to Monday night. It was only the beginning. The following year it was Tuesday night. The next year Monday, and the next year Tuesday. Fortunately our audience was loyal enough to find us.

Later, after Natalie had returned to Chicago, "Bigger than a Bread Box" appeared on television. She called me the day after.

"Thank you, darling."

"What for?" I asked.

"I've been getting phone calls all morning. I'm a star."

We had shot a dozen shows and the studio and network were very pleased with them. Jorja and I were at a friend's house for dinner when I received a telephone call from Barbara Eden.

"Sidney, I have to see you."

"Fine, Barbara, I'll be in the studio in the morning and—"

"No. I have to see you tonight."

"Is something wrong?"

"I'll tell you when I see you."

I gave her the address.

She arrived an hour later. I took her into the den. She was near tears.

"You'll have to replace me."

I was stunned. "Why?"

"I'm pregnant."

It took a moment for this to sink in. "Congratulations."

"I'm sorry to do this to you."

"You haven't done anything to me. You're staying on the show."

She looked at me in surprise. "But how—"

"Don't worry about it," I said. "I'll take care of it."

The following morning I asked Gene Nelson to come to the office. "Gene, we have a problem."

"I heard," he said. "Barbara's pregnant. What are we going to do?"

"We're going to raise the camera higher. We'll shoot her above the waist, cover her with more veils, and use long shots. We can manage. I don't want to replace her."

He was thoughtful for a moment. "Neither do I."

And we managed to finish the season from the third week to the eighth month of her pregnancy.

There were storm clouds brewing in the east, so I flew back to New York to see if I could help calm things down.

John and Ethel Ross had found out that Patty and Harry Falk continued to secretly meet. Determined not to let it develop into a romance, the Rosses arranged for the show to be moved to California for its third season. In a sense it was a good move for me, because I no longer had to be bicoastal. But trouble was looming.

When I came back to California, I found a beautiful house for Jorja and me to rent in Thousand Oaks. I knew Patty and the Rosses were looking for a place, so I suggested that they look at the house I was going to take, and if they liked it, I would let them have it. They did like it and they moved in.

NASA was very cooperative with the *Jeannie* production. We toured Edwards Air Force Base and the Kennedy Space Center in Florida, and met several of the astronauts. Many of them watched the show and were fans. They let us use their facilities at Edwards, where I took a flight in a Gemini simulator and sampled the dehydrated food. It was terrible.

The ratings for *Jeannie* remained high the first year, but all was not well on the set. The problem was Larry Hagman. I planned to use more guest stars, but Larry was always antagonistic toward them. He would be sullen and ignore them, and spend time sulking in his dressing room.

He wanted to be the star and he wanted it *now*. It was Barbara who was getting all the magazine covers and interviews. Larry wanted to show the world that he could be as successful as his mother. The result was that he put himself and everyone else under tremendous pressure.

I was not aware of it then, but every morning Larry opened a bottle of champagne and began drinking. It never affected his work on the set. He always knew his lines and was never less than adroit. But the pressure began to show.

One morning, after a reading, I asked the actors if there were any problems. All of them said they were satisfied. When I got back to my office there was a call from Gene Nelson.

"I need your help, Sidney. Larry's in his dressing room, crying. He won't come out."

I went to Larry's dressing room and we talked for a long time. Finally, I said, "Larry, I'm going to do everything I can to help you. I'll write scripts where the plots will revolve around you."

And so, I began to write scripts to build up Larry's character and make him more prominent. But when an actor is in a show with a scantily dressed actress as beautiful and enticing as Barbara Eden, it is very difficult for him to become the star.

Larry became more and more miserable, and it was upsetting everyone on the set. Barbara was very patient with him. I finally had another talk with Larry.

"Larry, do you like this show?"

"Sure."

"But you're not happy doing it?"

"No."

"Why?"

He hesitated. "I don't know."

"Sure you do. You want to be in a show where you're the star."

"I guess so."

"You're a very important part of this show, Larry. But if you want to stay in it, you have to take the pressure off yourself. I think you should see a psychiatrist. And I wouldn't wait."

He nodded. "You're right. I will."

A short while later, he told me he had made regular appointments to see a psychologist. It helped to a degree, but the tension was still there.

CHAPTER

32

At the start of the second season, *Jeannie* went to color. I was hiring other writers to help me carry some of the load, but I was dissatisfied with many of the scripts they turned in. A lot of writers believed the best approach was to pile fantasy on fantasy. They wanted Barbara to meet a Martian or some other fantasy character. I felt that the success of the show depended on a bedrock of reality: the incongruity of putting Jeannie in ordinary, everyday situations.

As an example, I wrote a script with the following premise: Tony was away at work, and a man from the IRS came to his house and was greeted by Jeannie. To impress her visitor, Jeannie blinked in wall-to-wall genuine Rembrandts, Picassos, Monets, and Renoirs.

"See," she told a stunned tax investigator, "my master is very rich."

Tony had to get out of it.

In another sequence, Tony was having Dr. Bellows over for dinner. Jeannie thought the house was too small, so she blinked in an enormous ballroom, an ornate dining room, a huge garden, and a large swimming pool. Tony has to explain the transformation to Dr. Bellows.

From February 1966 to April of the following year, I wrote thirty-eight consecutive scripts under my own name. In Hollywood, screen credits are the criteria by which a writer exists. Everyone fights to get a credit because that leads to the next job. I had a problem. I felt that I was getting too many credits. My screen credits on *Jeannie* read: "A Sidney Sheldon Production . . . Created by Sidney Sheldon . . . Produced by Sidney Sheldon . . . Written by Sidney Sheldon . . . Copyright by Sidney Sheldon." It felt to me like an ego trip. I called the Writers Guild and told them I was going to start writing for the show under three different pseudonyms: Christopher Golato, Allan Devon, and Mark Rowane. From then on, my doppelgängers wrote many of the scripts, and I had one fewer credit.

After the first year of *Jeannie*, Gene Nelson had other offers and decided to leave the show. I knew I was going to miss him. I used a variety of directors, most often Claudio Guzmán and Hal Cooper.

And the show went on.

Sammy Davis, Jr., was over at our house one night for dinner.

"Sammy, have you ever watched *I Dream of Jeannie*?"

"All the time. I love it."

"Would you be interested in doing an episode?"

"I'm in," he said. "Call my agent."

The next morning, I called his agent. "Sammy wants to do *I Dream of Jeannie*," I said. "Can we set it up?"

"Sure. How much are you paying?"

"A thousand dollars. That's all we pay our guest stars."

I heard a snort. "You must be kidding. Sammy tips his manicurist that much. Forget it."

"Call Sammy."

One hour later, the phone rang. "When do you want him?"

Sammy did the show and was wonderful.

We also used Michael Ansara, Barbara's husband, in the show as the Blue Djinn.

Groucho Marx called me. "It's too bad you don't have an eye for talent. I know a guy who would be great for the show. He's young and handsome and brilliant."

"Who did you have in mind, Groucho?" I asked.

"Who else? Me."

"Why didn't I think of that?"

A week later I wrote an episode for Groucho called "The Greatest Invention in the World." As usual, he was dazzling.

One night, when Mary was in a play at school, Jorja and I were going to see her. I asked Groucho if he would like to come with us, and to my surprise, he said yes.

After the show, Mary had some of her classmates back to our house. They were fascinated by Groucho. One of my fondest memories is of Groucho Marx sitting in a chair in our den, with the boys and girls sitting in a circle on the floor, listening to him talk to them about show business.

The first year of *Jeannie* had been very successful and the merchandising was tremendous. There were *Jeannie* dolls and *Jeannie* bottles. *Jeannie* even had her own magazine, *The Blink*. The fan mail was enormous, but nearly all of it went to Barbara Eden. Larry could barely conceal his anger.

Jeannie was going fairly smoothly, but I was constantly putting out fires. Meanwhile, there were big emotional problems on the set of *The Patty Duke Show*. Patty had reached the point where she refused to let the Rosses control her. There was constant friction among the three of them.

One evening, they had a heated argument and Patty moved out of the house and found an apartment. Harry Falk flew to California and he and Patty were married. That was the end of the Rosses' power over Patty.

But on the set, the conflicts continued, and it finally got so bad that at the end of the year, even though the ratings were satisfactory, the network decided to cancel the show.

In 1967, during the second season of *Jeannie*, I was nominated for an Emmy. At the awards ceremony, I met Charles Schulz, who was also nominated for writing *Charlie Brown*. I was a big fan of his and his friend, Charlie Brown. Charles and I started talking, and he turned out to be a warm and wonderful pixie. He said that he was a fan of *Jeannie*.

I mentioned to Charles that I had a favorite *Peanuts* cartoon, where Snoopy is at his typewriter, typing: *His was a story that had to be told*. There is a panel of Snoopy vainly thinking. Then he types, *Well, maybe not*, and throws the paper away.

Shortly after the Emmys, a package arrived from Charles. It was the original strip, signed to me. I still have it hanging in my office.

Incidentally, neither of us won that year.

In September of 1967, I received an alarming phone call from Cedars Sinai Hospital in Los Angeles. Otto had

had a major heart attack. Outside his hospital room, the doctor told me that there was very little chance that Otto could live. I went inside and stood at his bed. He was pale and I sensed that his vitality had gone. I was wrong.

He motioned for me to come closer, and when I leaned over him, he said, "I gave Richard my car. I could have sold it to him."

Those were his last words to me.

During the fourth season of *Jeannie*, the show that followed us was an enormous hit. It was a one-hour show called *Rowan & Martin's Laugh-In*. I called Mort Werner, the head of NBC, and suggested that for one night, we combine the two shows. I would write a *Jeannie* script, using the *Laugh-In* characters, and immediately after that, I would have the *Jeannie* cast appear on *Laugh-In*. Mort thought it was a good idea.

At one time there was a lot of speculation going on in Hollywood about Barbara Eden being forbidden to show her navel. There were half a dozen different theories, but what really happened was the following:

I wrote a script called "The Biggest Star in Hollywood." Judy Carne, Arte Johnson, Gary Owens, and George Schlatter (*Laugh-In*'s executive producer) appeared in my script interacting with the *Jeannie* characters.

Then George Schlatter showed me the script that the *Laugh-In* show writers had prepared for our cast. The opening scene had Barbara Eden in her *Jeannie* costume slowly coming down the stairs with a spotlight shining on her navel. I told George that I thought that was in bad taste and I refused to let the cast of *Jeannie* go on *Laugh-In*.

So, what we finally ended up with was the *Laugh-In* group in our show, but none of our cast in their show.

*   *   *

I Dream of Jeannie was completing its fourth year, ready to go into its fifth. We had not received our official pickup for the fifth year. I received a call from Mort Werner.

"I think Jeannie and Tony should be married."

I was taken aback. "That would destroy the show, Mort. The fun of *Jeannie* is the sexual tension between Jeannie and her master. Once you marry them, that's gone. You have nothing to work with."

"I want them to get married."

"Mort, that doesn't make sense. If they—"

"Do you want the show picked up for a fifth year?"

There was a long silence. I was being blackmailed, but it was his network. "Can we discuss this?"

"No."

"I'll get them married."

"Good. You'll be on the air next year."

When the cast heard the news, they were horrified.

"Businesspeople shouldn't be allowed to make creative decisions," Larry said.

The entire cast called Mort Werner, but it was no use. He thought he was smarter than any of them. He knew what was good for the show.

For the fifth year of *Jeannie*, I wrote a wedding scene.

We filmed the wedding at Cape Kennedy and a lot of the Air Force brass attended. I tried to make the script as interesting as possible, but with their marriage the relationship had changed and much of the fun went out of the show. At the end of the fifth year, *I Dream of Jeannie* was canceled. Mort Werner had taken a hit show and destroyed it.

We had produced a hundred thirty-nine episodes. In

its sixth year, *Jeannie* went into syndication. That was in 1971. And it played in syndication for five years.

Today, forty years after *Jeannie* first aired, it has been revived and is playing all over the world, still bringing laughter to millions of viewers. In color. Columbia is planning to make a movie of it.

During the time I was producing *Jeannie*, I got an idea that I thought was exciting. It was about a psychiatrist whom someone was trying to murder. What intrigued me was that as far as he knew, he had no enemies. But if he was a good psychiatrist, he would have to figure out who was trying to kill him and why.

The problem with the idea was that I felt it was too introspective. You had to get into the psychiatrist's head to see how he solved what was happening. I decided it would be impossible to do in the dramatic form. It would have to be a novel where his inner thoughts could be explained to the reader. But I knew I was not capable of writing a novel, so I dropped the idea.

Groucho called me to tell me that a play about the Marx Brothers and their mother, called *Minnie's Boys*, was opening on Broadway, at the Imperial Theatre. He asked if Jorja and I would fly back east with him to see the show. Though I was busy producing at the time, I said yes. We flew to New York, saw the show—which was well done— and attended the cast party afterward.

The next morning, we went to the airport to catch a plane home. There was an air traffic controllers' strike. Our plane started to taxi and the pilot's voice came on the loudspeaker to announce that there would be a one-hour delay because of the strike. We taxied back to the gate, and two hours later, the pilot came on the loudspeaker again, to announce that there would be a three-hour delay.

Groucho rang the stewardess.

"Can I help you, Mr. Marx?"

"Yes. Is there a minister on board?"

"I don't know. Why?"

"Some of the men are getting horny."

The great poet T. S. Eliot was putatively anti-Semitic. Groucho had a framed picture of Eliot on one of the walls of his home.

When I asked him about it, he said, "Eliot wrote to me, asking for an autographed picture. I sent a photograph to him and he sent it back to me. He wanted one with my cigar in it."

Eliot respected Groucho so much that, in his will, he had written a request that Groucho preside over his memorial, which Groucho did.

Shecky Greene was another one of the comedians we'd see at Groucho's famous dinner parties. I once asked Shecky the difference between a comic and a comedian.

He said, "A comic opens funny doors. A comedian opens doors funny."

Shecky was one of the top nightclub acts around the country. What was interesting about him was that he had no act. No two shows of his were ever the same. He would walk out onto the stage and ad-lib for a hysterical forty-five minutes.

One night, when we were at one of Shecky's shows at the Sands Hotel in Las Vegas, Shecky told the audience, "Frank Sinatra saved my life. When I walked out the stage door onto the parking lot, three hoodlums started beating me up. After a while, Frank said, 'Okay. That's enough.'"

After the show, we went backstage to Shecky's dressing room.

I was puzzled. "What was all that about Sinatra?"

"Well, I go on before Frank. A few nights ago, I made some jokes about Frank's family. After the show, Frank said, 'Don't do that again, Shecky.' Well, you know me. I don't like anyone telling me what to do. So the next show, I told some more jokes about Frank's family. When I finished the show, I went out to the parking lot and these three hoodlums started to work me over.

"Finally, Frank said, 'That's enough.' And they disappeared."

I first met Frank in 1953, when he was down and out, before he made his comeback. His studio contract had run out, his record deal was canceled, and no one wanted to book him for personal appearances. But with his talent, he quickly got his career back.

Frank Sinatra lived by his own rules. Actually, there were several Frank Sinatras and you never knew which one you were going to get. He could be a warm and generous friend, and he could be a bad enemy.

Sinatra was engaged to Juliet Prowse, a talented dancer and actress, and when she mentioned the engagement to a reporter, Sinatra called it off.

When lyricist Sammy Cahn flew to Los Angeles and checked into the Beverly Hills Hotel, Sinatra had Sammy's luggage moved to the Sinatra home. During an interview, Sammy Cahn mentioned Sinatra and soon after found that his luggage had been moved back to the Beverly Hills Hotel.

Frank had never met George C. Scott, but he admired

his work, and when Scott had a heart attack, Frank arranged for medical care and took care of all the bills. Frank was also generous in contributing to charity.

Sinatra had married and divorced Ava Gardner, but he never completely got over her.

Carl Cohn, the manager of the Sands Hotel, and I were in Frank's apartment, getting ready to go out to dinner to celebrate Frank's birthday. Ava was in Africa, shooting *Mogambo*.

Frank made no move to leave.

Finally, I said, "Frank, it's ten o'clock. Carl and I are starving. What are we waiting for?"

"I was just hoping that Ava would call and wish me a happy birthday."

Every Thursday night for years, a group of us who called ourselves "The Eagles" would gather at our home for dinner and a few hours of interesting conversation. Each week it was the same group, along with their wives. Sid Caesar, Steve Allen, Shecky Greene, Carl Reiner, and Milton Berle. Through the years, we had the pleasure of watching all their careers skyrocket. These were the giants of comedy, and as decades passed, I realized they were all getting less young. Soon their voices would be lost, as though they had never existed. But I had an idea.

I thought of a way to preserve the image of the incredible talent and at the same time aid colleges with their financial problems. I had been involved in education, and had served as national spokesperson for the Coalition for Literacy, so what I had in mind seemed like an exciting plan.

I broached my idea to the group at dinner one evening.

"Friends," I said, "I would like to put a show together

with all of you on the future of comedy. I would be the interlocutor. We would travel to colleges around the country, sell tickets for our show, and donate all the money to the colleges. How many of you would like to get involved?"

The hands started to go up. Sid Caesar . . . Steve Allen . . . Shecky Greene . . . Carl Reiner . . .

"That's great," I said. "Let me make some arrangements."

I decided to do our first show in Hollywood, as a test, and the city of Beverly Hills was delighted to have us. The first-ever "Future of Comedy" panel discussion was held on July 17, 2000, at the Writers Guild Theater in front of an overflow crowd.

Our reception was wonderful, and I could see that my idea would work. Sid, Steve, Shecky, Carl, and I had a ball, and so did the audience. The laughs were nonstop. The panel members kept interrupting one another with one-liners. We were really on to something, and we were all looking forward to our new adventure together.

But shortly after that evening, fate stepped in, and everything began to fall apart. Steve Allen died, Sid Caesar was not able to travel long distances, Shecky Greene had some emotional problems, and Carl Reiner became heavily involved with movies. It was not meant to be.

But I will never forget the generosity of my friends.

In 1970, I created another television show. I called it *Nancy*. It was a story of the sophisticated young daughter of the president of the United States who, while on a vacation at a ranch, met and fell in love with a young veterinarian. They married. And the scripts were based on the disparities between the two lifestyles.

I cast the leads with three very good actors: Celeste

Holm, Renne Jarrett, and John Fink. The pilot was shown to NBC and they bought it.

The show was a sweet, romantic comedy and the cast brought it to life beautifully. The network canceled it after seventeen episodes. At the time it was canceled, the Nielsen ratings ranked *Nancy* as number seventeen, which is more than strong enough to keep a show on the air. I have no idea whether the White House was displeased by the show or whether any political pressure was ever brought to bear, but I know that the cancellation was a big surprise to all of us.

CHAPTER

33

Several years later I decided I wanted to do a black-tie show with sophisticated people in elegant backgrounds. I created *Hart to Hart,* and it went on the air in 1979, with Aaron Spelling and Leonard Goldberg producing. We were fortunate in obtaining Robert Wagner and Stefanie Powers as our stars. The show was a hit and ran for five years.

In the midst of my doing other projects, the idea about the psychiatrist kept coming back to me. I could not seem to get rid of it. It was as though the character was demanding to have a life. I had no confidence in my ability to write a novel, but in order to get the psychiatrist off my back, I decided I was going to write his story.

Mornings I dictated the novel to one of my secretaries. Afternoons I put on my producer's hat and worked on other projects.

The novel was finally finished and I had no idea what to do with it. I did not know any literary agents.

I called a dear friend of mine, the talented novelist Irving Wallace.

"Irving, I have a manuscript of a novel here. Who do I send it to?"

"Let me read it," he said.

I sent it to him and waited for his phone call saying, "Don't send it to anybody."

Instead, he called and said, "I think it's wonderful. Send it to my agent in New York. I'll tell him to expect it."

The novel was called *The Naked Face* and it was turned down by five book publishers. The sixth one to read it was Hillel Black, an editor at William Morrow.

My agent called. "William Morrow wants to publish your book. They'll give you a thousand-dollar advance."

I was filled with a sudden sense of excitement. I was going to have a book published. William Morrow did not know it, but I would have gladly paid *them* a thousand dollars.

"Great," I said.

Hillel wanted a few minor changes made and I quickly took care of them.

The novel was published in 1970. The day *The Naked Face* came out, I panicked. I was sure it was going to break every publishing record: that it was not going to sell one single copy. I was so certain of it that I hurried to a bookstore in Beverly Hills and bought one copy—a tradition that I have continued to this day.

It is customary when a book comes out for an author to travel around the country, publicizing it, making the public aware that the book is in stores. Authors appear on television shows, attend book parties, and go to literary lunches to publicize their books. I called Hillel Black.

"I just want you to know," I said, "that I'm willing to go on a book tour. I'll do all the television shows you can set up and—"

"Sidney, there is no point in sending you on a book tour."

"What are you talking about?"

"Outside of Hollywood, no one knows who you are. None of the shows will book you. Forget it."

But I did not forget it. I called a public relations man and explained the situation to him.

"Don't worry about it," he said. "I'll handle it."

He booked me on *The Tonight Show*, with Johnny Carson, *The Merv Griffin Show*, and *The David Frost Show*, as well as half a dozen others.

He also arranged for me to go to a literary luncheon at the storied Huntington Hotel in Pasadena, California. The procedure was for the authors to talk briefly about their books, have lunch, and then the people in attendance would buy the books, which were at the back of the room, and come up to the dais to have the author sign his or her book.

Next to me on the dais that day were Will and Ariel Durant, the popularizers of world history who spent a lifetime writing *The Story of Civilization*; Francis Gary Powers, who had written his book about his experiences of being shot down in a U-2; Gwen Davis, a well-known novelist; and Jack Smith, who wrote a popular column in the *Los Angeles Times*.

During lunch, each of us was introduced and we briefly talked about our book.

When lunch was over, members of the audience bought their books at the back of the room and then lined up in front of their favorite authors. There was a line in front of Will and Ariel Durant that ran clear to the back of the room. The line in front of Jack Smith was almost as long. Gary Powers had a long line, and so did Gwen Davis.

There was not one single person in line for my book. Red-faced, I took out a notebook, pretending to be busy writing. I wished there was some way I could have escaped. The lines for the other authors got longer and I sat there, writing gibberish.

After what seemed like forever, I heard a voice say, "Mr. Sheldon?"

I looked up. A little old lady was standing in front of me. She said, "What is your book called?"

I said, "*The Naked Face.*"

She smiled and said, "All right. I'll buy one."

It was an act of mercy.

That was the only book I sold that day.

A few weeks later, I flew to New York and met with Larry Hughes, the president of William Morrow.

"I have good news," Larry said. "We've sold seventeen thousand copies of *The Naked Face* and already went into a second printing."

I looked at him for a long moment. "Mr. Hughes, I have a television show on the air that's watched by twenty million people every week. I'm really not thrilled with selling seventeen thousand copies of anything."

When the reviews of the book came out, I was pleasantly surprised. They were almost all favorable, and the topper was the *New York Times* review. The reviewer said, "*The Naked Face* is clearly the best first mystery of the year." And to top it all off, at the end of the year I received an Edgar Allan Poe Award nomination.

When I returned to Hollywood, I was still working on *Nancy,* but I could not stop thinking about writing another novel. *The Naked Face* had not been financially successful. In fact, I had spent more on publicity than the book had made. But there was a more important element involved in writing the novel. I had experienced a sense of creative freedom that I had never known before.

When one writes a screenplay or television show or a play for the theater, it is always a collaborative effort. Even if you write alone, you are working with a cast, a director, a producer, and musicians.

The novelist is free to create whatever he or she wants. There is no one to say:

"Let's change the scene to the mountains instead of the valley . . ."

"There are too many sets . . ."

"Let's cut out the words here and create the mood with music . . ."

The novelist is the cast, the producer, and the director. The novelist is free to create whole worlds, to go back in time or forward in time, to give his characters armies, servants, villas. There is no limit except the imagination.

I decided that I was going to write another novel, even though I had no expectations that it would be any more successful financially than *The Naked Face*. I needed an exciting idea, and I remembered a story of mine that Dore Schary had refused to buy at RKO, *Orchids for Virginia*. I decided that that was the story I wanted to tell. I turned the screenplay into an elaborately textured novel, and changed the title to *The Other Side of Midnight*.

The book was published a year later and it changed my life. It stayed on the *New York Times* best-seller list for fifty-two weeks. *The Other Side of Midnight* became a phenomenon, an international runaway best-seller.

Bea Factor's prediction that I would become world-famous had finally come true.

Afterword

Of all the varied writing I have done over the years—
motion pictures, theater, television, novels—I prefer
writing novels. Novels are a different world, a world
of the mind and the heart. In a novel, one can create
characters and bring them to life. The transition from
playwright and screenwriter to novelist was easier than I
had expected. And the advantages!

A novelist travels all over the world doing research,
meeting interesting people, and going to interesting
places. If people are affected by something you wrote, they
let you know. I sometimes get mail that is very emotional.

I received a letter from a woman who had had a mas-
sive heart attack and was in the hospital, and would not
let her parents or her boyfriend come in to see her. She
wrote me that she just wanted to die. She was twenty-one
years old. Someone left a copy of *The Other Side of Midnight* on her bedside. She started to skim through it. Intrigued, she went back to the beginning and read the
book. When she was through, she had been so caught up
in the characters and their problems that she forgot
about her own, and was ready to face life again.

Another woman wrote to tell me that her dying daughter's last request had been that all my books be spread around her hospital bed, and she had died happy.

In *Rage of Angels*, I let a little boy die and I began to receive hate mail. One woman wrote to me from the east, gave me her phone number, and said, "Call me. I can't sleep. Why did you let him die?"

I got so many similar letters that when I did the miniseries, I let him live.

Women have told me that they had become lawyers because of Jennifer Parker, the heroine of *Rage of Angels*.

My novels are sold in one hundred eight countries and have been translated into fifty-one languages. In 1997, the *Guinness Book of World Records* listed me as the Most Translated Author in the World. I have sold over three hundred million books. If there is one reason for the success of my books, I believe it's because my characters are very real to me and, therefore, real to my readers. Foreign readers identify with my books because love and hate and jealousy are universal emotions that everyone understands.

When I became a novelist, one of the things that struck me was how much more respect a novelist gets than a screenwriter working in Hollywood. Jack Warner said, "What are writers but schmucks with typewriters?" A sentiment shared by most studio heads.

One day when I was writing *Easter Parade*, I was in Arthur Freed's office when his insurance agent came in. We were talking when the secretary announced that the dailies were ready to be seen. Freed turned to his insurance agent and said, "Let's go look at the dailies."

The two men got up and walked out of the room, leaving me sitting there, alone, while they went to watch a picture I had written.

Not much respect.

* * *

I enjoy traveling around the world doing research for my novels and I have fun doing it. In Athens, I was researching *The Other Side of Midnight.* Jorja was with me. We passed a police station and I said, "Let's go in."

We went inside. There was a policeman behind the desk. He said, "Can I help you?"

"Yes," I said. "Can someone here tell me how to blow up a car?"

Thirty seconds later we were locked in a room. Jorja was panicky. "Tell them who you are," she said.

"Don't worry. There's plenty of time."

The door opened and four policemen with guns came in. "You want to blow up a car? Why?"

"I'm Sidney Sheldon and I'm doing research."

Fortunately, they knew who I was, and they told me how to blow up a car.

In South Africa, I was doing research for my novel called *Master of the Game,* which is about diamonds. I got in touch with DeBeers and asked whether I could go into one of their diamond mines. They gave me permission and I had the rare experience of exploring a diamond mine.

An executive of DeBeers told me about one of their mines that was a beach with diamonds lying on the surface, in full view, protected by the ocean on one side, and a patrolled gate on the other. I felt challenged, and figured out a way for one of my characters to get inside and steal the diamonds.

For *If Tomorrow Comes,* I checked on the security of the Prado Museum in Madrid. I was told it was impregnable, but one of my characters figured out a way to steal a valuable painting from there.

In *Windmills of the Gods*, I went to Romania, which was one of my locales in the book. Ceauşescu was alive at the time, and there was a paranoid feeling in the city. I went to the American embassy and I was in the office of the American ambassador when I said, "I would like to ask you a question."

He got to his feet. "Come with me." He took me down the hall into a room guarded by Marines twenty-four hours a day and said, "What do you want to know?"

"Do you think my room is bugged?" I asked.

"Not only is your hotel room bugged, but if you go to a nightclub, they will bug you there."

Three nights later, Jorja and I went to a nightclub. The maître d' seated us. The air-conditioning was hitting us and we got up and moved. The maître d' came running back and put us back at the first table. That was obviously the table that was bugged.

The next day I had lunch at the ambassador's home and I said, "I would like to ask you a question."

He got to his feet. "Why don't we go for a walk in the garden?"

In Romania, even the ambassador's home was bugged.

For *The Sands of Time* I went to Spain to research the Basque separatist movement. I had the driver take the two routes that the nuns in the book would take. We ended up at San Sebastian. When my driver pulled up in front of the hotel, he said, "I'm leaving now."

"You can't leave," I said. "We're right in the middle of doing research."

"You don't understand," he told me. "This is the headquarters of the Basques. When they see the Madrid license plates, they will blow up the car."

I met with some of the Basques and heard their side of the story. They felt that they were displaced citizens. They wanted their land back, along with their language and their autonomy.

These are a few of my experiences. I am very grateful for them. I love to write, and I'm lucky to be working at something that I care about. I believe that no one can take credit for whatever talent they may have. Talent is a gift, whether it's for painting or music or writing, and we should be grateful for whatever talent we have been given, and work hard at it.

What I enjoy most is the actual process of writing. My business manager once gave me five hundred dollars worth of tennis lessons as a birthday present. A tennis pro came to the house once a week and gave me a lesson.

One day he said to me, "We've used up the money. Do you want to continue?"

I enjoyed playing tennis very much. I started to say yes, and then I thought, *I don't want to be here. I want to be in my office, writing.*

I haven't been on my tennis court since, and that was twenty years ago.

Four years after Cary Grant's last movie, *Walk Don't Run*, Cary called to say the Academy was giving him an honorary Oscar in New York, and he asked if I would join him there. I was happy to. His award was long overdue.

I was very pleased to see that over the years, Bob Russell and Ben Roberts had a series of successes.

My brother Richard eventually divorced, and in 1972 he surprised us all when he met and married an attractive businesswoman named Betty Rhein.

In 1985, my lovely Jorja died of a heart attack. It was an unbelievable loss and there was an emptiness in my life that I felt would never be filled.

It was a little over three years later when it happened. I met Alexandra Kostoff and my life changed. She is all the women I had written about—intelligent, beautiful, and amazingly talented, and it was love at first sight. We had a private wedding in Las Vegas, with only family there.

As a surprise, my buddy Marty Allen and his wife, Karon, appeared. The multitalented Karon played a wedding march on the piano that she had written, and the wedding went on.

Alexandra and I have been married now for sixteen wonderful years.

To my great delight, my daughter, Mary, has become a writer. To date, she has had ten novels published. My granddaughter, Lizy, had a novel published when she was sixteen. I expect ten-year-old Rebecca to be next.

My manic depression—today commonly known as bipolar syndrome—has slowed me down the last four years, but it is pretty much under control now with the help of lithium. I am planning a new novel, a nonfiction book, and a play for Broadway. I have just celebrated my eighty-eighth birthday.

I treasure the roller-coaster thrill ride that my life has been. It has been an exciting and wonderful journey. I am grateful to Otto, who convinced me to keep turning the pages, and to Natalie, for her unshakable faith in me.

I have had an incredible career with great successes and king-sized failures. I wanted to share my story with you and to thank you—because you, the readers, have always been there for me. I am deeply grateful to every one of you.

The elevator is up.

Sidney Sheldon's Credits

Broadway Plays
The Merry Widow

Jackpot

Dream with Music

Alice in Arms

Redhead

Roman Candle

Gomes (London)

Film Screenplays
South of Panama

Gambling Daughters

Dangerous Lady

Borrowed Hero

Mr. District Attorney in the Carter Case

Fly-By-Night

She's in the Army

The Bachelor and the Bobby-Soxer

Easter Parade

The Barkleys of Broadway

Nancy Goes to Rio

Annie Get Your Gun

Three Guys Named Mike

No Questions Asked

Rich, Young and Pretty

Just This Once

Remains to Be Seen

Dream Wife

You're Never Too Young

The Birds and the Bees

Anything Goes

Pardners

The Buster Keaton Story

All in a Night's Work

Billy Rose's Jumbo

Producing Credits—Film and TV

The Buster Keaton Story

I Dream of Jeannie

Rage of Angels

Rage of Angels: The Story Continues

Memories of Midnight

The Sands of Time

Directing Credits—Film and TV

Dream Wife

The Buster Keaton Story

Television Series—Creator

The Patty Duke Show

I Dream of Jeannie

Hart to Hart

Nancy

Novels

The Naked Face

The Other Side of Midnight

A Stranger in the Mirror

Bloodline

Rage of Angels

Master of the Game

If Tomorrow Comes

Windmills of the Gods

The Sands of Time

Memories of Midnight

The Doomsday Conspiracy

The Stars Shine Down

Nothing Lasts Forever

Morning, Noon & Night

The Best Laid Plans

Tell Me Your Dreams

The Sky Is Falling

Are You Afraid of the Dark?

Memoirs
The Other Side of Me

Children's Books
The Adventures of Drippy the Runaway Raindrop

The Chase

The Dictator

Ghost Story

The Money Tree

Revenge!

The Strangler

The Twelve Commandments

The Adventures of a Quarter

Films Based on Sidney Sheldon Novels

The Other Side of Midnight

Bloodline

The Naked Face

TV Movies and Miniseries Based on Sidney Sheldon Novels

Rage of Angels

Master of the Game

If Tomorrow Comes

Windmills of the Gods

A Stranger in the Mirror

Nothing Lasts Forever

The Sands of Time

Memories of Midnight